Pro Butter Side Up

by
Wally Morgan

Everyone who has ever worked in a kitchen knows that the first rule of culinary-thermo-dynamics is that an accidentally dropped piece of buttered bread or toast must fall face down, so much so that "Butter Side Up" has become shorthand for unexpected good fortune. The stories that follow attest to the fact that while some things don't always go right for probationers, their success is more widespread than is generally believed and they land "Butter Side Up"...

What they said about
Probation: Butter Side Up...

"Warm, kind and insightful – this is a book that tells us how much has been lost in successive probation reforms. And yet, for anyone starting work in the Probation Service today, this book is still immensely relevant. It's not the targets and the back covering forms that are truly important even today, it's the life changing human contacts between probation officer and client, and you will struggle to find a better account anywhere of how it should be done. Read and learn."

Nick Hardwick
Professor of Criminal Justice,
Royal Holloway University of London
and former Chief Inspector of Prisons

"This book is really, really good. I have tried hard to find something wrong with it but couldn't. It would be immensely valuable to anyone thinking of going into the Probation Service or just wanting to know what it was all about. It is life-affirming and tragic."

Jeremy Cameron
Author - Former Probation Officer

Probation: Butter Side Up "illustrates the imagination, creativity and the courage needed to provide this kind of opportunity for clients which is the real contribution probation has to offer to the pursuit of social justice for so many who come before the court. It needs a team that is committed to that goal too. A point it makes clearly.

These days there is some interest in what have been described as community hubs for the delivery of modern day probation practice aimed at desistance. Sadly, though unsurprisingly, there has been little research in that context to support the importance of the relationship between client and officer. Morgan's reminiscence, although intended as that rather as an academic study, illustrates how careless we were to allow practice of the kind this account exemplifies to be down graded in favour of excessive obeisance to the questionable gods of risk management and public protection with their algorithmic rituals. If we are ever able to revive the Service as a social, as opposed to a criminal, justice agency, I'm sure this book will help inspire that resurrection."

Christopher Hignett
Former Senior Probation Officer

ISBN 9798759748380

To
Ellen, Jeremy, Charlotte, Andrei,
Tim and Nancy

and to Lucy –
thanks for your
vital part in it!

Design and illustration
Jon Everitt
www.joneveritt.net

"Il n'y a ni mauvaises herbes ni mauvais hommes. Il n'y a que de mauvais cultivateurs."

"There are neither bad plants nor bad men. There are only bad gardeners."

Victor Hugo, *Les Misérables*

Contents

About the Author

After spending half a lifetime in business, Wally Morgan used his broad experience to re-train as a probation officer. What prompted him to take such an absurd step is open to conjecture. When, after a two year full-time course, he took his first probation job in an impoverished North London borough, he was treated to a view of urban life that few people see up close and personal.

This volume shows what now seems impossible in the modern world of criminal justice. Though not perfect, an earlier system worked better for many more offenders, until the turn of the millennium when it was then supplanted by an unwieldy structure based on targets and tick-boxes, monitoring and control, on cost/benefit analysis, economies of scale, privatisation and government contracts and by performance-related profits earned for global corporations by committed staff, over-worked but underpaid. Whatever their advantages, present-day penalties and punishment do not change lives for the better and do not reduce crime.

Despite his light-hearted, informal approach, the author urges a return to some of the values our society has cast aside, forgotten or overlooked. The recommended re-emergence of humanity, listening, encouragement, persuasion and convincing, is here shown to yield greater benefits than the principles that have guided the service in the last two decades. The abolition of probation officer discretion incorporated in the privatised 'offender management' system has resulted in policies now publicly acknowledged as failures. Can we learn from the past to improve our future?

Acknowledgments

Who, in a right state of mind, would choose the field of crime for a mid-life career change? Though baffled by my barmy intentions, my family supported me throughout. They are still baffled, but our family remains intact, stronger than ever. In her editing and helpful comments, Ellen was tireless – I almost wrote tiresome – but she was, of course, like most wives, always right.....

Many, many people endured agony to create these tales. Their lives, experiences, stories, are those of the forgotten people, victims of ineffective schooling, of flawed government policies, of poverty and ill-equipped parenting, of malicious officialdom, or of people who just didn't know how to live without drugs, alcohol, or even power, in an over-crowded world. But most, eventually, found their way and learned to avoid that conduct which brought pain, loss, disappointment and even injury to others. By telling their stories but changing names and other details as a mark of respect, I thank them for their frankness with me for their sometimes inhuman efforts and I applaud the myriad accomplishments of all clients whose lives provided these stories (many of whom maintained friendly contact long after their statutory reporting ceased).

But many others were also generous with their help and encouragement during the period covered by this book – and long after – not just those whose stories are related here. Clients and colleagues, family and friends urged me to record them.

My life has been enriched by those dear long-suffering team members whom I would particularly like to thank. It was an immense privilege to have started my probation career with the teams at Englefield Road. While working with my caseload, I turned incessantly to colleagues who tirelessly supported, guided, encouraged me (and often, wisely, gently suggested I curtail some of my over-zealous but perhaps ill-advised ideas). Their first names appear as a token of my admiration and respect.

In retirement I went back to school! I joined a writing group in U3A London (University of the Third Age) where classmates write short pieces which, over many months and years, are read out in our weekly classes. Their comments, enthusiasm and friendship have given a new dimension to life in retirement – and their urging, too, led to this volume.

Asked for his ideas on a cover illustration, my good friend Jon Everitt generously exceeded the call of duty and designed the entire book.

Thank you, every one of you.

Wally Morgan

1. Escaped Prisoner

You Mr. Wally?" Puzzled, I must have scowled. "You are, aren't you? Mr. Walter Henry! You can't deny it – I'd recognise you anywhere." He said with a smile.

"Erm, yes, hello." I said hesitantly, walking toward my always-open front garden gate.

———

Early retirement on grounds of ill-health had prompted a change in lifestyle: we had moved house. Our new home needed plenty of work which is why I found myself foolishly trying to sand the floor in the front room. Through the window, I saw a large car draw up outside, black, smart, top-of-the-range, a Mercedes saloon – extravagantly out of place in this modest urban corner of Victorian Inner London. Parking at the kerbside beyond the small front garden directly in front of our living room and unaware of his audience, the driver, a tall, handsome, smartly dressed man in a dark suit, opened the door, removed his official-looking cap which he tossed onto the driver's seat, closed the door and walked purposefully up the road remotely locking his vehicle as he did so. My half-sanded floor beckoned.

A while later, maybe an hour or so, as I took a sack of sawdust – the spoil from the sanding machine – to place beside the rubbish bins in the front garden for later collection, I saw the same man returning to his car. Looking at me intently as he approached, it was then that he'd stopped to speak. He continued:

"I can see you don't recognise me, Mr. Henry. I'm Marcus, Marcus Benjamin." My mind went blank, totally blank. "You came to see me when I was in prison an' wrote me a report that got me parole.

You were my parole officer. You told me you were new at the job and I said 'That's cool, cause I'm new at stayin' away from drugs."

"I bin clean for ten years since you 'elped me get that college course in motor mechanics. Then I got started as a private hire driver. Now I got my own car. I'm doin' OK. I bin to see my baby-mother nex'-door-but-one to you." He held out his hand and shook mine warmly and vigorously before opening the door of his car. Still speaking, he got in, placed his chauffeur's cap back on his head and, lowering the window, continued "Glad to see you're OK. You changed my life. I escaped from all them drugs 'n that. You showed me what I could have and how I could do it," he said through the open driver's door window. As he turned the ignition key to start the engine, he beamed with a broad grin, slightly familiar, I thought, when he screwed up his nose as he did so.

"Oh, an' I got a receipt for this!" In a flash, I remembered – but he was gone....

Back in the house, wearing protective earmuffs in a futile attempt to block out the awful din from the rented sanding machine, I reflected morosely that refurbishing my living room floor was not so very different from my earlier occupation as a probation officer: with a little work on my part, one hundred and fifty years of scuffing and warping of the original floorboards could be removed to reveal the beautiful wood that had always been there, and merely needed a little help to show itself.

Those men and women I worked with, influenced, manipulated or damaged whether by birth or by life experiences, were still ordinary human beings with all the promise and potential which that implied. All it took was a little effort. In practice, though, just as I was finding with my wooden floorboards, it always seemed to take a great deal more effort than I initially anticipated.

It was then I decided to write this book covering my first two years in the job.

It took some time, during which successive governments changed the whole nature of probation into an unrecognisable profit-making industry for major commercial organisations. Probation became an exercise in a box-ticking, target-centred, time-limited activity eradicating any realistic chance of changing people's lives for the better. My hope is that one day, perhaps in my lifetime, the role of probation officer might once more return to a profession that encompassed flexibility, creativity and humanity.

Since the time I began to write, I have encountered several people with whom I had a professional relationship, who were proudly or modestly able to display their various levels of subsequent accomplishment. The following stories show some of the effort it took to achieve those goals.

There were, of course, challenges, ghastly errors and miserable failures. You will find those here too.

—

2.   ...And We're Off!
A New Career

Going back to formal study at the age of forty-six had been a jolt. I found the two-year Home Office-sponsored course a struggle – but persevered, with patience from the lecturers and encouragement from my wife, Ellen. Before I knew it, I was qualified and eligible to apply for a post as a probation officer. Interviews over, acceptance confirmed, I awaited a suitable vacancy. Word was, it was not a good idea to work in one's home borough.

"You don't want to keep running into your probation clients every time you go to the shops, the pub or the cinema," people would say – or words to that effect.

"Or, worse, their wives and girlfriends" someone would chime in.

"Or even worse than that – their mums!" another would add – always someone wanting the last word.

After half a lifetime in business, it seemed strange on that first day of my new career. Even after a two year full-time intensive training course I felt, for some reason, inexplicably naïve, even ignorant. Never one for remembering people's names (I have been known to go completely blank when introducing my wife) I knew I would have difficulty remembering those of my dozen or so main grade probation officer colleagues and a similar number of secretaries and support staff.

Naturally, I was welcomed by my supervisor – a female senior probation officer (SPO), Jackie, who exuded eagerness with a warm personality and a northern accent. The other officers were cordial too, if a little curious and even cautious in varying degrees. At forty-eight years old, I was perhaps the second or third oldest in the office. It must have been unusual for some of them to have a new boy who looked older than their fathers. The officers were organised into two teams, each led by a senior probation officer.

The SPO of the other team was Chris, a man closer to my own age than most of the others, who radiated wisdom and intellect, generosity and good humour. It was not expected that we would have as much contact as I would with Jackie. Chris, naturally, had his own team of officers to manage.

Despite my apprehension at starting a completely new career in my late forties, I somehow felt safe among these colleagues. Their confidence and enthusiasm were infectious and helped to blot out my initial nervousness..... until next day when my phone rang. It was June, our much loved receptionist. Her educated antipodean voice calmed everyone.

"Wally, Allan Barfield is in reception asking to see Sylvia, but he doesn't know she's leaving and I see the case has been allocated to you. He doesn't have an appointment. Will you see him?"

"Certainly, June. Will you explain to him that I'll be taking over the file and I'll be down in a moment?" My first day and already seeing clients – I didn't expect that quite so soon...

His bulky file, dumped on top of a heap of about eight files of varying thickness, came to me as a gift from Sylvia, a colleague along the corridor who was soon to be leaving the office for pastures new. I thought I detected a look of relief on her face and assumed it was because she was leaving Hackney. As I quickly leafed through the file, I realised that it was more likely because she had handed over Allan Barfield's case. He was an injecting heroin user, she wrote in her summary, who was dishonest, manipulative, smelly, unappreciative and was never satisfied no matter what anyone did for him. He always failed to turn up for appointments, but then insisted on being seen when 'in crisis' which usually meant he needed money. He had a miserable upbringing; little was known about his history, and the main purpose of the probation order was to keep him alive. This gave a new twist to the job. An appointment letter had already been sent to him for an interview a few days hence but he had turned up in reception on my second day.

I descended the stairs to the reception area. He ignored my outstretched hand. He would be the first of my clients to be invited to my office.

"I never met a probation officer I liked," he grumbled as we climbed the stairs to the first floor. "You're all tossers!" Then, arriving at my office, "Bloody 'ell! Who did you upset to get given this room? My last prison cell was better than this!"

"Mr. Barfield, what brings you here today?"

"I din' get no probation letter. I ain't seen Sylvie for a while so I thought I'd report to her. Keep up my probation, like. I'm lookin' for somewhere to live."

"Where are you living at the moment?"

"At me gellfriend's, wiv er mum and dad but it ain't that convenient. I can't bring me mates back, an' I can't, well, you know..." Perhaps I should try the oblique approach, I thought...

"So, you've got a girlfriend? How do you come to be living with her family?"

"Look, I'm on probation. You're supposed to be 'elping me. How'm I going to stop crimes if I ain't got nowhere to live? All you want to do is talk about my girlfriend. You some kind of pervert or something?"

"Mr. Barfield,"

"Allan"

"Allan, I'll do whatever I can to help you but I'd like you to tell me what you think you might be able to do to help yourself."

"Oh, I see, it's all that social work crap is it? I've been managing to help myself all these years and I don't need you."

"The file says you were arrested for helping yourself to alcohol in a supermarket. It doesn't seem to have got you far."

"Very funny. Look, I've got to be somewhere. Can I go now?"

"I'm beginning to wish you would. Here's a card with your next appointment on it. I'll need at least an hour. Leave enough time."

"What about me noo flat? Can't you get me somewhere on me own?"

"Well, when you come on Monday, we'll see what we can do. See you next week."

"O-o-o-o-oh Yeah, I know what that means." He stood up. "Another job you're gonna kick down the road. Fuckin' waste o' time. An' people wonder why I don't like probation officers." This last comment came over his shoulder as he left the room. A few moments passed before I thought I'd better see him off the premises and decided to follow him along the corridor. He couldn't have heard me because, turning the bend in the corridor, I was just in time to see him pause at a colleague's open empty office and duck inside as if to see if there was anything worth taking. Hearing my footsteps behind him he stepped back out and ambled down the stairs. I said goodbye in the reception area but he left without any further word. *(Well that went pretty well, I chided myself.)* I was miserable for the rest of the day and wondered whether I had made a mistake with my career change.

The letter confirming acceptance of my application for a post as probation officer invited me to choose between north and south of the River Thames for my base. Not a difficult one, really, since I lived in Islington, the epitome of "Norf Lon'n" and before long a telephone call from Head Office sent me for interview in the next-door borough: Hackney. Robin, the Assistant Chief Probation Officer – ACPO – for Hackney and Islington, was someone I'd met before my probation training so I was pleased to be directed to his office upstairs in the building of Thames Magistrates Court at 8.30 one Thursday morning. We met previously when I did some voluntary work accompanying offenders' families to summer camps, once in Wales and once in Devon. He was an agreeable man of approximately my age.

"Good to see you again, Robin," I said. "I'm relieved that traffic on the journey didn't make me late."

"Well, Wally, our appointment was actually for yesterday morning," he replied without a smile. I thought then that I preferred him at camp in shorts and tee-shirt. However, though I at first insisted I had taken the date down correctly, I eventually apologised and the tone of the meeting improved. At the end of the half-hour chat Robin invited me to join an established Hackney team in Englefield Road, Dalston, towards the end of September, which is how I came to be here.

Jackie's welcoming chat outlined my job and explained that it was normal for newly qualified probation officers to have a protected caseload, at least for the first year. I was to be "on probation" until formal acceptance after one year. Main grade officers normally prepared eight to ten "Social Enquiry Reports" (SERs) each month and hold around forty cases. As a generic team, we would each have a varied caseload covering anything from milk bottle thieves to muggers to murderers.

To start with, I would inherit about six to eight cases and be allocated one or two reports a month while I learned the ropes. Though initially restricted, my caseload of offenders would increase as I accumulated my own 'clients' as a result of successful recommendations for probation orders in my court reports. If I proposed a probation order and the court concurred, that offender would be added to my caseload of probationers. In addition to writing reports and supervising my own clients on probation orders I would be expected to attend court for a day and a half each fortnight and eventually participate in the office duty rota.

"You will find the word 'client' is frowned on by some," Jackie told me. "I have no personal objection to it." At the earliest opportunity I checked several dictionaries and adopted the same view.

Wednesday mornings, Jackie told me, were reserved for joint team meetings and all officers were expected to attend so that, where possible, appointments, interviews, prison and home visits should be so arranged as not to clash with this regular event. She planned that I should have a small number of "through-care" cases: people who had been sentenced to imprisonment but who elected to maintain contact with the home probation officer. Thus, in addition to attending prisons for social enquiry report SER interviews, I would be required to visit sentenced clients in custody as well, partly to help them maintain links with family and the local community and partly to prepare them for a productive life on release.

'Too much detail too soon....' I thought to myself as Jackie regaled me with her expectations. I must have begun to look a little blank

by this time. As though reading my thoughts Jackie assumed, correctly, that this was all too much to absorb in one bite.

"Don't worry," she assured me, "You'll pick it up as you go along. Anyway, everyone here is so pleased to get a new colleague that they'll all pitch in if you need any help. We've been short- staffed for eight months and on top of that one of our team has just taken long term sick leave and another is due for a transfer to another office soon."

Then, with finality "We'll have a meeting like this every two weeks. We call it 'supervision' and we can use the time to review your cases so that you can tell me about any problems that may arise and what you're doing to solve them. A lot of officers regard their supervision sessions as a kind of insurance. When your SPO knows what you're doing, your back is partially covered and responsibility is shared." I began to realise that, just as passing the driving test qualifies you only to begin learning how to drive, my intensive Home Office probation training qualified me merely to start learning what it really means to be a probation officer.

The following stories are some of those I shared with Jackie, my boss. I have, of course, changed almost all names and in many cases, places and nationalities. Any similarity to any other person, living or dead, is, as they say, purely coincidental.

3.   Getting Started

Allan Barfield had a point. As last one in, I had been allocated the smallest office – a wedge-shaped room at the end of the curved first-floor corridor. There was just room for a desk and swivel chair, two easy chairs for interviewing (with no room even for a small coffee table between them) and a tall four-drawer filing cabinet which blocked daylight from the small window, a high price for only eight files. Jackie suggested I read the files and talk to the officers who had last managed them.

Three of the files were fat and heavy. They came to me from other officers in the building whose brains I would be able to pick for further details and background if required. Two more files were of people who had re-offended but had not been subject to recent supervision. Any probation correspondence older than three years would have been destroyed if there was nothing more recent on the file. The remaining files were, as I recall, very thin, of first offenders, not previously known to the probation service. Their offences were considered comparatively minor matters. Thus, with a caseload of eight, counting the report allocations, I began life as a probation officer.

I started reading. The bulging files were a little tedious at first. It was difficult to get used to the standard forms containing abbreviations and jargon, which I feared would take me years to comprehend. Some of the older contents were carbon copies of pre-computer typewritten reports and records of contact that had become dog-eared and yellowed with age. They were of recidivist characters who repeatedly appeared in court on relatively minor matters – trivial thefts, bungled burglaries and other offences of dishonesty that seemed to have been dealt with in what I thought then was a rather routine and uninspired way. I tried to conjure pictures of what the men might be like from the many mixed messages in the file: it was too early in my career to realise that any preconceptions I may have had would all be wrong. The other four files, new probation orders, contained little more than a request from the court for an SER, a list of the previous convictions and the latest report, which the court had used as a guide to sentencing. I eagerly drafted appointment letters to my new protégés with the idea of offering interview dates the following week. By now it was already Tuesday, my second day. I began to wonder how I would fill my time....

The office opened at nine o'clock each weekday but by that time most colleagues were already in the staff room drinking coffee. The day would begin with chatter and banter, with general laughter about current news, national, local and professional. The Senior Probation Officers (SPOs), Jackie and Chris, would participate equally in the general mêlée. I remember wondering if their willingness to take their turns in making tea or coffee was an attempt to make me feel at home. I later realised that this was probably not the case: they were always as willing as the rest of us to take an equal share in the staff catering. Much later, I reflected that it was most likely because making tea or coffee, washing up the crocks and tidying the staff room was probably more interesting than the normal work of an SPO. At least their efforts were greatly appreciated by the rest of us.

An extra file appeared in my tray: Craig Denham. It was another fat file. He was a drug user. The file came from a colleague no doubt glad to lighten his heavy caseload. A note from Jackie was pinned to the front cover. 'Wally, you don't have to take this on, as he's no longer on probation. This man maintains voluntary contact but Terry is leaving our team and there's no-one to see him after he goes. Talk to Terry about it."

"Craig is a most likeable young man," Terry told me, "with a tragic childhood. His father was an intermittent but serious drinker who would leave home and live as a vagrant during his binges. He and some other drinkers broke into a church in Canonbury and tried to keep themselves warm by burning some rubbish. When the fire got out of control, the church burnt down and they all died. Craig has never been told this. He was seven at the time, worships the memory of his father and it would destroy him if he knew the truth. There is no mention of it in the file and I urge you not to write it down. Contact is currently voluntary. He is not on a probation order. His last order was revoked after he breached the conditions. He was given a prison sentence instead and started seeing me voluntarily after his release."

After such hopeless handling of my first client interview on day two, I felt a little less eager to meet the remaining caseload, let alone purely voluntary clients.

'A bit late now to change your mind' I told myself.

'Appointment letter.' I wrote on the contact record sheet, again completely forgetting to indicate when the appointment was to be. As instructed, I took the files to the admin office where, without a word, Jean, the supervisor, placed them on the desk of Ayesha, who, after a couple of hours, called me from the admin room where she was typing my appointment letters.

"Shall I pick some times when you're free?" she asked, "Can I have your diary or would you like me to come back to your office and make some dates with you?" Ayesha, I was to learn, was always full of fun and *double entendres.*

———

4. In at the Shallow End

It was my second week. Craig Denham appeared on time in response to his appointment letter. He was tall, thin but well turned-out and had clearly gone to some trouble to make a good impression. We shook hands and chatted for a moment and I offered him a cup of tea. He waited in reception while I produced two mugs of steaming hot sweet liquid which we took to my office.

"What do I call you"

"Craig's fine. And you?"

"Wally will do, or Mr. Henry. Anything as long as it's not too insulting."

He giggled, slightly embarrassed. Wally had become a synonym for an idiot, thanks to Ken Dodd, the television comedian, who applied the North Country affectionate word for a pickled gherkin as a term of derision. I'd had time to get used to it.

"I'm glad you've come. I read that your last order was revoked so you are not obliged to attend. I've heard some nice things about you."

"That must be from Terry. Not everyone has the same opinion I'm afraid. It depends who you talk to."

"So, what do you want to talk about?"

"There's a lot of offences I've never been arrested for. I'm about to hand myself in to the police to get all my old cases cleared up so I'll be in court again in December for several old matters and I've got to go back to the police station to be charged for some other old burglaries I told them about. I want to get everything tied up together. It's no good trying to clean up from drugs if I'm always going to be looking over my shoulder to see if they're going to nick me for something I thought they'd forgotten about. I wanted to ask Terry to do me a report."

"He will have left Hackney by then, I'm afraid."

"Will you do it?"

"I don't know how reports are allocated at this office. I've only been here a week. I could ask my boss. Anyway, how do you know I'll write you a good report if opinions about you are so divided?"

"I figured that one out before we came up the stairs."

"Nice of you – but could be a ghastly mistake on your part!" A short while later we were back downstairs in the reception area. We shook hands and he left. Later Jackie said it would be acceptable for me to do the report, since he was well-known and several other officers had already declined. I sent a letter inviting him for interview the following Monday morning.

The telephone on my desk rang. I had made several calls but not received many. June, our gifted receptionist spoke: "Mr. Henry, Allan Barfield to see you."

"His appointment isn't until next week."

"He says it's urgent."

"Is he drunk?"

"No. He seems OK." I heard him whining in the background "Oooooh pleeease!"

"Tell him I'll be down."

"What is it Allan?" I asked curtly, trying unsuccessfully to sound warm and caring.

"Can I talk to you for a moment?"

"Yes, go ahead."

Glancing around uneasily, he said "No, not here." We went up to my room. Climbing the stairs I remembered my colleague's words... "He always insists on being seen when 'in crisis' which usually meant he needed money."

Even before he sat down, he said "Look, I want to apologise for yesterday. I'd had some coke in the morning and I was in no mood to be polite to anyone. Can we start again?"

"Give me your appointment card." He handed it over with a puzzled look. I tore it up.

"What are you doing?"

"Go back down and wait for me in reception. I have something I need to attend to first." I finished a small job I'd started earlier then made some tea for both of us and called him back in. He seemed far more responsive with a mug of tea in his hand.

"Look, I've been taking drugs for years but at the moment I'm not using anything. Yesterday for some reason I just caved in when I ran into some old friends who gave me some Charlie (cocaine) I wish I hadn't."

"My girlfriend's great," he continued, "and her family are very kind to me but I'm a junkie and it's not right that I should be sponging off them. I'm twenty-seven. I should be looking after myself in my own place. I've got a flat but I can't live there."

"Why's that?"

"It was my mum's. She died a couple of years ago. They said she had heart disease, but I think she topped herself because I became a smack-head (heroin user). Anyway, my lifestyle could have caused her to have a heart attack. Why did I do it? I hate myself. If I didn't have to take drugs, I'm sure she'd be still here and I could live in the home I grew up in. When she went, I vowed I'd never go back there. Whenever I did, I got the creeps – as if she was asking if I'd cleaned myself up yet. I want to do the right thing and my girlfriend knows about it but doesn't understand how to help. Her family have no idea I'm a junkie. I hate it. I hate it!"

His face slowly screwed up and years of pent-up frustration began to trickle from his eyes. "I'm sorry," he continued, wiping his eyes on his sleeve "But you're the first person I've been able to talk to in a long time. I'm upset that Sylvie's going. She was great."

"Would you like to tell her that? I'm sure she'd get a kick out of knowing how much you admire her."

"No, not while I'm like this." I proffered a tissue.

"Allan, I'm sorry you're upset today. It's too late in the day to talk to housing department but why don't you come over on Tuesday morning and we'll have a session on the phone. I can give you a letter of introduction and perhaps we can start the ball rolling. Here's an appointment card to remind you of the time."

"Honestly? That's great. And sorry about, well, you know..."

Monday morning came. Craig Denham didn't. I wrote again, checking that I had put the right address. Next day Allan Barfield was due at ten thirty. He arrived out of breath about fifteen minutes late and was still panting when I went downstairs to greet him.

"Sorry I'm late gov. I had to..."

"It's OK, it's OK. I was in the middle of something." He'd forgotten his appointment until almost too late. I didn't want him to have to lie, especially over something so trivial.

Back in the office – "What have you done about finding somewhere to live?"

"Well it's impossible. There's no housing available."

"How do you know?"

"What planet have you come from? Everybody knows it."

"Have you checked that out?"

"Of course not. It's a waste of time."

"Do you know where housing department is?"

"Yes. Next to the Town Hall. You can't get in there."

"So what do they do all day if no-one goes in?"

"Fuck knows. They certainly don't help the likes of us."

Looking up the number I muttered "Let's call them." I dialled.

"Hackney Housing."

"Hi, my name's Walter Henry. I'm a probation officer and I would like to try to help one of my clients find accommodation."

"You need the Homeless Persons' Unit (HPU). Lines are open until 11.30 a.m." She gave me the number.

"Aren't you able to put me through?" Click, brr-r-r-r-r. I dialled the number she'd given me.

"HPU." Try saying this a hundred times a day and not sounding bored.

"Hi my name's Walter Henry. I'm a probation officer and I would like to try to help one of my clients find accommodation. Could you tell me first of all what the procedure is? I've only just come to Hackney and I need to learn how you do things here." I felt a real creep saying that.

"Homeless people need to come here in person for initial interview," said Miss Bored. "They take a number then form a queue outside in the street and we see the first fifty people each day. Today's numbers won't work for tomorrow, so if you got fifty-one today you don't go to the 'ead of tomorrow's queue unless you get the first ticket – that's about 5.45 in the morning."

"Are you able to deal with other agencies in Hackney, like Social Services, Probation, Mental Health Services and so on."

"Yes of course. Just turn up 'ere at 5.45 a.m. with your client and we'll give you ticket number one. Apart from that, no."

"Can you send housing forms to this office so they could be completed before our client turns up?"

"No."

"What about someone who has literacy difficulties or other problems?"

"Look mister, all our applicants got problems, that's why they're 'omeless. We 'ave to deal with everyfink 'ere. No-one gets any different treatment OK? It's what they're calling equal opportoo-o-o-onities."

"I was suggesting that I could be of some help and reduce the amount of paperwork you have to do when my client turns up."

"Look, we're very busy here and we don't have time to talk on the phone. Either come 'ere in the morning or don't."

"Maybe I should talk to the head of the HPU. Who's your supervisor?"

"Look, Mister, don't cop the needle with me. If you want the supervisor, you phone up and ask for 'er like anyone else."

"What's her name?" But she'd hung up. I was hopping mad but trying not to show it. Allan had only heard my side of the conversation. I looked to him for sympathy.

"Well fuck you, first you don't believe me, then you say I'm mentally ill then you call me illiterate. You obviously got a bollocking 'cause you've gone all red. And I've come here expecting you to help me? I must be fucking mad."

But I was already dialling the HPU boss. It was a long wait for the call to be answered.

"HPU"

"Supervisor, please."

"Line's busy, will you hold?"

"Yes." *(Get out of this,' I thought, I've got an irate client, Housing*

Department won't help me and I'm stuck on the phone for God knows how long.) ....

"Oh... Hi, my name's Walter Henry, I'm a probation officer and I would like to try to help one of my clients find accommodation. I asked one of your colleagues some questions she couldn't answer so she suggested I ring you. It occurred to me that it may be helpful to your staff if I complete some of the paperwork for clients who wish to apply for housing. That way your counter staff wouldn't have so much to do when the client arrives. It might just have public safety benefits as well."

"Sorry, where did you say you're from?"

"Inner London Probation Service. I'm a probation officer in Hackney."

"And who are your clients?"

"Well, could be anyone really, people on probation, on parole or life licence."

"You mean criminals?" she asked with undisguised concern. "What sort of crimes do people on your books commit?" I didn't like the way this conversation was going. I was beginning to lose my composure.

"Well, as a matter of fact they could be anything from milk bottle thieves to robbers, rapists or ritual killers. I believe we have several perpetrators of violent offences, many drug addicts, a couple of rapists and some people on life licence for murder. Many of them are homeless and could come to your office any day now. From what I understand tensions run high in your office and it seemed to me that any steps you or I and my colleagues could take to reduce the anxiety level in the public area might be appreciated by you, your colleagues, my colleagues, me, and my client who's sitting with me in the office now."

"Mr. erm...."

"Henry." (*Oh terrific, I thought to myself, I've done it now. She sounds mad at me....*)

"Mr. Henry, that seems an interesting proposal, and one I haven't considered before. Would you be willing to come to my office to discuss it?"

"Wouldn't you rather see the Senior Probation Officer? On the other hand of course, if it's just an exploratory chat I could relay it to our management."

"That sounds an excellent idea. When would you be available? I don't suppose you could come this afternoon; I have a cancelled meeting?"

"As a matter of fact, I could."

"That'll be fine. Shall we say 2.30?"

Mr. Barfield had had little difficulty in understanding that little exchange.

"You're fuckin' brilliant. Right from the first time I saw you I thought 'This bloke's fucking marvellous'."

"Yes, but you were being sarcastic."

"Look, I may have said a few unfortunate things but that was before I knew you. Right, I have to go Hackney Hospital. I'm registering at the Drug Dependency Unit. Can I see you at this time next week?" I gave him an appointment card confirming the date and time.

Mrs. Bond greeted me warmly. I explained that I was having difficulty negotiating the correct procedures for my client Allan Barfield. She understood my argument that offenders were more likely to offend if they had nowhere to live. She knew that homelessness was a trigger to drug misuse, alcoholism and crime. She also knew that whenever her staff had difficult dealing with applicants, the police would be called – an almost daily occurrence – and those bureaucratic formalities would cause further disruption and delays in an already overburdened system, not to mention the added burden if charges led to arrest which meant court appearances necessitating her staff to appear as witnesses, causing interminable absences from work. Anything that might relieve that stress was worth exploring.

She walked me through the existing system. Today's fifty applicants were still being dealt with. Ticket holders were allowed in and told to wait in rows of chairs until their ticket number was shown on an illuminated indicator board. At that point they would approach a booth for interview by a housing officer. The area was bedlam. Children of all ages were running all over the place, walking, shouting and shrieking as only neglected children can. Someone was changing a baby's nappy. She left the smelly, soiled one on the chair next to her. Groups of people at several booths were having conversations in unidentifiable languages, varying from demanding, crying, pleading, complaining, to screaming. Only then, after the initial interview was completed, would each applicant be invited to go back to the rows of chairs to fill in a complex, and poorly designed, application form. If the information given was, in the eyes of the housing officer, wrong or incomplete, the person would be sent back to the chairs to correct the error. The whole procedure would take two or three hours, at the end of which the applicant, if successful, would be put on the housing list.

For those homeless people for whom English was a second

language, the problems were greater. Some forms had questions in several languages, some had completely foreign language versions, but of course many applicants were unable to read and write even in their mother tongues. Interpreters were available by appointment and at great cost to either the council or applicant. Single males had to fend for themselves but any single women or homeless families would be offered temporary accommodation in a bed and breakfast hotel until a suitable flat became available.

It's an interesting word, 'suitable'. If a flat is available, i.e. untenanted, and has the requisite number of bedrooms for the applicant family, then by definition it is 'suitable'. This is regardless of its location, state of repair, cleanliness, décor, ease of access (for example for the elderly or disabled). The housing shortage in Hackney at the end of the nineteen-eighties and beginning of the nineties was so acute that no-one would refuse any offer of accommodation, whatever the standard. It may be a little better today.

Homeless families, then, did get the chance of accommodation, first in a hotel paid for by the local authority and eventually – thousands of pounds later – in a flat. Single people, though, fared rather less well. Women could be referred to hostels, or if thought by the housing officer to be particularly vulnerable, to a bed and breakfast hotel. Males, on the other hand, would be given a list of landlords prepared to take state-funded tenants/residents. Of course, like all landlords, they would demand a security deposit. Though the state would eventually pay rent, by way of housing benefit, the state would not provide the deposit, which was a matter strictly between the landlord and tenant. And neither did the housing office provide a telephone to call the landlords to see if they had vacancies. This depressing picture was exactly what Allan had been referring to but had not been able to articulate.

Yet the wonderful Mrs. Bond was aware of all this and was

determined to try to improve it. One thing beyond her control was the unavailability of housing accommodation in the borough. It must have been an awful job to be housing manager for the homeless and to have no houses to manage. Yet she seemed to face each day bravely and had plans for the future.

"What would be helpful for Mr. Barfield," she said to me "would be to get him on the housing list first. When he is on the list, we can refer him to housing associations with specialist client focus. For example the biggest housing association in the borough has an offshoot, a subsidiary, which specialises in flats for ex-offenders."

"I do know there are three vacancies coming up and if you help him complete the forms, we can put his name forward. The houses and flats are supported, which means they have wardens and key-workers who would be able to help residents cope." We talked a little longer and I took a supply of forms to make available to colleagues in my office.

5.   Silence in Court

A magistrates' court is not permitted to be in session without a probation officer present or available. My inclusion in the court duty rota required me to attend Old Street Magistrates' Court for one and a half days a fortnight, but to start with I attended more often as an assistant to my colleagues to get acquainted with them and with the procedures, the court staff and the surroundings.

Old Street Magistrates' Court was a fascinating place. An imposing late Victorian building, it was not designed to be a friendly place. The cold marble floor of the wide entrance hall, the stately stone staircase to the upper courtrooms, the hard, oak public benches all conspired to instil fear into any visitors, whether defendant, witness or public.

It was like taking part in a relentless television drama. What I did not enjoy was all the bureaucratic procedures that went with it. Every step, it seemed to me, needed another form or a notification.

For one who never found it easy to walk and chew gum at the same time, taking notes was a particularly difficult chore because I often found the outline of the case so interesting that I forgot to write. Then I would pull myself up, pay attention and write copious notes only to find that the case was to be adjourned or remanded and no action was called for.

Just occasionally the case history would reveal some dire family situation where children's safety was at risk. In these circumstances the Social Services department would need to be notified and this was one of the extra jobs for the duty probation officer. It might be the first indication they received that this, or that, particular family – or child – was in crisis or at risk.

But court duty was not without its occasional lighter side. Back in the office, the coffee room was the place to regale colleagues with stories of mirth or disaster without fear of damage to one's career. Richard and Michael, two of my close colleagues had been on court duty one morning. One of the gaolers came over to the probation bench between cases and asked for a probation officer to come to the cells. In the safety of the staff room one lunch hour, Richard told the story:

Michael had volunteered to attend to this one, he told us . . .

Edward Fernwood, 30, had arrived at court to answer a charge of theft. It was not a serious matter in the wider scheme of things and he expected to receive a fine and be on his way. The magistrate thought differently, reminding him caustically of his several previous offences, and that on the last occasion, just two months ago, in front of the same magistrate, Fernwood had been given a conditional discharge for two years.

A conditional discharge meant that, provided Edward did not re-offend within the stated time (in his case, two years) nothing further would happen. In the event, he committed another offence in two months, so he was punished for the original matter as well as the new one. It's a legal version of double or quits. She gave him an immediate prison sentence of twenty-eight days.

So why did Edward Fernwood want to see a probation officer? Through the hatch in his cell door he explained to Michael that last night he had been out at a club in the West End and had met a beautiful young woman whom he had taken home to his flat. She stayed the night and he left her in bed, expecting to be back by her side in a couple of hours.

On the way out to court this morning, he double locked the front door, for her own safety, of course, not to keep her prisoner. Would someone please go round and let her out? Mr. Fernwood gave his address and, signed a written authority for the gaoler to release the front door keys to the incarcerated man's high-rise flat. As he said goodbye to Edward, Michael asked him what the woman's name was. "That's just it," he replied, "I never found out."

The morning court session finished at one o'clock. Michael thought it would not be a good idea to go alone so persuaded Richard to go with him. They took the lift to the eighteenth floor of a local tower block and found the flat.

Michael knocked. No reply. Again, more loudly. Nothing. So they used the keys to open the door. There appeared to be no-one at home but loud music was coming from one of the rooms. They knocked hard on what appeared to be the bedroom door. Still no response. Opening the door they found a very startled woman dancing completely naked to the music. She let out a blood-curdling scream as she saw them enter. The two men hurriedly cried "Don't be alarmed, we're probation officers." At which point she screamed even more loudly in total alarm.

Michael and Richard beat a hasty retreat to the hall and, when the music was lowered, explained that Mr. Fernwood was unavoidably detained and she should leave. They waited until she emerged in her previous evening's glad rags looking totally inappropriate on the eighteenth floor of a concrete block of flats on a grey day in Hackney Wick.

"Where am I?" she asked in an estuary accent.

"You're in Hackney Wick."

"Where the fuck is that?"

"It's East London. Where are you from; don't you know London?"

"I'm from Luton. How do I get home?"

"Bus and a train. Easy."

"You don't understand, I haven't a bean on me. I can't walk to Luton. He was supposed to pay me for an all-nighter, then he was going to pay for my cab home." Richard and Michael pooled their resources and came up with just about enough to get her home - but certainly not by taxi. Then they returned to Old Street Magistrates' Court to return Edward Fernwood's keys to the gaoler and resume the afternoon court session. They dined out on that story for years.

6.   A Straightforward Case

When I arrived back at the office there was a new file in my tray, a request from Snaresbrook Crown Court for a Social Enquiry Report (SER). When a court finds a defendant guilty – or when a defendant pleads guilty – it is often the case that a sentence is not made immediately. As one of the principles of the justice system, it is not important merely that the punishment fits the crime, but also that the punishment is appropriate to the perpetrator. The judge or magistrate will often wish to know more about the background of the offender before passing sentence and so will adjourn, or 'remand' the case while a report is prepared.

If remanded on bail, the offender (now no longer the defendant, since he or she is guilty and is thus convicted) is called to the probation office for interview. If the remand is in custody, the officer will need to make a prison visit to interview the person in the visits area. Prisons usually, though not always, have interview rooms for these "legal" visits. The interviewing officer will prepare the document which the bench will use as an aid to sentencing. I am self-critical now, looking back at some of my earlier reports. I cannot help thinking they would not have been much help. My hope is that they improved over the years.

Living at home on bail, Gary Howard received my appointment letter offering two interviews for an SER. Good practice in those days demanded two interviews, and we were given four weeks in which to arrange them and produce the report. That has long since changed. The brief account of the offence on the court papers showed that this man had pleaded guilty to common assault on a female (his girlfriend at the time) when an altercation got out of control, and to assault occasioning actual bodily harm (assault/ABH) on a male who tried to intervene on the woman's behalf. Both offences occurred more than a year previously.

Gary Howard arrived punctually for the first session. A softly spoken man of twenty-six, he had clearly gone to some trouble to look smart for the meeting. When I came downstairs to reception to meet him, I offered my hand which he shook apprehensively. We did not speak further until we were seated in my office with the door closed. We talked for a while about his living arrangements, his employment, his social habits and his aspirations.

Asking Mr. Howard to explain the offences, I observed that they were committed fourteen months ago and wondered why they had taken so long to come to court. He had also been puzzled by this. He had already made friends with his girlfriend, though they were no longer living together, when he was surprised some months later to be summoned to the police station to be charged with the two offences. He seemed a reasonable man, though he acknowledged he needed to control his temper, especially when he was tired from work. I was yet to learn about the possible effects of hypoglycaemia: in adults not suffering from diabetes, low blood sugar can cause irritability or irascibility – among the less serious of the possible symptoms.

I was to learn soon enough that it was fairly unusual for offenders to be in employment. Gary Howard said his boss knew about the offence. He gave me his consent to call his employer who told me that he was an able and respected employee who worked long and hard hours. A second interview with Gary Howard seemed superfluous, but I wanted to see if he struck me as positively on second meeting as he had on the first.

He was due in on the same day as Allan Barfield. I thought that some time with Gary Howard might be a relief after an hour with Allan. Allan didn't show up, however, and fortunately Gary Howard came early. After firing off a letter to Allan I went down to greet Gary. He arrived this time in his working clothes, and the conversation, while still cordial, was more relaxed than before.

He disclosed more information about himself and his family and I formed the view that though he had had previous convictions as a younger man, his lifestyle and demeanour made him an unlikely candidate for recidivism.

There had been a significant chance that Gary Howard could have received a prison sentence. The courts do not like people who commit acts of violence, especially if it is towards a person who intervenes in an altercation. And domestic violence – once thought to be unimportant ("It's just a domestic" was the usual local Bobby's refrain) – was by this time attracting the attention it deserved. The judge did not agree with my recommendation entirely, though my notes from court suggested that the Court gave Gary Howard some credit for his willingness to accept responsibility and for his apparent remorse. Without these factors he would certainly have gone to prison.

For the blow to Mr. Verwood, Gary Howard received an order to pay a fine of £250 with an alternative of fourteen days in prison if not paid on time, plus 60 hours of community service. He was also ordered to pay Mr. Verwood £400 in compensation. For striking his girlfriend, Gary Howard was fined £100 (or seven days imprisonment) and ordered to pay her compensation of £100. He was also ordered to pay £450 in costs to the court. I did not hear from Gary Howard again and so far as I know he did not reappear in court.

I was to discover the hard way that the court did not always follow the proposal in the report. Frequently the magistrate or judge would voice an opinion about the report. If they were encouraging comments, the court duty probation officer would include them on the results sheet. It was always good to have some positive reinforcement for your efforts included in the information on the file. If the comments were negative, the officer would merely telephone the author of the report concerned and have a quiet word.

7.   Irving Jensen

The chance to go to court one day per week was in my view a privilege. It was like being a bit-part actor in a TV show, part of a long running soap opera, an invisible director calling the shots, where everyone knew his or her part, words, actions and where even the magistrate sometimes worked from a well-worn script.

My workload in those early days had hardly reached fever pitch and I was keen to experience as many aspects of the job of probation officer as possible. Being present at court also enabled me to learn about some of the community health and welfare resources and meet the lawyers who conducted the defence.

Each day in court would see a new duty solicitor. The local legal practitioners formed a rota among themselves, taking it in turn to cover the court each weekday and Saturday morning. Defendants who came to court without a solicitor were permitted to ask the duty solicitor to speak on their behalf. If the case looked as though it justified further professional representation, the defendant could ask for time to see his or her chosen solicitor or could instruct the duty solicitor who would then, in almost every case, apply for legal aid.

I often heard offenders say that they would never take a duty solicitor because he was appointed by the police or the court and couldn't be trusted. This was, of course, false and still is. It was an efficient way to generate business in criminal law. Most of the local solicitors became very good at what they did and knew how to conduct their clients' cases.

On one of my early visits to court I saw a striking looking man enter the dock. Aged forty-something, I guessed, he was over six feet tall, fair haired with a full beard hiding rugged good-looks.

When he was asked by the clerk to state his name, I detected an American accent: "Irving Jensen, Ma'am." He volunteered the correct spelling.

"Mr. Jensen, you were supposed to be here yesterday. Can you please tell the court why you are here today and not yesterday? I notice that a warrant was issued for your arrest not backed for bail which means you could be remanded in custody."

"Yes, Ma'am," he replied in a clear drawl to the clerk, "I am a patient at the Hackney Hospital Drug Dependency Unit (DDU). Yesterday was my appointment there. If I missed the appointment, I would not receive medication for another week. I would die before then. I telephoned the court from the doctor's office and left word I would be here today." The magistrate and clerk each looked through papers in front of them. The magistrate nodded to the clerk.

"Very well, the court has withdrawn the warrant," the clerk continued, then explained to him he could be tried in the magistrates' court or in the crown court before a judge and jury and asked him to choose.

"This court please, your honour." It was the first time I had heard anyone use the term 'your honour' in a magistrates' court; inappropriate, of course.

The clerk then proceeded with the charge: "On the 20th August this year you did steal a quantity of meat, value fourteen pounds thirty pence, from Tesco supermarket in Hackney. How do you plead, guilty or not guilty?"

"Guilty Ma'am."

"And on the same date you did steal from Tesco supermarket a bottle of whisky, value eighteen pounds and eighty pence. How do you plead, guilty or not guilty?"

"Guilty Ma'am."

The prosecutor stood and read the facts of the case: "On the 20th August at about two fifteen in the afternoon a security guard noticed Mr. Jensen and another person behaving suspiciously. They were observed to take a packet of frozen meat which they did not put in the Tesco customer basket they were carrying but hid in their clothing. They then proceeded to the wines and spirits department where they took a bottle of spirit. After some minutes they discarded the wire basket and left the store without attempting to pay. They were then apprehended by the security guard outside the entrance to the store and asked to accompany him to the manager's office which they did without resistance. Police were called and they were arrested and transported to Hackney Police station. The goods were recovered in saleable condition. No one has permission to remove merchandise and take it from the shop without paying for it. Mr. Jensen was in possession of eighty-nine pence."

The defence was invited to address the bench.

"Mr. Jensen is apologetic for this offence. He and his partner, who appeared at this court yesterday, are patients at the Hackney Hospital Drugs Dependency Unit. Although they insist they were not using the money for drugs, they had spent all their money on alcohol and were left with no food to eat. His girlfriend pleaded guilty to these offences in this court yesterday." The solicitor sat down, his peremptory explanation finished, his fee earned. Or so he thought.

The slow, questioning "Ye-e-es?" by the magistrate indicated that she did not think the defence had done a very good job. Those in court all knew she meant: "Is that it? What then? What else do you have to say?" The solicitor rose weakly to his feet again and asked the magistrate to remand the matter for reports. A list of Mr. Jensen's previous offences was requested and a copy handed to the magistrate. It showed a series of theft offences over the last twenty years.

"This record is disgraceful. I am minded to give an immediate custodial sentence." In truth she was saying "Dammit, man, do some work for your fees!"

"Sir, Mr. Jensen's co-defendant was remanded on bail for reports yesterday. She is to appear four weeks from then. Perhaps you would consider remanding Mr. Jensen until then so they can both be sentenced together?"

"Are you requesting that they serve a custodial sentence together? I assure you that would not be allowed." There was some stifled giggling from the public gallery at the back of the court. The sarcasm appeared to be lost on the solicitor, as was the magistrate's indication that the defence continue with mitigation.

"Very well," she sighed after what seemed like a long pause, "I'll have a social enquiry report on the 16th October. I'd better see a medical report as well. All options are open." The magistrate leaned to one side as if to peer at a book open next to the court papers in front of her, a diary perhaps... and to the dock she said: "Mr. Jensen, I shall be sitting on that day: don't think that I've changed my mind about sending you to prison."

My colleague on court duty hurried out to interview him briefly and tell him to expect a letter from the probation service with an appointment for interview which he should be sure to attend. I asked the prosecutor for a copy of the list of previous offences. It was several pages long.

Next afternoon I found a new file in my tray. It was fat and frayed. I had been allocated a request for a Social Enquiry Report . . . . . . for Irving Jensen.

"Mr. Irving Jensen is here for his appointment." June told me on the phone a few days later. I went down to meet him. His firm handshake was slightly clammy. Back in my cramped office he took one of the easy chairs. I sat at the desk but swung my swivel chair round to face him.

"As you read in my letter, I have to prepare a report for your next visit to Old Street Magistrates' Court. One of the reasons is to make a proposal for your sentence. I'm going to ask you a lot of personal questions, and it's up to you whether you tell me the truth or nothing at all. I can say that you will have the chance to see what I've written and if you don't agree with anything in the report, you will have the chance to get it erased, or even the whole report withdrawn, but I don't think that will happen. You will probably form the view that this could be the best chance you have of avoiding custody."

"Let's go for it."

"Tell me your full name and correct date of birth."

"Irving Jensen." He spelt the surname. "May nineteen fifty- three." He was thirty-seven. He looked about ten years older.

"What day in May"

"I said it, nineteen."

"Where are you living?"

"You got the right address on the appointment letter."

"Is there someone close to you, a relative, a partner?"

"My girlfriend, Kathryn, same address." He gave the name of his co-defendant.

"Where were you born?"

"I don't know. I may have been born here – my mother was English but we lived in the USA. I have an English passport issued in Washington DC."

"Was?"

"She died in Tennessee ten years ago."

"I'm sorry to hear that. Were you close to her?"

"I was all she had. She had rotten luck. She took me everywhere she went. We went to almost every state in the US. She'd work in clubs and bars, meet a man, go with him – you know what I mean – then take off with me and meet another man. Same thing all over again. She'd get into trouble in a town, spend a night in jail, me too sometimes, then off we'd go. 'Sbeen like that since I was a small kid."

"How did she die?"

"Drink." Then after a pause, "We both used drugs since I can remember. Heroin's no bad thing but it's the alcohol. It'll be the alcohol that gets me too, you wait and see." I said I hoped to have to wait a long time but he didn't hear.

"She'd pick a man up in a bar, then stay in his hotel room. I'd sit outside usually on the floor of the corridor and then when they'd finished, the man would fall asleep and she'd lift his wallet and we'd leave. Usually jumped on freight trains. It's a good way to travel. She could look after herself – and me. I admired that."

"When did you come to England?"

"First time? More than twenty years ago. She was from here but couldn't make a go of it. I tried my hand but wasn't too smart. Got caught. We went back after a couple of years. Then the alcohol really took hold. She only lasted about five or six years after that. I've got a brother still there. He's older. Didn't know him too well."

"And what happened to you then?"

"I tried stealing but wasn't much good at it. I already had a record in several states. Got deported back to England."

"From the look of your list of previous you haven't got much better at it have you?"

"Well I wouldn't say that. It doesn't show you all the ones I got away with. But I am careless, yes, I get tripped up by the little things."

"Is there anything you are good at? Something you enjoy doing?"

"I learned the guitar from some of the musicians in the clubs my mum worked in. They were real cool guys and brilliant musicians. An' I got a lot of practice on the trains. The hobos would teach me too. Some of those guys are real good. They taught me a lot. Will I need to see you again? I'd like to bring my guitar to play you some." I wasn't sure how to respond to that. 'What's the protocol?' I wondered.

"OK" I heard myself say. "We'll see. How much heroin are you using?"

"About eighty pounds worth a day."

"Chasing or injecting?"

"Used to inject, 'til I blew all my veins. Now I'm just chasing the dragon."

I had not yet made the connection between rotten teeth and chasing heroin. People who chase drugs develop ugly tooth decay. The teeth turn black, deteriorate into spiky stumps, then if the person is lucky, they fall out. Otherwise they turn septic. Internal infection develops. It can be a slow death over many years characterised by intensely painful stomach and intestinal cancer or other ailments.

"You said 'Now I just chase' but in court your solicitor said you no longer used illegal drugs."

"He said that, I didn't. He never asked me. I wouldn't have lied."

"So how much do you use and how often?" I asked again. He paused before answering. I thought he was weighing up how much to tell me, or deciding whether to lie.

Irving Jensen drew a long breath. "If I can get it, I would use eighty pounds worth. But then there's my girlfriend. We're pretty well known in the supermarkets now. Instead of taking food and selling it we found it's easier to steal spirits and drink them – it cuts out the middle man. I try not to use heroin more than about once or twice a week now. In any case, I go to the DDU every week for my methadone and they do a test so they can tell when I've slipped up. I'm going back tomorrow for my next script."

"How long have you been going there?"

"Only since August. I started after I was arrested. Figured it might help my case."

"What happens at the DDU?"

"You arrive for your appointment. You give a urine sample. The clinical nurse sees you for counselling or you see the doctor, or both. Sometimes you get to see the boss, the consultant. Matter of fact, he's a really nice man, Dr. MacKay. He's got a good team."

"So you've gone to the DDU to stay out of prison, not to clean up?"

"That's how it started, yeah, but now I'm on a reducing methadone script I'm beginning to feel better."

"In what way?"

"Well, as you obviously know," (I definitely did not. This was better than training college.) "when you are addicted to heroin and you stop taking it your body reacts violently. You get flu symptoms, temperature, pains in your stomach, and you know that the only treatment for this condition is heroin. It's a physical dependency for which there is only one cure: heroin."

"There must be a second cure – you just said you're feeling better."

"It's methadone, synthetic heroin. It treats the symptoms without giving you the same buzz."

"How do you take it?"

"The DDU gives me a prescription every Tuesday and I take it to the chemist. Seventy-five milligrams a day. She makes up a glass of linctus – well a tiny paper cup actually – and I take it right there, in the shop. I go there every morning and evening. Supposed to take it once a day but she agrees to split it up for me. I can't sleep at night if I've taken it all in the morning. It makes me very drowsy during the day but need it to get to sleep at night."

"So if I want you to come back to see me, I'd better make it an afternoon appointment? OK. Come on Wednesday at two. I want you to ask the doctor to telephone me and to tell him that you agree to him discussing your case with me. Would you like me to give you a note to remind you, or shall I write a letter to him?"

"No, I'll remember......"

And he did. Dr. Lindbergh telephoned late the next day and introduced himself. He told me that, amazingly, Irving's urine tested negative for opiates for the first time. A few other things in there, but no opiates. Apparently, he reported, Irving was keen to build on his brief period of success and had asked for a report for court.

Dr. Lindbergh chatted warmly for a while then suggested I might like to visit the Drug Dependency Unit and meet the consultant, Dr. MacKay and his other colleagues. The team there had much to gain from informal liaison with probation officers, he said, and it was widely felt among his colleagues that they should be more open to collaboration with allied services. In the long run it could only serve to help their patients. I concurred, and though I was inwardly worried about exposing how little I knew about drugs and drug users, this seemed a good way to rectify the problem.

Mr. Jensen arrived for his next appointment carrying what I took to be his guitar in an extremely shabby case. I had completely forgotten about that. I made some tea and we went up to the office. He didn't take it out of the case immediately but put it on the floor next to him and sat dangling his arm over the side of his chair all the while fondling it as a person might idly stroke a cherished pet.

"Dr. Lindbergh called yesterday. Well done for remembering to ask him. He seemed very nice."

"Did he tell you? Did he tell you the result?" Irving asked proudly.

"He certainly did. You must be very pleased with yourself."

"I'm particularly pleased because my girlfriend used, (heroin) and I didn't. She's the cause of all this."

"Oh, come on, Irving, you already told me you've been doing drugs since you were twelve and drinking heavily since you were sixteen. You can't have known her for that long?"

"Oh yeah, I forgot. Well, I mean, like, I really want to quit now but she's got no willpower at all."

"And you have? For how long? Look, you can't put it on her. A few weeks ago you weren't even serious about cleaning up. You've had a good result for one week now she's the one who's holding you back."

"I guess I'm just nervous about stopping."

"Irving, you have every reason to be nervous. You've been dependent on heroin longer than most people have been married. It must be frightening to be facing a future without heroin. That's why you have a friend at the DDU."

"But I only see him once a week and sometimes it's not even the same person."

"It's another three weeks before you go back to court. Do you think you could keep it up till then?"

"Yes, but after that? I'll go to prison, lose my prescription, then a month or two later get released and thrown out onto the street. What's the first thing I'm going to do with my discharge allowance? Right – get some gear. I'll use all my money to buy heroin and alcohol. It's happened before and it'll happen again. What a great way to stop people offending."

"Who said you're going to prison?"

"The judge."

"It's within your power to make her change her mind."

A look of disbelief: "Get outa here!"

"No, really. If you think you could hack it, I could recommend probation in my report." He began to look interested. "There would, of course, be a few strings attached..."

"I'd do anything not to go to prison."

"Anything? That might be a little rash."

"Well, what then?"

"I want to see you at least twice more before I write that report. You must be here on time, sober and drug-free. You must continue to get negative test results at the DDU and you must tell Dr. Lindbergh that I can have any information about you that I ask for. If we go for a probation order, you must know that if you commit another offence during the probation, if you stop your treatment at the DDU, if you come here drunk, if you don't do what I tell you, I can take you back to court and have you re-sentenced for this shoplifting. You know what that will mean."

Irving laughed. "Are you crazy? I could never sign my name to all that."

"Well, from what I've seen myself and heard from the DDU you have already made a pretty good start. You've managed to get here twice in under a week. Your urine test was negative. How about starting to believe in yourself like some other people seem to believe in you?"

There was a long silence. It seemed like minutes. The stroking stopped as his fingers slid over the guitar case searching for the catch on the lid. He flipped it open and lifted the guitar to his lap. Without stopping to tune it he played a few chords, then, almost as if he was warming up, Irving played some of the most stunning blues I had ever heard. It was rapturous.

This must have lasted for four or five minutes when suddenly I realised this had to be very distracting to my colleague in the next office. I excused myself. I wanted to go next door to apologise but didn't want Irving to stop. The sound was magical. As I opened the door, two colleagues were standing there, ears bent to the door. They were as surprised by my bursting out as I was to find them nearly fall on top of me. They were beaming from one ear to the other. Irving just went on playing.

"Should I get him to stop?"

"No, no, no. This is the best thing that's happened in the office for months."

We listened for a while, but eventually he did stop. I returned to my desk as he put his guitar away wistfully. "If you get me a probation order, I can't promise I'll succeed, but I'll sure as hell try."

"Good. If you're open for business, there's a lot of work to do before then."

The phone rang and I answered. "Irving, the next person is here. I'm going to let you go now but I'd like to see you before the weekend. Could you pop in on Friday, say 2.30? Before then I'd like you to tell your girlfriend that I'll be making a home visit. It can be any day except Tuesday or Wednesday next week."

Friday came. June, our receptionist was on the phone. "Mr. Jensen to see you. He knows his appointment isn't until this afternoon but if you're free would like to see you now." It was not yet ten o'clock."

"Thank you, June. Ask him to take a seat. I'll be right down."

"Erm, he's not in very good shape."

I wondered what that meant as I descended the stairs to reception. Irving's handshake was as firm as before but clammy. His speech was slightly slurred. He looked much scruffier than the last two times I saw him. His healthy growth of hair had not been combed and with his full beard he looked frightening. I asked if he wanted to take a visit to the washroom and clean himself up a bit. He thanked me. I went off to make some coffee. When I returned with two steaming mugs Irving was dozing in a chair in reception.

Later, in my office, Irving explained. "We had a row last night," he growled, "and she threw me out. I didn't take my tablets with me so I had to drink to keep warm. I slept in the park. I had to wait until the chemist opened for my methadone and now the medication and the alcohol are taking their toll." I offered him some fruit from the big basket on my coffee table. I kept it well stocked from Ridley Road Market in Dalston for clients in exactly these circumstances.

Devouring a banana, he continued. "She brought heroin home and I got angry. There was a fight."

"You hit her?"

"Had to, self-defence. She's crazy. She beats me all the time. I left to save my own skin."

"Irving, I think I have to tell you. Assaulting your partner is not allowed. It's a crime of violence and, much more than other assaults, is likely to get out of hand and lead to serious injury. In any case, violence in the home is regarded seriously by the courts and could land you in the dock with no chance of bail. Added to that, I don't like it and I would add my weight to any conviction. Do we understand each other?"

"I'm sorry." Then, after a short pause "But –"

"Don't give me any buts. Violence is not allowed. Capiche?"

"What am I to do?"

"You could try apologising to her and saying you will try not to let it happen again. You could discuss why you get so angry. You could work out ways in which you both might avoid inflammable situations in the future. And you could stop hitting her. In any case, you have to make it up soon because I'm making a home visit on Thursday. I'll be there for eleven o'clock."

"Don't come. The flat's a mess and she's out of control."

"I'm coming, Irving. You'll straighten things out."

"Is that it? Shall I go now?"

"I think you should." I said, handing him an appointment card for the home visit on Thursday and an office interview the following week. I realised I had become rattled and that was not good. It's hard to remain impassive when a six-foot man tells you he's beating his wife.

———

The address was a flat on the top floor of a brick-built 1960s council block. The entryphone security system was broken so I walked in. A plastic rubbish bag sagged against a discarded washing machine in the down-at-heel lobby. The lift smelt of urine.

I was surprised therefore, on leaving the lift at the eighth floor, to see a gleaming floor and a large pot plant in the hall by the east facing window. I walked over and looked out at the stunning views across East London to Essex and Epping Forest, south to the City and, slightly eastward, to Docklands, where Canary Wharf and its surrounding buildings looked like a small army intent on challenging the power of the City. I was surprised to see the window ajar. I looked down eight floors to the area of untidy waste bins below. It was a swivel window hinged at the midpoint of each side, so that the outside could be cleaned from the inside. Someone had made a brave attempt at cleaning the urban grime from it so that it looked incongruous, clean but streaky, against its grey obscured neighbours.

There were four front doors facing onto the eighth-floor lobby, a door at each corner. I wondered which tenant was responsible for its beautiful appearance and how the other three tenants felt about having such a couple as Irving and his girlfriend on their floor. I couldn't hear any sound from the bell when I pushed it. Irving answered the door when I knocked. He looked good – completely different from the last time we met at the office.

"This is Kathryn." He said pointing toward a tiny woman holding a small houseplant watering can.

"Nice to meet you. Irving's said a lot about you."

"Likewise." I realised I was tongue-tied. I didn't know what I was expecting, but Irving had described someone very different from Kathryn. She was petite – perhaps fifty kilos – around five feet one, well-turned out and well-spoken with a marked Swansea accent, with that little Welsh pause in the mid-dle of words. The flat was immaculate.

"I was just about to water our plant in the hall when you knocked. I'll do it later is-n't it?" She went into the kitchen and put the watering can down. "Would you drink a cup of coffee?"

"Thanks, yes." There was little idle chit-chat. I gathered that Kathryn knew I was coming but did not know why. "I'm writing a report for Irving's next court appearance."

"Yes, I have to have one as well. When I turned up for the appointment the probation officer was ill. They've given me another date."

"Who is it with and when?" She told me. I knew from conversation in the staff room that Joanie, the officer, was unlikely to be back for that appointment.

There was considerable intolerance for colleagues who were constantly sick with minor ailments. Joanie only had to sneeze and she would leave work to take to her bed. That would be the last we'd see of her for two weeks and everyone else would have to carry her caseload. Most members of the two teams at our office would come to work no matter what – head-splitting, eye-streaming colds, limbs hanging off, you name it – but there was always the odd one whose commitment was in doubt. I said nothing.

As Kathryn brought the coffee I told her: "Irving said he'd put you in the picture that I'm thinking of proposing a probation order for him. That would mean he would have to come to see me regularly and would have to continue with his drug treatment. It could be quite a strict regime. What would you have to say about that?"

"I think it's exactly what he needs. If I were in the same situation, I would really use it well."

"Do you go with Irving when he goes to the DDU?"

"We usually go together because I've been having treatment there longer than him. I always see Dr. McKay. I've been trying to persuade him to start treatment for ages, but he didn't do it until he got arrested. I think he's finding it difficult. I'm on a reducing script – they cut down my methadone by five milligrams every fortnight so now I'm down to forty-five.

"How much are you on, Irving?"

"Seventy-five. I thought I'd told you. I'm on a maintenance script. I won't start reducing until they know I'm stable."

"I nag him when he brings gear (heroin) into the home. It disrupts me terribly when he's using in front of me. But at least he's stopped injecting. I used to hate that. I never did it myself. Always chased." She smiled revealing more bad teeth. I still hadn't made the connection. "I'm very luc-ky, reeeelly. I've been here two years. There's not many people in Hackney with a home like this. Would you like to see it?"

Without waiting for me to answer she beckoned me to follow her into the hall where she pointed out the bathroom, neat and clean, the bedroom, likewise, with a pretty view over the park – London Fields – surrounded by trees colourfully preparing to shed their leaves, and back into the kitchen. The whole place was simply and cheaply furnished with no frills. Posters brightened up the walls which still had the previous tenant's wallpaper. An old person, I thought.

While I was being shown around the flat, I could hear Irving busying himself in the kitchen. As we returned to the living room, I thought I could smell burnt toast.

"I feel slightly embarrassed being shown around your home. It's Irving I've come to visit, not to inspect how you live. But you've made it very nice. And such terrific views!" We arrived back in the living room and I noticed a pile of spirit bottles behind the settee as though hastily shoved there. She saw me glance at them.

"It was nicer before Irving moved in. I get upset with his whisky bottles all over the place. Don't get me wrong, we're a good couple. Oh, we have our difficulties but we understand each other. But sharing is hard when you're used to being alone. And sharing with someone who has the problems he has is especially hard." Irving was still busy in the kitchen. I heard the pop of a toaster and the sound of burnt toast being scraped, then a plate falling, perhaps breaking on the floor.

"Will you have a piece of toast with your coffee? I've made it." It sounded as though he'd made some more. A toaster popped again... followed by more scraping and the sound of buttering. "Oh shit!" I saw him pick something up from the kitchen floor and place it on a plate. "It's OK," he explained, "it landed butter side up. I'll have that one. Might be a good omen." We talked a little longer, then I thanked them for the coffee and toast and left, reminding Irving that we had one more appointment on the tenth of October.

Outside, in the fresh, bright autumn sunshine I silently gasped. Well, talk about life's little surprises. Who is the liar, Irving or Kathryn? She's no more capable of beating him up than flying. Who is using the heroin? Who's drinking the hooch? If she's still on a reducing script, her urine tests must be negative. She's not out of control by any means. Or is she in denial? And Irving hardly said a word. The flat looked nice – almost too nice... are they dealing? These and a thousand other thoughts and questions made me wonder, not for the last time, whether I was in the right job...

It should be said that four meetings and a home visit merely for an SER is extravagant in the extreme. No probation officer with a whole caseload to supervise would have been able to devote that amount of time to a report designed to assist the court in sentencing. Yet my early caseload was light and I was eager to get the maximum amount of experience in the field.

I had not yet learned the coffee room protocol: it was not encouraged to talk business in the staff room. When I did – which was often because all this was new and strangely exciting to me – I received discouraging or even resentful comments from some of the other officers. They were getting reports heaped up in their in-trays while I was able to luxuriate in one or two a month. I soon took the hint.

———

"Mr. Jensen is here. He's staggering." I told June I'd be right down. There were four people in the waiting area.

"Hi, Irv..."

"Mr. Probation Officer, you're a bastard. You come to my home. You flirt with my wife. You're plotting to send me to prison so you can make yourself comfortable with my wife in my house. I'm not going to be on probation to you. I'd sooner go to jail." This outburst was at full volume.

Two officers came to the window in the door separating the reception area from the staffroom corridor. Their initial looks of alarm turned to what I interpreted as mild laughter, and they returned to the staff room, from which I deduced that the situation was an everyday occurrence.

But in the reception area I was safe. The bemused onlookers outnumbered Irving and their body language suggested they appeared to be sympathetic with me. On the other hand, if I was to engage with this man, the waiting area was not the place to do it.

"You look as if you need some coffee Mr. Jensen."

"If I wanted coffee I'd stay home." Of course, it was I who needed the coffee and I wanted use the opportunity for momentary escape to check with my colleagues. This kind of outburst was pretty normal really, they thought. "If you really need to talk to him, take him up to your office. We're around. If you need reinforcements phone June and ask for two more cups of coffee. It's code for 'Help!' "

On the way up the stairs to my office I spilled some of the coffee over my hand. In doing so I burnt my hand and, worse, trying not to scream while changing the over-filled coffee mug to the other hand, spilled more coffee down my leg. I must have looked as though I'd wet my pants. This was not a good start.

"Nice of you to come, Mr. Jensen. What can I do for you?"

"What the fuck are you talking about? You wanted to see me."

"But you obviously wanted to see me. From what you say, you have no reason to report if you don't want to be on probation. I won't push it if you'd really rather go to prison. It would be your choice. A great pity of course, after you've done so well, but never mind."

Irving drank his coffee while I was talking. I was making it up as I went along, but I'd run out of ideas. I opened a file – not Irving's – on my desk and began to read, hoping I might find something inspiring on the page. I didn't and the room fell silent for a while. I turned pages occasionally to break the silence.

Irving finished his coffee. "I've blown it, haven't I?" He was no longer shouting.

"Blown what, Irving?"

"My chances."

"Chances of what, Irving?"

"Of getting on probation."

"Is that what you really want?"

"Of course it is." He was calmer but his speech was very slurred.

"You have a funny way of showing it. Are you aware that you frighten people when you get mad?"

"I frighten myself sometimes. I shouldn't drink but I do, and when I do, I can't stop till the bottle is empty."

"Have you tried drinking from smaller bottles?" There was a long pause.

"I can overlook today, because you are not under my supervision, you are here voluntarily and, most important of all, you are here exactly when we arranged. If you get probation, you will not be seen if you are drunk. And if you create the kind of disturbance you made downstairs the police will be called. Is that something you can agree to?"

"Yes"

"Yes what?

"Yes...erm... sir?"

"No, Irving, 'Yes, what?' means is there anything else you'd like to say to me?..." He looked puzzled. "...perhaps, about your behaviour in the waiting area?"

"Oh, of course, yes."

"Yes what? Go on."

"Did I say something rude?"

"You don't remember, do you?"

"Not really, no. But if I did, I'm really sorry about it." I was really exasperated. I didn't want to feed him lines but it would have been nice to hear him retract his comments. I knew I should never expect clients to thank me or apologise.

"Irving, I'm going to write your report this week and send it to court. If you want to come to see what I've written you can call in on Monday. You have to be in Court on Tuesday morning. With luck you should still make it to the DDU by lunchtime, or you could tell Dr. Lindbergh that you're in court in the morning and won't be able to see him till the afternoon. He'll know you're in court anyway because he's writing a report as well."

"If you don't make it here to read the report, Irving, that's OK because you still get the chance to read it before you go into court. If there's anything you don't agree with in the report you can ask your solicitor to get it struck out or changed. OK?"

"Yeah, thanks. Talking of changing I want to change to Kathryn's solicitor. He was brilliant. Mr. Brendan, I think his name was. Mine was crap." I gave him the address and telephone number.

"Make sure you do it right away. Good luck at court." He didn't come in on Monday.

Weeks earlier, when Craig Denham did not show up for his appointment the week after our first voluntary meeting, I had written another appointment letter; then, when that was fruitless, offered another appointment a couple of weeks later. Jackie told me I shouldn't worry about it, since he was not a statutory client and had probably decided he didn't need help and there was plenty of other action to keep me occupied. I nevertheless sent another subsequent appointment letter for the same Monday as I had invited Mr. Jensen.

I found Irving Jensen's case absorbing and, in a strange way, enjoyed writing his report, which I shared with Jackie in supervision prior to his expected visit to discuss it on the Monday before his appearance at court for sentencing. Her response to the report was encouraging but she urged me not to get too optimistic over my recommendation of a probation order because he appeared to be a recidivist and he was likely to face a prison term.

In fact, Mr. Jensen didn't come to the office on Monday, but, as if out of the blue, I received a notification form telling me that Craig Denham, whom I was expecting, had appeared in Court on Friday for the old offences he had mentioned to me when he was here weeks earlier.

The matter had been committed to the Crown Court for sentence and to that end he was remanded in custody for reports and was currently in Brixton prison. Since I had the file, I would have to do the report. I tried to make an appointment to go to HMP Brixton.

After what seemed an interminable time waiting for the telephone to be answered I was told that unfortunately there were no free slots in the legal visits diary for the rest of this week. Asking if I could make a date for the following week, I learned it was not permitted to make legal visits appointments more than seven days in advance. I would have to telephone again tomorrow. I made a note to do so and went on with other things. I promptly lost the note and forgot all about it. Instead, I was distracted from my plans by a call from June in reception...

8.   First Supervision

"Morning, Wally. Allan Barfield to see you" "Thank you, June, I'll be right down."

"Allan, nice of you to come. What happened to you last Tuesday? We had an appointment."

"I've been kicked out. I'm sleeping rough." Rough would have been a very mild way of describing his appearance. "I wanted to finish filling in that form for housing."

"That was weeks ago, Allan. It would have been better if you'd come when you had an appointment, or even if you'd called in to let me know and fix a new date. Still, now you're here we'll see what we can do. I have to see my boss shortly but, in the meantime, we'll get something done. Go and have a wash while I make some tea."

Minutes later in my office, as we completed the form for the housing department, I realised that Allan was having difficulty writing. His spelling was not very good but I noticed that his mis-spellings were inconsistent. He was left-handed and his writing was a scrawl. It didn't deserve any comment from me but I dictated a covering letter to Housing Department and assured him the completed form would go off that evening.

"The next step is an interview at the housing office. They'll write to you here – probably around a week from now so make sure you keep coming back. Where are you going to sleep tonight?"

"I just met someone I used to know. He said I could kip down there for a few days. Could you give me something for a cup of coffee?"

"I'm allowed to give you fares, but no more. You'll have to sign for it."

When he'd gone, I went back to putting the finishing touches to my report for Irving Jensen before my supervision appointment with Jackie. The largest office on each floor situated at the western end of a short curving corridor was occupied by a senior probation officer. Jackie's was on the second floor and commanded a leafy view of urban Victorian houses and gardens.

Jackie has just made herself some coffee and welcomed me with an invitation to fetch my own mug so she could share her fresh brew. Regular supervision was to be a feature of probation work, she told me, and though eventually it would take a more structured format, to begin with it would be a broad-brush look at the justice field, my own learning needs and where and how my caseload fitted into it all.

We talked for a while about my caseload. I was not finding it too taxing and if I was stuck on anything tricky, I was able to find enough support in the staff room without troubling her. We soon dealt with the small number of cases and conversation turned to broader issues.

Crime today, Jackie told me, was at the highest level in living memory and increasing. Prisons were full to overflowing – there were almost fifty thousand people in prison, up from below forty thousand when I had commenced my training in 1988, two years earlier. The courts had become clogged with bureaucracy and the justice system, from the police service to the courts, probation service to prisons, was virtually bankrupt.

Morale was on the floor and sinking, she continued, while people who worked in the system complained that they spent more time on procedures designed to absolve them from responsibility than on serving their target community. Despite promises of further injections of government money, the Home Office was seeking even more ways of reducing escalating costs of services already strapped for cash. The almost laughable result was that each new strategy and procedure introduced into an already congested system exacerbated the situation and produced the exact opposite to the desired effect. Crime was not reduced: it increased.

Why was Jackie telling me this? Perhaps she just wanted to open my eyes to reality before I became too stressed to see the truth. But she must have known that I had already been exposed to these views in the staff room. Perhaps she was venting her own frustrations to make herself feel better – treating me as the therapist, so to speak.

But although either argument might have had some substance, I suspect neither of these was the main reason. She knew I was full of enthusiasm for the job and, with hindsight, I believe she was throwing down the gauntlet by saying "...if you can't do the job, don't start. There's a great deal wrong with this whole field and if you let it grind you down, you'll perish. I think you can do this job; I just want to see you prove it."

Rightly or wrongly, that was how I took it. I did not discern that Jackie was tired of life or that she was any less keen than I. Moreover, I felt safe in her team. She conveyed that though she may not know all the answers, she knew a lot of questions and would tolerate discussion, debate, even argument. Eventually, I showed her Irving Jensen's report.

9.   Getting Active

As a newcomer to Hackney – and to the job – I had already begun to investigate the local resources. It always seemed to me a pity that there were so many people with nothing to do during the day and there was no constructive activity they could hook into. On one occasion I called at the local leisure centre to ask what facilities existed for the unemployed to enjoy. I asked to see the centre manager. The uninterested attendant asked me who I was and what was my business. Tearing herself reluctantly away from painting her fingernails, she then made a short phone call:

"There's a man here who says he's a probationary officer wants to see you," after which she told me that the manager was "too busy preparing for privatisation to get involved with the probationary service." She advised me to write for an appointment. I decided instead to telephone from my office when the opportunity arose.

"Yes, someone from your office came here. I told our receptionist to get rid of him. I'm not a criminal and I'm not on probation." He sounded about as pleased to hear from me as his receptionist the day I called in.

"I was the one who called. I hoped to get the chance to talk to you."

"What about?"

"I have many people in my care who are unemployed and have little to do during the day. I figured they might usefully occupy their time in the gym, the swimming pool or doing some kind of physical activity for health and pleasure."

"Are you trying to get them in free?"

"If you put it like that, yes, why not?"

"Because it costs a lot of money for Hackney to provide these services and we need to recoup it from the entrance fees we charge."

"But it seems to me that the money is already spent, whether people turn up to use it or not. Your pool has lifeguards, your gym has attendants and the lights are on however many people are there to use the service. Why not open up the place as a morale booster to local residents who are not working. People who feel good about themselves are more likely to get jobs and stay healthy.... and probably stay out of trouble, too."

"I don't think so. Not for the kind of people you're talking about."

"To whom should I talk if I want to pursue the idea?"

"Write me a letter. I'll see about it." I didn't feel confident that my enquiry was in the right hands, but I wrote the letter.

10. Craig Denham's False Start

I forgot about Craig Denham for a couple of months but when I received a notification that he was in Brixton Prison on remand for reports I had tried unsuccessfully to book a visit. Since the file was still in my cabinet, the task fell to me. After my first attempt I was distracted and missed a few days' opportunity so I again set about making an appointment to see Craig Denham in Her Majesty's Prison, Brixton. When I did, they told me they'd never heard of him and demanded his prison number, which I did not know. When I eventually reached the department that could provide it – which proved he had been there – I couldn't get back to the legal visits extension.

A day or two later provided more success: "Where is he, remands or convicted?" asked an officious voice. I had no idea.

"He's been remanded for reports so I guess he's in remands." Remand prisoners have slightly different conditions from convicted prisoners. They are usually kept separately from sentenced prisoners, are not compelled to wear prison uniform and have the right to more visitors.

"Well you're wrong. If he's waiting for reports then he's guilty and has therefore been convicted. He may be unsentenced but he'll be with the convicted prisoners," the officious voice said smugly. I made the appointment to visit a few days later.

It was my first visit to Brixton prison. Even on a bright day it is a long grey walk from the security barrier near the main road to the entrance in the side of a tall wall built over a hundred years ago from London stocks – those typically Victorian yellow bricks turned black through the ages with home fire smoke and now air pollution. But this morning, contrary to the optimistic weather forecast, the sky remained overcast with a threat of rain.

Showing my pass first at the gate, again at the office where I was instructed to leave all my belongings (except what I would need for the interview) and a third time when signing into the visits area, I was eventually allocated room 7 – a glass partitioned cubicle containing a small table and three tubular steel stacking chairs with plywood seat and backrest.

Everyone seemed to be in familiar territory. People coming and going, prisoners, solicitors, probation officers, prison officers – they all seemed to know what they were doing. I felt like an impostor and I felt it showed.

"Craig Denham? Room 7" shouted an unseen officer.

Craig appeared at the door while I was nervously reading the file. I must have been as pleased to see him as he was to see me. We shook hands and he took the chair opposite mine.

"Sorry about this, Wal. When I handed myself in, I didn't know they were going to bang me up. The police were surprised too because they weren't opposing bail but the magistrate said that half of the offences were committed while I was on bail for something else and he wouldn't listen to my brief. Anyway I'm here now and I'll just have to get on with it. The trouble is, it's harder to get a non-custodial once you're in. If you're on bail and the report says you got to have probation, you're more likely to get it. If you're already in custody there's not much chance. All my brave words to you about wanting to clean up are all out the window now. I just heard I'm not going back to Crown until after Christmas. Shit. I was so full of confidence and I was drug-free."

"But surely you must still be drug-free?"

"It doesn't follow. In fact, I am, but there's so many drugs in here it's worse than Hoxton. I've only got to go outside my cell onto the landing and I can score." He looked dejected. "Luckily I haven't yet, but it might be only a matter of time..." I gave him space to chat for a while; this was disheartening news. And almost ten minutes into the interview I hadn't had the chance to talk or ask questions. "But you are clean at the moment. And if you can keep it up, I can still propose probation." He shook his head dejectedly.

"Craig, I know things don't look good, but when you think of all the progress you've made over the last few months it doesn't get wiped out just because you're in here. And don't forget, you handed yourself in – that has to count for something." *(You're struggling Wal.)*

"I missed my first treatment appointment at the DDU and I bet they won't see me now. I'll have to start at the beginning again and that takes at least six weeks."

"I didn't know you were going there. Who do you see?"

"Dr. MacKay."

"Would you like me to phone him?"

"Yeah, could you?" He began to show some enthusiasm. "See if I can stay on the programme if I get released. I really want to do it this time. If I can stay clean in here, I can do it anywhere."

"OK, I'll do it if you'll write to him as well mentioning our conversation and authorising him to talk to me about your case. I know it would help. Otherwise we can't talk about specific patients because of confidentiality. But you must write first." It was as if I had just lit the blue touch paper of a firework.

"I'll do it today." He started to brighten. I got him to talk about his life, his work, his health, his mum, his girlfriend, why things had gone wrong for him, and what he thought he could do to improve his prospects for the future. He talked movingly and animatedly with only little prodding and guidance from me, but I got what I needed for the report. It was as though he didn't know he was being interviewed. It was a conversation in which he did not have to say things that weren't true. It seemed as if the truth about his life and his mistakes suddenly spilled out. He was as off guard as I was. There was a loud knock at the door. Startled, I looked up and saw a prison officer holding up his hand spread out to indicate there were only five minutes left. Craig ignored it. He just went on talking and raising his own spirits as he did so. The room brightened noticeably as a sudden shaft of bright early winter sunlight illuminated the visits area.

"Finish up now please." The same officer. And we did. Craig thanked me profusely for coming. Slightly embarrassed by his gratitude, I told him that actually it was my job.

"Ah," he said, "but you didn't have to take my case over, did you?" I had forgotten that. On the drive back to the office from interviewing Craig, I tried formulating the report in my head. It was not the way to do it. I thought of good things to say, then forgot what I'd just thought, then remembered I had appointments that afternoon with Irving and Kathryn, then thought of other tasks and chores I had planned or forgotten to do. All this before the Elephant and Castle roundabout.

I was looking forward to a sandwich lunch with colleagues in the staff room but when I arrived back Irving and Kathryn were already waiting. They were sitting on opposite sides of the waiting room. I began to hum to myself "There may be trou-ble a-head..." I decided to see them at once. It was a tricky interview but at least they were on speaking terms when they left hand-in-hand.

The telephone interrupted my reflections. Inner London Crown Court was on the line to say Craig Denham's appearance for sentence had been brought forward since all outstanding matters at other courts had now been joined up with the matters for which I was writing the report. Could I send it in the next few days please? I had better get on with it. Craig had told me he was going back to court after Christmas so after failing to write the report in my head on the way back to the office I had put all thoughts of it out of my mind. I needed to speak to Dr. MacKay and had to check with the Crown Prosecution Service on details of some of the offences.

Dr. MacKay remembered Craig Denham. He had taken a shine to him despite his false starts. Dr. Mackay explained that in his view, relapse was part of the natural path of rehabilitation: it was as if the body needed to remind itself what it was escaping from. The power of guilt – not failure – was a force for good, he told me. He offered to write a note to the court confirming that in his opinion Craig Denham made a good candidate for treatment while on probation and that he would admit him to the programme immediately on his release from custody. A letter to the court from a doctor is always a powerful tool for the defence. Over the next couple of days I wrote the report and took it proudly to the staff room.

Each day, one officer would be assigned "office duty" which meant he or she would cover any urgent tasks for absent colleagues. It became customary for that officer to cast an eye over reports completed on that day and offer helpful comments before the report was despatched to court. By doing this we managed to avoid any howlers, correct any typing errors and gain feedback on sentencing proposals or treatment plans. This routine of "gatekeeping" as it came to be called, was highly unpopular with many of the probation officers who regarded the opinion of others as an intrusion into their own mode of practice. As a new boy, I was usually grateful for any help I could get and was eager to learn how to improve my report writing in any way I could.

Today's Duty Officer was Marnie: though still under thirty, she was an experienced probation officer with well-formed opinions.

"Wally, you're wasting your time." I had asked Marnie to read my work. She knew Craig Denham. She thought he was beyond redemption.

"I can see you mean well," she continued, "but he's an injecting heroin user and likely to stay that way until he dies, which probably won't be long." I began to feel gloomy. "Every time he appears in court, he says he won't do it again, then he does. You've been taken in, Wally."

Though Marnie didn't mean it as such, her strident manner made me feel I was being attacked. The staff room fell silent except for munching noises. Mick had a penchant for crunchy muesli on which he poured orange juice. He stirred it vigorously while reading my report on Craig Denham which Marnie had brutally criticised before cruelly discarding it on the coffee table.

But Marnie continued. "You mustn't lower your guard, Wally. Your trouble is you're too nice for this job. These people need controlling and you can't do it if you're nice." I had felt, during my interactions with Craig Denham, that he had some admirable qualities which could somehow be released. Now I was beginning to doubt myself. Perhaps I was too soft. Perhaps my perceptions were inaccurate. Maybe I am unrealistic. The phone rang and Richard answered. "Telephone call for Marnie," he announced.

"I'll take it here" she said reaching her hand across the coffee table towards Richard.

"Put it through to the other room please, June. Marnie knows we don't have business calls in the staff room." He looked at me and winked as Marnie left the room. When she'd gone Mick looked up.

"Go for it, Wal," he said, "It's a good one. I hope you get the result you're proposing."

Those few words of encouragement brought me to my senses. I had lowered my guard, just as Marnie had warned, but as a result I had allowed her to puncture my enthusiasm and was beginning to feel dreadful. Luckily Mick and Richard were there with exactly the right support. Richard's neat way of securing Marnie's exit, with Mick's endorsement of my efforts, together managed to restore my confidence – and my appetite. I ate my sandwiches.

.

11. Meeting the Champion

A few days after that exchange in the coffee room, my office phone rang.

"Hi. I had a call from the centre manager at Britannia Leisure Centre. He asked me to get in touch with you. My name's Sylvester Mittee." said a cheerful, mellow voice.

"Thanks for getting back to me so quickly. Did you see my letter to him?"

"No. He wasn't too helpful. I had asked him how I could drum up some support for Hackney's new programme of community activities and he said there was some nut came in trying to get free rides for convicts. Ha-Ha-Ha! So he suggested I ring you. What did you have in mind?"

"Did he explain I'm a probation officer?" There was a short silence.

"No, he told me nothing, just your name and phone number."

"OK. At this office we supervise offenders in the community, most of whom are unemployed, fit and restless. It occurred to me that sports related activity might be a more constructive use of their time than sitting around using drugs or drinking alcohol. It may not sound appealing to you, but it's an idea I'd like to explore."

"This sounds great. Can I come round and talk about it?"

"As soon as you like."

"I'm free on Wednesday afternoon. What about two o'clock?"

"Perfect."

Mr. Mittee to see you, Wally."

"I'll be right down, June."

We shook hands warmly. It was hard not to like this man on sight. I could not help thinking that his broad grin, stocky but agile frame, must be the antithesis of the centre manager I had spoken to on the phone – but never met. Sylvester, I later learned, had been Commonwealth Welterweight boxing champion, though he modestly never alluded to it himself. He exuded confidence – and why not – and personality to match. We shared the same views about the need to occupy disenchanted, unmotivated and disenfranchised people constructively and how best to do it. The method centred on fun. Enjoyment was to be the key.

Sylvester had been engaged by Hackney Council as outreach worker for the sports and leisure department. He seemed to have the ability to think positively in any situation. We talked about how we might try to motivate probationers and parolees to participate in activities and discussed what activities we could dream up. And, boy, did he have some terrific ideas!

He seemed to think that the council would allow him to work with us for one afternoon every week. In fact today, Wednesday, was the time slot he had available to fill every week and he was able to get an old council minibus for our use. In a very short time we had made a list of several activities. These included swimming, tennis, squash, badminton, football, basketball, weights, sauna/ steam room, canoeing on the canal, rock climbing, ice skating, pitch and putt golf, and more. I conceived the idea just for my own caseload, but as we chatted it dawned on me that I probably didn't have enough people to fill a minibus every week and, in any case, my colleagues almost certainly had dozens of clients among their caseloads with the same level of needs and every bit as much chance of benefitting from the same scheme.

By the end of our meeting we had produced a poster on the word processor in the spare office next to the coffee room and sent a note to the two senior probation officers telling them of our plans. (I forgot to ask first!) The first session was booked for one week hence. Interested people were to come to reception at 1.30 with trainers and a towel. As he was leaving, I asked Sylvester why he hadn't asked me about the client group. "People are the same everywhere," he replied. "I'll see what they're like when they turn up. If they don't come, I don't have to worry. Anyway," he grinned, "I'm not scared. I'll have you to look after me!"

I put small copies of the poster in all my colleagues' pigeonholes and hoped for the best. The response was pretty immediate. In a day or two several of them had telephoned to ask for more details or to refer their clients. I was optimistic but anxious.

Wednesday arrived – and so did Sylvester with the minibus. It had been raining on and off all day but now it was pouring. This did not augur well. Attendance was bad enough when probationers were threatened with court action for failure to attend. What chance did we have in a downpour?

Visitors such as Sylvester, who were here for reasons other than reporting were invited into the staff room where they were welcomed with tea and conversation. Probation officers liked visitors, people from the real world, and usually eagerly engaged them in conversation. I kept getting up nervously to see if anyone had arrived and when the first two people were there, even though they were late, I thought we should proceed.

"No, no, no, not yet." Sylvester insisted.

"Why not? It's pouring down. No one will come out on a day like this."

"You seem to forget. Anyone who wanted to come will have started out an hour ago. It was only drizzling then. When the rain increased it made more sense to finish the journey than to go back. Anyway for these guys it's probably worse being at home on a wet day than being somewhere else." This man wasn't even a probation officer – yet he had more understanding of people than I had yet learned and he was two-thirds my age.

One by one, eight men of varying ages arrived to take part. Three of them were my own clients, but did not know each other and the remainder had been referred by my colleagues. They waited uneasily in the reception area as if listening for their names to be called for sentencing. Reception was not normally an animated place. The lobby was inhabited by people whose only apparent common ground was that they had been ordered to attend by the court. Conversation was rare and today was no exception.

The first booking was a trip to Clissold Park Leisure Centre for an introduction to weightlifting, followed by a sauna, followed by a swim. The silence during the short drive to the centre was almost painful and I began to wonder whether this really was a good idea. No-one spoke, except the irrepressible Sylvester who seemed to be either oblivious to everyone else's apprehensiveness or masking his own anxiety.

But I malign him. With hindsight I tend to think that in his supremely confident way, he knew this would turn out OK. Like the rest of life for him, this was an adventure. He chatted the whole way there, asking questions, making comments about places, people, drivers, everything and was completely unperturbed when no-one replied. On arrival at the Victorian swimming pool and leisure centre we were directed to the archaic and draughty changing rooms. Some of the men did not bring swimming shorts or towels, though luckily Sylvester and I had thought to bring some spares.

There were some interesting surprises. One or two of the

men were already acquainted with weights from their time in prison, yet not one of them had ever been in a sauna before, while three of the group were almost non-swimmers but, after an hour and a half together, the group melded so well that the more accomplished swimmers helped try to teach the others. At the end of the session we all returned to the office and had a celebratory cup of tea or coffee in my room. By this time the atmosphere in the minibus was electric. Everyone joked and chatted as though they had been friends for life. They wanted to know what was planned next week and some wanted to bring friends who weren't even on probation.

Sylvester stayed behind after the others left. "How do you think that went?" he asked when we sat down, each with another cup of tea, in the staff room.

"Sylv, I thought it was terrific. And you?"

"I had no idea what to expect. It was great. I think they really enjoyed it. We'll soon know. If no-one turns up next week, we'll know something's wrong. I'll bring tennis racquets and balls. That'll be a good winter activity and if it's raining, we can go inside and learn badminton and squash. Squash'll wear 'em out good and proper."

These events, of course, overlapped with other matters, and I was beginning to understand the need to juggle erratically attended appointments with clients along with meetings, report-writing, record-keeping, training courses and other activities, in order to develop a workable routine. Juggling was a good metaphor, since (being male) I never found it easy to keep several balls in the air at once. The more organised officers (mostly female) would poke fun at their male colleagues when lack of attention to detail left them vulnerable to jokes of the walking and chewing gum variety.

12. Irving and Kathryn

Towards the end of the lunch break in the coffee room, the phone rang. Someone answered it and handed me the receiver: "It's June for you, Walter."

"Mr. Jensen to see you. He has a woman with him."

"Sit them down. I won't be long." I had been in the middle of making tea and coffee for colleagues. I put out two more styrofoam cups, finished the job and as I went out to reception, took with me three cups of coffee on a makeshift tray.

"Mr. Probation Officer, I got probation."

"And so did I," said Kathryn.

"This calls for a celebratory cup of coffee. Come on up." And later, when sitting down in my office I asked "So what did the magistrate say?"

"We were in the main court with that woman magistrate from last time and she was really fierce," said Irving excitedly. "There was a long list of cases and they were all big ones. People were trying to get bail and she was refusing them and locking them all up. By mid-day she'd only heard about six or seven. Someone came in from another court and spoke to the clerk. Then they called out lots of names, including ours and told us to go up to Court Two. It was three magistrates. Our case was moved with loads of others."

Kathryn took over: "I didn't have a report. The letter from the Senior Probation Officer said that my probation officer was off sick and had been expected back which is why they didn't ask someone else to do it but at the last minute she didn't come back so no-one did it. The magistrates said that Irving's would do for both of us. Our solicitor said it was irregular and I could complain if I wanted to but I thought better of it. The middle magistrate, a woman, gave us a bollocking and said Irving was lucky to have a good report and if he hadn't done well during the remand period he'd have gone to prison. She gave me probation because she thought it was right we both had the same punishment. So you're our punishment Mr. Henry. She said we had to report to you straight after court."

"Wait a minute, I won't be your officer, Kathryn."

"She seemed to think you would be."

"Well the magistrates don't decide on that. Anyway, I'm not sure that would be a good idea. In any case, Joanie was allocated your report."

"...whoever she might be." joked Kathryn. "No-one seemed to know when she's coming back if ever – if she even existed in the first place." I gave them appointments for the following week and went straight to Jackie's office. I related the circumstances and the conversation to her.

"Can you take it over Wally? I know it's unusual to have partners or married couples on probation to the same officer but we're so terribly overburdened that there's no-one else I can allocate this to. It looks as though Joanie's likely to be away for some time. If you find you're overwhelmed by it, she can take the case back when she returns... whenever that might be." I agreed. My caseload was growing at faster than the projected rate but I didn't mind. I was falling in love with the job.

A week passed quickly by: "Mr. Jensen and Kathryn Lewis here to see you."

"Sit them down, June. I'll be right there."

They were early, but I was relieved they had come at all. Having stated my opinion to the court that Irving was a sound candidate for probation I would have felt disappointed if he hadn't shown up for his first appointment. I greeted them and we all went upstairs to my office each carrying a polystyrene cup of tea. There was not the same vitality as the previous week when they had just got back from court; it turned out they had just had a row. Was Irving a little drunk? I couldn't tell for sure but reminded him that I would not see him if I thought he had been drinking heavily. There was sufficient doubt on this occasion for me to let the interview proceed.

We talked about what it meant to be on probation. Irving had many more previous convictions than Kathryn, though he had not been on probation before. The problem was, he observed, that once a magistrate sees you've been to prison for shoplifting it was easy to send you there again. The more times you've been, the easier it was to send you back. The more you go to prison, the more tricks you learn and the more likely you are to do it again and so it goes on. It was a tale I was to hear again and again and it would take very little time to learn that it appeared to be true.

I explained that they would have to come to see me at least once a week. I wanted to know the outcome of their urine tests and treatment at the DDU and to liaise with Dr. Lindbergh. I wanted to know when their methadone prescription was altered, which way – up or down – and why. They agreed to this without demur. I would expect to make the occasional home visit and to be told if they moved home, separated, changed address or obtained employment. There was no opposition to this. I expected them to keep their appointments, to telephone me if they could not make it or wanted to re-arrange. No objections.

Kathryn asked a few questions, which I was able to answer, but after a while, conversation flagged. I glanced at Irving and realised he was asleep. He had slid down to an almost prone position in the easy chair.

"It's normal." Kathryn said in her beautiful Welsh brogue. "He can't take alcohol and methadone, but at least he's docile."

She had made comments like this before. "What exactly do you mean Kathryn?"

" 's obvious. He hits me."

"I think he and I have had a conversation about this but I wanted to talk to you on your own to find out more."

"Oh it's OK, he'll not hear until I shake him and tell him it's time to go home. But he has been better lately. I didn't know you'd discussed it with him. He didn't say anything. Now I can see it worked....... a little."

"What prompts it?" I hardly expected her to say 'I drive him crazy actually' so I was astonished when she said:

"Well, I think I probably drive him crazy; I talk a lot, you see? And if he's got a lot of alcohol inside him, he goes over the top."

"What do you do about it?" (Meaning 'Do you talk about it afterwards, do you seek help, do you discuss it at the DDU?')

"I hit him of course."

"But you're half his size."

"I haven't let that stop me up until now. Anyway, I'm more agile than he is especially if he's drunk. I've landed some good ones,

I'll tell you. I even gave him a black eye once. He didn't come near me for weeks after that." Irving stirred slightly then jumped in his sleep.

"See? I only got to talk about it an' he gets scared is-n't it?" I felt out of control of the situation. This wasn't covered in the training.

"Irving, wake up. Come on." He blinked, slowly appearing to realise where he was. When he spoke his speech sounded sleepy but not slurred. "Irving," I said in a loud voice, "this is no good. I can't talk to you if you can't stay awake. If you arrive drunk again I will refuse to see you and take you back to court for non-compliance. I'm going to make next week's appointment in the morning. It'll be the day after your DDU appointment so I'll want to know all about it. I think it may be better if I see you separately."

So, for a while, Irving and Kathryn patched up their differences, resumed their probation appointments and for a few months all went smoothly. My attitude to their relationship was reinforced by the title of one of my probation training course textbooks "The Situation is Hopeless - But not Serious" It seemed to fit their incompatible personalities.

13. 'I' for Idleness?
or Initiative?

There were times when I felt I was beginning to get my feet under the table. The six-month mark was still a little way off, but I could see that time spent seeing 'clients' was rapidly expanding and reducing the time available to explore the resources of the borough.

The staff at the Drug Dependency Unit seemed to welcome involvement with the probation service, and though my own colleagues were unable to make the time to visit the DDU with me, they were encouraging and wanted to hear all about it on my return from visits. But there were also alcohol advice services, housing, mental health team, social services – and a host of other resources I didn't even know about yet.

Clearly there was a great deal more to this job than met the eye. But clients came first: that was the purpose of the job – to supervise offenders. Yet what did that mean? Was I supposed to lecture them from the moment they arrived to the moment they left? Definitely not: they would never come back for a second meeting. My caseload was growing as a result of new allocations from Jackie and also from some of my court reports producing probation orders.

My court report on Craig Denham yielded a probation order which my colleague Marnie certainly didn't expect, and I think one or two others in the office had grave doubts about some of my recommendations for probation. Naturally I had to maintain contact with all the clients, each one of whom came with his or her own set of challenges, from personal problems to personality disorders, from homelessness to worklessness, from illiteracy to innumeracy, from drugs to alcohol, sex to violence - the list was endless – and at times I felt I was foundering....

Not all clients were on weekly reporting. People nearing the end of their orders often found jobs as their lives stabilised, and so long as there were no danger signs – retrograde changes to circumstances, family dysfunction, dependency relapse or even just an intuitive hunch on my part, clients would be permitted to report to the officer at longer intervals – perhaps fortnightly. Of course, if there were ever a problem, and the client wanted help with something specific, my door had to remain open – and there was always the duty officer to help with emergencies if I happened to be out of the office.

Knowing about the problems was one thing; motivating the offenders was, in many cases, quite another. But how could I help the clients if I didn't know the resources or services available to them? I had helped one chap get a flat. I wondered if I could get him to tell the others. But how? Client confidentiality was sacrosanct. It was even frowned on to introduce one client to another – even if I knew they bought drugs from each other!

Every day was a new story, some less gripping than others, but the demands on my time were, as for all probation officers, relentless. If clients failed to keep their reporting appointments, I had to fire off a letter and if necessary, another, clearly suggesting that failure to attend could – no, would – have serious consequences back in court.

Yet I had to see clients regularly to check that they were not heading for risky conduct and I soon realised that even when clients had little to report, I was spending too much time with them, since I felt I still had much to learn from them. After several months in the job it dawned on me that long routine appointments were not a prudent use of that most valuable resource: time.

Some of the clients I inherited when I began my job in Hackney were approaching the end of their probation orders as were one or two others I'd been asked to take over in the meantime through staff absences. It seemed to me that if, instead of allocating half an hour to each of these interviews, I could arrange for them to visit me together, that would free up some time for other productive activities. I decided to run it past Jackie so at my next supervision session I asked her if I could try something new.

"What do you have in mind?" she asked cautiously.

"Well, I have several clients now who are reporting satisfactorily. Their lives are relatively stable, and they are no longer in need of many of the specific resources available to them. I'd like to invite them to come to my office all at the same time. We would have a kind of 'open access' reporting period, say on Tuesday mornings, where anyone who did not have specific issues to discuss could show up, contribute - or not - to any discussion, and leave, knowing that he or she was keeping to the requirements of the order. It wouldn't matter how long they stayed, as long as June recorded their names on arrival and they actually made it up the stairs to my office." Jackie thought for a moment.

"Though I have no objection, Wally, some of your colleagues might take exception. They will argue that we don't have a culture of group-work at this office." She must have seen me visibly deflate.

"Forgive my naiveté, Jackie, but what's it got to do with anyone else how I arrange my probation practice or organise my time?"

"You have a point, of course. But it could be argued that seeing your clients all together could be viewed as idleness - just being lazy, cutting corners. For my part, I think it shows initiative and it'll free up more of your time to devote to more needy and pressing cases. It's a good strategy. I've seen nothing since your arrival at this office to suggest that you're idle but if you want to try it out for a few weeks go ahead. Perhaps you'd like to report back on it in, say, eight weeks' time?" and, reaching for her diary... "Shall I put you down for a presentation at the team meeting?" This last sentence was spoken as a question, but I knew it was a statement.

So, I began to explain my new system of reporting to my clients. The first occasion only two turned up, so we were able to accommodate them without any manoeuvring. The following week there were four, and we had to import two chairs, but the week after that no-one came. The clients continued to report to me, but some would phone to decline the group meeting and re-arrange another time to report. So much for my big idea.

By now, a member of Chris's team had moved to another post. A widely recognised ingredient of good career development was to move offices every three years or so. The theory was that you'd learn the job as well as the quirks and foibles of the locality in the first year, do a superb job in the second and either make a name for yourself or burn out in the third. With a dozen or so main-grade officers in our building that meant that a person should move on – and be replaced – every few months. That was the theory, at any rate.

What I came to understand through meeting other officers on training courses, social events, union meetings and other gatherings was that our office was almost unique in its high level of morale. Whatever their differences in personality, Jackie and Chris seemed to work well with each other and their two teams pulled together as one. Chris was as accessible to me (or my team colleagues) as to any member of his own team. The two seniors joined in the tea-making, the staff-room banter and the washing up just as much as anyone else. It was no surprise, then, that people moved away only very rarely – and then usually reluctantly.

So, when the second-floor room next door but one to Chris became vacant I asked if I could take it. He offered no objection but thought it would be both polite and prudent to first offer it among the more established members. Luckily for me they seemed to think the effort of moving outweighed the benefits of a slightly larger room so after a few days of suspense I was very fortunate to get a new room, larger than most of the others, located on a front corner of the building with windows facing in two directions. There was no need for me to move furniture as it was already amply furnished. The filing cabinet here was only two drawers – the same height as my desk so I placed them together to enlarge my workspace. I was a little overwhelmed by the size of my new office to start with and tried several configurations for the furniture. Even with five easy chairs, a coffee table and a separate work table there was still so much space I felt I would rattle around.

Apart from my files and the contents of my desk drawer there was only one other item to move. Ellen, my wife, had wanted to dispose of an enormous shallow African wicker basket that was too big to fit anywhere useful in our home. Not wanting to throw it away, I took it to my previous cubby-hole office and sat it on the filing cabinet, occasionally placing in it the odd piece of fruit I'd brought for my lunch. It looked absurd.

But almost by accident I hit on a different arrangement for the furniture. I placed the easy chairs in two rows facing each other – and purloined an extra one from the meeting room – and positioned the long coffee table between them. Then I went over to Ridley Road market to buy some fruit – apples, oranges, bananas and grapes – to place in the basket on the coffee table. Now my office looked like home.

One by one my clients continued to report to me, and when they saw my new abode they were amazed. Queenie asked me who I had to sleep with to get this. Allan Barfield said it was better than his new flat and asked if I wanted to swap. Kathryn brought me a flower which I put in a glass of water on my desk. I bit my tongue when about to ask where it came from. Gradually the Tuesday groups swelled. The icebreaker came when Allan prefixed something with "When I was in prison..." after which Jake and others opened up. As people became more familiar with one another the camaraderie grew.

Each week I would prepare a subject for discussion and created a folder I called my 'Toolbook' to be kept in a handy place I could reach if conversation flagged. I don't recall ever referring to it during a group – though I did use the topics on several occasions. But it was easy to guide conversation to health, personal hygiene, AIDS, pregnancy and abortion, drugs, the justice system, education and dozens of other hot topics of the day, not to mention the raison d'être for the group: drugs, alcohol, deception, theft and violence. By the time the date of my presentation arrived I had plenty of material. The original point of the group, to my mind, was to use my own time more economically, but interestingly, some useful by-products emerged, most notably the apparent greatly increased self-esteem and confidence among the members.

For new clients under supervision, whether probation order or release from prison on parole licence, it was always necessary to have a few individual consultations. It was often fruitful to go over the offence and discuss ways in which things might have been different to avoid recurrence. Several sessions were often required to enable the client to understand that a change in his or her behaviour could have resulted in a very different outcome. I gradually learned that getting people to accept the part that their own behaviour played – not necessarily in their offence, but in their wider experience of life, such as poverty, unhappiness, dissatisfaction – could be a turning point in their personal development. Recognition of culpability was seldom a strong suit. But when it did happen, the effects were remarkable.

All too often there were drug or alcohol issues that could be addressed, either through our own probation resources or by referral to other agencies. Either way, it was common to see new clients on their own for a spell to get the probation order 'up and running'.

But when the difficulties of the initial part of the order had been overcome, or, even more appropriately, when I determined that it could be helpful for clients to see positive results in others, an invitation to join the group worked a treat. It came to be regarded almost as a 'graduation.' Best of all, I learned a lot from it too.

So, after the initial period of weekly reporting with personal supervision, they had three options to meet their continuing obligation for weekly attendance: they could come to the Tuesday morning group between ten and one o'clock, they could attend the Wednesday sports activities, or, if they needed one-to-one advice, they could still see me alone in the office by calling up (or dropping in) to make an appointment. Numerically, it meant that in the time it would have taken me to see two or three clients, on a Tuesday morning, between nine and twelve people could have passed through my door. And on a Wednesday, with the group averaging eight to ten, only a few of whom would be on my caseload, it meant that my colleagues were relieved from having to see their clients if I sent a (pre-printed) note to confirm their attendance, which their client would countersign.

But getting members to come – and to keep them coming was the main task and I had to find a way to do that. I remembered an old story about the iconic jazz musician and band leader, Duke Ellington. He was known for giving interviewing journalists a difficult time with his reluctance for personal publicity and his consequential monosyllabic replies to the journalist's questions. Anticipating this, one reporter tried his luck using a complex question he had prepared beforehand, that required a long answer.

"Duke, you and your crazy guys in the band have such a punishing schedule. You seem to spend more time on trains and buses than anywhere else. One night each in Chicago, Rochester, Albany, Boston, New York, Philadelphia, then Washington, New Orleans and St Louis. Tell me Mr. Ellington, how on earth do you get all your unruly musicians to stick with it, practise, show up and do exactly what you want?"

"I give 'em money." he growled.

Although I clearly couldn't pay people to report, some other kind of encouragement was not out of the question. It occurred to me to bring in an old kettle from home so that tea- and coffee-making facilities were available in my room. Clients gradually came to know they could dip into my fruit basket at will – but anyone who took something without asking would be immediately admonished by another member, without any word from me.

When people had a question or a problem they were willing to discuss openly, I – or they – would put it to the group, some of whom might say they needed that information as well, or someone might know an answer, an approach, a useful name or a word of advice. This way I learned about housing, drugs use and misuse, pharmacists who short-changed on methadone prescriptions, alcohol counsellors – and quacks – and employment programmes – or people to avoid, bent coppers and police violence. The list became longer every week. They didn't teach me this in college.

There were of course house rules: learn not to interrupt one another, attack what people say, not the people who say it, no racism and if there happens to be any unfinished business among rival members, they have to leave that at the door. No violence would be tolerated, especially among rivals. The spirit was usually upbeat and good-natured, often with people telling riotously funny anecdotes about themselves. A little poetic licence was always tolerated for the sake of a good story. But occasionally when someone was feeling down, perhaps through bereavement, re-arrest or relapse, the atmosphere would turn serious but supportive. People were learning to think of others and act as a community, a new experience for some of them.

So that, broadly, was the content of my team meeting presentation. But if colleagues showed polite interest in my ideas and were mildly supportive, it was certainly not going to change their practice. Some officers were, however, quick enough to see an opportunity to shed work and asked if they could send their own clients to the Tuesday group. Declining made me feel guilty, but I reminded them their clients were welcome on Wednesday activity afternoons.

It wasn't enough for some of my workmates. My reluctance to accept their clients was read as competitiveness, arrogance or, worse, hostility. There was even a comment (from one of those who had asked to send his clients to the group) that it was a lazy way of running a caseload. I looked at Jackie. She frowned slightly and shook her head in a way that told me to disregard the critics.

14. Irving's Hiccup

Irving and Kathryn had been keeping their appointments impressively well. After a period of stabilisation, Irving began a programme of methadone reduction so that his daily dose reduced by five milligrams every fortnight. Already ahead of Irving when we first met, Kathryn 's intake continued to reduce steadily. They had each given consent for the hospital to communicate results to me and their urine tests were, according to reports from the DDU, consistently satisfactory. They were both doing well.

Arriving at the office around lunchtime after a visit to HMP Pentonville, I joined colleagues in the staffroom for sandwiches and banter. Richard always sat by the phone in the staff room. Now he was handing me the receiver.

"Mr. Jensen in Reception."

"Thanks June. I'll be right out." I was still chewing.

"I think he's drunk. He's got someone with him" she added.

"Is it Kathryn?"

"No. A man. Looks rather nice. Mmmmm."

"Now, now, June! Ask him to give me a few minutes."

"Mr. Jensen!" I shook his hand while he was still seated. It was very clammy. He'd clearly been giving the alcohol a bashing.

"Yeah Mr. Wally, cool. I need to see you."

"Here I am."

"No I need to talk to you in your office."

"Irving, you know very well that I won't see you when you're drunk. I've told you not to come here when you have been drinking."

"I only had one."

"Irving, I'm not interested in how many you had. You are very drunk and not allowed in here. Please go." He stood up. Wow, that was easy. Half way to the door he turned and lurched toward me threateningly. He looked very big and very angry. The other man who had been sitting there quietly immediately got up and stood between us. He was even bigger than Irving, very broad with a gentle face and blue eyes. *(Boy, am I glad you're here!)*

"Jus' wanted to say this is my friend Martin. He's been very good to me."

"Good to meet you Martin."

"And you. I've heard a lot about you from Irving. He says you're better than his father."

"Can I have a drink of water?"

"Before you leave? Yes." Irving went to the washroom for drinking water.

"How do you come to know Irving?" I asked Martin.

"I've seen him around a lot. He's basically pretty harmless and he plays wonderful guitar. His wife's kicked him out so I've been trying to help him."

"What happened?"

"He seems to have been drinking a lot lately. I think they were rowing a lot."

"How long has this been going on?"

"Three days. He insists on sleeping rough but I let him come to my place to clean up. In any case I'm not keen to let him stay because of the drugs."

"Oh yes, of course." Irving returned. They left. I went back to my office. Glancing out of the window minutes later I saw Irving sitting on the pavement asleep, propped against a tree. His friend Martin was never far away.

About an hour later June called me to say Irving was still outside the office. He was sitting on the wall across the street having finished his nap. He did not appear to be troubling anyone and was still there a further hour later when I finished what I had been working on. Martin had remained with him so I went out to speak to them. Irving saw me emerge from the office and clambered to his feet. He spoke first.

"I said I wanted to talk to you. You didn't say you wouldn't talk to me, only that you wouldn't talk to me if I was drunk. I'm waiting 'til I'm not drunk."

He seemed more sober now. I relented. "Do you want some tea?"

"Yes please. Can Martin come too?"

I nodded. "Two teas?"

"Kathryn's thrown me out." Irving told me matter-of-factly when we reached my office. I couldn't tell if he was trying to elicit sympathy or criticising her. "We had a fight. I think I hurt her."

"Then she did the right thing. Is she badly hurt? Did she call the police? We've talked about this before. Why do you do it? What did you do to her?" *('Wait, wait, wait, Wally, don't panic, one question at a time....)*

"When she drinks, I drink. We don't talk, we just drink. Then she gets argumentative and the fighting starts. She picked up a knife, I struck out. Left her on the floor."

"You said she told you to go."

"I came back an hour later to make sure she was OK. She looked terrible. I'm ashamed for what I did to her. She must have been in awful pain. It was then she said it's all over. I had to go. Didn't even take my things, just my guitar."

"Have you been back since?"

"Yes, but she won't open the door. I have a key but the security chain is on."

"Has she put your things out for you to take?" "No."

"Where have you been staying?"

"There's a block of flats near Martin's house. It's easy to get into the boiler room at the bottom of the stairwell. It's warm and no-one disturbs me. Martin lets me go to his place for a wash."

"What are you doing for money?"

"Kathryn's got my benefit book. I'll have to sign on again. I'll go tomorrow. But Mr. Wally, that's not what I want to talk to you about."

"Oh?"

"I'm sorry Mr. Wally, I've been arrested again."

"Oh terrific! ....What for?"

"Shoplifting. I stole a sandwich from the supermarket."

"Is that it?"

"Yeah, that's all. The police knew I had just been put on probation and told me the order would probably be revoked and I'd go to jail."

"Oh, for God's sake!"

"I'm in court tomorrow. Could you write a letter to court saying I'm doing well and to let me off?"

"No, Irving, I won't do that. Number one I don't tell lies to the court and number two the secretaries are going home now."

"Tomorrow first thing, then? I could take it to court with me?"

"No Irving, I'm not in tomorrow." Irving looked crestfallen and Martin, who had remained silent throughout the conversation looked disappointed as well. "On the other hand I agree you had been doing very well indeed for a while and since I am on court duty tomorrow, I will be able to tell the magistrate myself how you've been trying to overcome your difficulties."

Court next day was routine enough. The list was short and it looked as though we could be finished before the end of the morning session that normally lasted till one o'clock. This would be unusual since the tail-enders normally spilt over to the afternoon. There was the usual string of overnight charges – those who had been arrested the night before and held in custody until court this morning.

After collecting a list of cases from the clerk's office I began the morning's work by visiting the cells to see if any of the incumbents were known to the probation service. If someone on probation or parole is arrested and brought to court it was a matter of courtesy to notify the supervising probation officer.

There were none that morning, the only overnighters being local drinkers placed in custody for their own – and public – safety as much as anything else. I didn't enjoy this part of the task. Though some of the jailers were decent enough, there were those who were easily identified as bullies. They would treat all but their own with derision – prisoners, solicitors, probation officers, doctors, no-one was exempt from their carping. I checked the four occupied cells. None of the inmates had any connexion with probation. One of the jailers made a contemptuous comment, which I ignored.

While waiting for proceedings to begin, I sat at the probation desk to one side of the court reading through the reports of two people remanded three or four weeks previously after pleading (or being found) guilty. The magistrate had adjourned their cases for the probation service to prepare SERs, each with a proposal for sentence. The standard of writing was generally very high and the reports often made fascinating reading. Sometimes this was less true and occasionally the report was more damaging to the defendant than no report at all.

"All stand", called the usher. The door to the rear of the bench opened for this morning's magistrate to enter and seat herself behind the imposing raised bench. It was the same magistrate who had threatened to send Irving Jensen to prison.

Although the overnight charges were normally heard first, the remainder of the list was heard in no particular order. From time to time the usher would go into the public area outside the courtroom and call out the next few names on the list. As people responded they would be ushered silently into court to wait in a line on an uncomfortable wooden bench behind the dock but in front of the public gallery. Anyone who arrived late would be reprimanded by the magistrate, or possibly even fined. Occasionally a defence solicitor would ask the list caller for a case to be heard before others especially if she or he had to be in another court the same morning. Sometimes a probation officer might ask for a case to be delayed by an hour or so if, for example, an SER was still awaited.

There were two reports this morning, neither of them mine. One was for an offence of drive-while-disqualified, the other for burglary of commercial premises. The first defendant was sent to prison for six months. It was his second disqualified driving offence within the period of the first disqualification.

One thing courts don't like is being disobeyed. When you are told not to drive, the courts expect you to obey the instruction. No-one checks on you daily to see that you haven't. On the other hand, the police officer who arrested you before you received the disqualification knows where you live. He knows your car. If, on his daily round, he notices the car comes and goes, it would be worth his while enquiring whether anyone else who lives at that address drives that car. If not, there's an easy arrest for him when business is slack.

"Arthur Ellis. Arthur Ellis?" From my probation desk in the court I could hear the name of the defendant for the second report being called out in the public waiting area. The call was repeated some minutes later, and once again even later. Eventually, when the queue of those waiting had dwindled, the list caller announced to the bench that he had called the name but there was no reply. The clerk asked if the man was represented and a solicitor jumped up. The magistrate spoke:

"Mr. Chapman, do you have any explanation of the whereabouts of your client, Arthur Ellis?"

94

"None at all, I'm afraid."

"Very well, warrant no bail." This meant that a warrant for the arrest of Arthur Ellis would be issued and signed by this magistrate. When arrested, the hapless Mr. Ellis would remain in custody until brought to court, since he was not to be given his liberty on bail.

Behind those waiting to enter the dock was a glass screen separating those seated in the public gallery from the courtroom. On this particular morning there were about half a dozen people watching. They were probably relatives, mostly mothers, wives or girlfriends of the accused, or in some cases victims come to see justice done. One woman, disfigured by an ugly facial bruise, I recognised. It was Kathryn. She neither looked in my direction nor acknowledged my presence though she must have recognised me milling around the court from time to time. The court worked its way through the morning list until, maybe two from the end, Irving Jensen was called.

"Please tell the court your name, and address." asked the clerk politely.

"Irving Jensen, no fixed address."

"Mr. Jensen, are you represented today?" "No Ma'am."

"Mr. Jensen you are charged with stealing merchandise from Tesco Supermarket, namely one egg mayonnaise sandwich, value one pound twenty pence. How do you plead, guilty or not guilty?"

"Guilty Ma'am."

"Please sit down while the court hears the details."

"Can I say something, ma'am?"

"No," intervened the clerk, "You will have your opportunity later."

The prosecuting solicitor rose to his feet. From a buff-coloured file, he read the details.

"On Saturday .... at Tesco Supermarket in Hackney, the store security officer noticed Mr. Jensen behaving suspiciously near the sandwich display. He observed Mr. Jensen select one sandwich, place it in his pocket and leave the store making no attempt to pay for his purchase. He was stopped outside the store and invited to accompany the security guard to the manager's office. Police were called and Mr. Jensen was arrested and transported to the police station where he was charged and bailed to appear this morning. He had no money in his possession. No-one has permission to take food from the store without paying. The loser asks for compensation of one pound twenty pence. Mr. Jensen has previous matters at this court and was placed on probation for two years here two months ago." With this, the prosecutor handed a copy of Mr. Jensen' previous convictions to the usher who gave it to the clerk who stood to pass it up to the magistrate. The magistrate was unimpressed.

"Mr. Jensen," Irving stood up instinctively on being addressed, "Normally I would not take a terribly serious view of someone who stole a sandwich. In your case I see that my colleagues went out on a limb and made a probation order under circumstances where I would most certainly have sent you to prison. I take a very dim view of someone who doesn't know when he's been treated generously. It shows an extreme lack of gratitude on your part and an absence of respect. Your probation officer should be told about this."

"He's in court Ma'am."

My turn to stand up. The probation bench is situated at the side of the court facing inwards, which is supposed to indicate that the probation service is neither judge, nor prosecutor, nor defence. The court duty probation officer must be seen to be impartial. The wooden seat on which I had been sitting was a tilting seat – like those in cinemas, though not upholstered – but one which did not lift up fully, so if one were required to stand up while at the desk it was impossible to straighten the legs. This was the first time I had been called upon to speak in court and while trying to address the magistrate I could not put out of my mind the idea that I must look completely absurd addressing the magistrate in what appeared to be a semi-curtsying position. Luckily the clerk of the court saw my discomfort immediately and invited me to go into the witness box. She asked me my religion.

"I have no religion. I prefer to affirm."

The magistrate said there would be no need for me to be sworn in and asked how Irving had been doing. I gave an account of his remarkable progress both leading up to and during his probation order and said that although we were experiencing a slight temporary difficulty, I was optimistic for the future. Even though there had not been a great deal of time for the probation order to take effect, I was satisfied that, broadly speaking, things were going better than might have been expected.

"Do you think stealing sandwiches is better than expected?" the magistrate asked gruffly.

"Like you I am disappointed, but Mr. Jensen appears to be contrite and his blood tests at the DDU show that his use of heroin has almost ceased. His methadone prescription is still at a high level and could, in my view, blur his judgment. He has recently become homeless which is, I think, what led to this offence."

"Did you know about this matter?"

"Mr. Jensen came to my office to tell me personally yesterday. I was unable to see him. He waited two and a half hours until I was free in order to tell me personally."

"Thank you, Mr. Henry. Do you have anything else to say?"

"No Ma'am, except that sometimes it takes a while for the probation supervision to take effect."

"Clearly," she said tersely and with finality. Then, after a pause, "Thank you" she added as an afterthought, meaning I was dismissed. She looked sternly at Irving.

"Mr. Jensen," Irving stood up formally, drawing himself up to his full height, almost like a soldier standing to attention. "This is the third time in recent weeks you have been in my court. On each occasion I was ready to impose an immediate custodial sentence. I see that the second time your case was moved to another court and this time, miraculously, someone was here to speak on your behalf. It will not happen again. Do you understand what I mean by that?"

"Yes Ma'am."

"Very well, I will make a conditional discharge for one year. That is all. You may go." The magistrate then spoke quietly to the clerk who said to everyone present,

"The court will rise."

At such a juncture as this it could mean the magistrate needs a natural break, she's just remembered to phone her husband, or any other reason. Often it might happen during a case when there is need for clarification by defence, prosecution or some other legal reason. Occasionally three lay magistrates may want to confer before agreeing on a course of action. I had no idea why court rose that day. Perhaps with the list nearly completed the magistrate merely felt like a cup of coffee. I went outside to see Irving. Martin was with him. Kathryn remained in the visitors' gallery.

"Gee, thanks Mr. Wally."

"Court is resuming". The usher called to those in the public area.

"Don't leave court without seeing me first, Irving."

15. Oliver Pollard

Old Street Magistrates' Court had not been busy that morning. Once again court was in recess for a few minutes – no explanation given – which gave me an opportunity to go into the public area to talk to Irving Jensen. When going back into court, I reminded Irving of my earlier instruction not to leave court without seeing me first. Returning to collect all my papers from the courtroom, now devoid of defence solicitors, with fewer members of the public in the spectators' gallery, I heard the list-caller speaking to the magistrate: "Another new case not on your list, Ma'am." There was a shuffling of papers being handed up to the magistrate by the clerk. "Oliver Pollard."

A door at the back of the court was opened and out shuffled a man in a white paper disposable overall, like a one-piece tracksuit. About thirty years old, he was short, black, portly, wearing very large and very thick glasses, and had a rather unprepossessing appearance and a noticeable squint. The words 'eye', 'pot' and 'chimney' came to mind. I remember wondering why I always used to think of old song lyrics at inappropriate times.

Mr. Pollard was accompanied by a jailer who led him to the dock and closed the door. The dock was a simple structure toward the back of the court. Constructed of stout oak, it was a rectangular barricade, about waist high, with a gate at one end and a bench seat inside across the back so the incumbent(s) could sit down facing the magistrate. If a person had arrived at court on bail, custom dictated that the gate was left open. If the accused was already in custody, the gate was closed and guarded by one of the jailers. In front of the dock were the defence solicitors' benches which faced the clerk's desk. Beyond the clerk, facing the court, stood the raised bench at which the stipendiary magistrate, now called the District Judge, or the lay justices (Justices of the Peace

– JPs to you and me) would sit to conduct proceedings.

"Stand up please." Mr. Pollard did so and grinned, beaming at the magistrate and turning from right to left, unselfconsciously showing everyone his only tooth, placed prominently in the upper top dead centre position beneath his voluminous nose. "Please tell the court your full name?"

"It's Pollard, Oliver Pollard, your ladyship." Mr. Pollard had a most extraordinary voice that matched his appearance. It sounded like a cross between a squeak and a bellow. There was nervous giggling in the public gallery and even some of the court staff smiled benignly to each other.

The clerk continued: "Mr. Pollard are you represented today?

"No, your ladyship"

"Do you wish to be represented? The duty solicitor is still available if you wish to see her." He declined her help.

"Mr. Pollard, you are charged that earlier today you conducted yourself in public in a lewd manner likely to cause a breach of the peace; namely you appeared naked in Hackney High Street. How do you plead, guilty or not guilty?"

"Guilty, your ladyship."

The clerk read the charge. "Mr. Pollard was seen by members of the public to be walking down Hackney High Street completely naked. Police officers were called and after being conveyed to the police station he was furnished with a garment and brought straight to court."

"Mr. Pollard can you tell the court what happened."

"Yes, your honour, it's because I've been made homeless," he wailed. "The council won't fix my front door. I spent some time in Hackney (psychiatric) Hospital and when I came out, I found my flat had been broken into and the front door removed. My flat is open to all the world and people walk in and help themselves to my stuff. Last night I woke up and there were three men smoking crack in my flat. I told the council this morning and they won't help me. I don't know how to get anyone to help me. I'm desperate. I don't want to harm anyone. I never done anything wrong. I jus' wanna go back into hospital. I was safe there. My house doesn't even have a front door any more." His high-pitched screech filled the courtroom; it sounded as though he was almost crying. Everyone was riveted. The magistrate spoke quietly to the clerk of the court.

"Is anything known about this man?"

"No, Ma'am. There are no previous convictions. Mr. Pollard is a man of good character."

"Very well...." and then aloud to the court she said: "This is not a matter for the criminal courts. This appears to be a mental health matter. I will not hear this in my court. Mr. Pollard, the matter is discharged. You are free to go but you must sort out your problem some other way."

"Thank you, ma'am, your honour, your ladyship." The jailer showed him back through the door to the cells. The low-level chit-chat which ensued was halted by the list caller calling yet another case – a latecomer from the morning list. Court life resumed. Later, the list completed, the court was finished early for the day. I saw Kathryn leave the public gallery in the direction of the waiting area. As I was packing up my things on my desk to take to the small probation court office upstairs, the custody area jailer whom I knew to be a sarcastic racist came toward me in the courtroom with a sickening smirk on his face. "You're gonna love this.... You 'elp people, don't you? Well I've got one for you to 'elp. We can't 'elp 'im cause 'e's not under arrest or on bail, 'e's discharged," he sniggered.

"What are you talking about?"

"Oliver Pollard. We've got to 'and 'im over to you."

"What am I supposed to do with him?" I tried to tell myself to stay calm knowing full well that he could already see he'd got me worried.

"Ca-a-a-an't 'elp you there, sire, we don't technically know anything about 'im you see? E's not guilty. 'E's not our job any more."

I left the court in the direction of the public waiting area. I realised I had forgotten that Irving was still waiting for me. As I came out, he stood up, as did his friend Martin. I noticed Irving's partner Kathryn a few seats away on the same bench. She looked away. I still couldn't figure out why she was being so hostile to me. At that moment, jailer Snide opened the door from the custody area saying, as he pushed Mr. Pollard towards me,

"...that man there. You'll be OK with 'im. He's the one who'll 'elp you. He'll get you a suite of rooms by tonight."

"Who are you?" asked Mr. Pollard.

"I'm Walter Henry. I'm court duty probation officer today and I'll see if I can help you."

"You gonna fix my door?"

"No, but I'll call someone who might help." His face was still awash with tears and his nose had been running. Mucous was streaming over his upper lip to his chin. Not a pretty sight. I wanted to flee.

"Who's your doctor, Oliver?"

"It's Dr. Barnes at Hackney Hospital."

"Would you like me to call him?"

"Yes please, but I don't have his number with me." As he said this he was patting where his pockets would have been if he'd been wearing normal clothes. He looked a pitiful sight in his disposable white paper overalls, like a person who had been wearing protective clothing that failed, resulting in dreadful disfigurement. I asked Mr. Pollard to wait there as I fled to my court probation office, looked up the hospital number and dialled. Before long I was through to Dr. Barnes.

"Yes I know Oliver Pollard," he said when I'd explained the reason for my call, "but he doesn't belong here."

"Why not?"

"Because he's not mentally ill. He's perfectly cognisant."

"But the magistrate indicated this was a mental health matter."

"Is the magistrate a doctor? Is he a psychiatrist? Has he talked to Mr. Pollard outside court? The answer is probably 'no' to all of the above. I can't offer him a bed just because he's homeless."

"But don't you accept that his behaviour is a little strange?"

"Mr. Henry," Dr. Barnes said patronisingly, "half the people of Hackney behave very strangely. We don't have room to admit them to hospital even if we had the grounds. Mr. Pollard is not mentally ill. He does of course, have a personality disorder but that is outside the realms of the mental health acts. I'm sorry I can't be more helpful. I don't know what more I can say. Please excuse me, I have to go. Goodbye."

Reeling, I called the housing department. They couldn't help. He already had a studio flat. If he wasn't homeless, he wasn't entitled to their services. Try estate maintenance.

"Look Mr. Henry, we've already given him one new front door two months ago. We can't go on fitting new front doors. We don't have the manpower or the budget." (*What's going on? I wondered.*)

"OK. Who's your supervisor? We're talking about public safety here. The court has instructed me to sort this out. You're telling me you can't. I would like you and your supervisor to come to court this afternoon to tell the court why he is not able to do what the magistrate has asked. Do you want to come voluntarily at 2.00pm or shall I get a warrant?"

"Okay, Okay, I'll look into it. Hold on." And after what seemed like several minutes, "We don't have any new doors in stock but we'll do a temporary repair on one and fit that by the end of the week. Friday."

"Why does it take three days to do an urgent job?"

"Believe me that's quick. It's the best you're going to get – and we have to put other things aside for that." I felt it probably was true. I went back to the public area. I was surprised to see Mr. Pollard and Irving Jensen, chatting like old friends. Irving offered Mr. Pollard a roll-up, which he accepted gratefully. Irving 's friend, Martin, was there too and offered Oliver a light. From the shoulder bag he always carried, Martin pulled out a huge red apple and gave it to Mr. Pollard who seemed to devour more than half of it in one bite, quite a feat with only one tooth! He looked up at me expectantly, apple juice escaping from his lips as he prepared to speak.

"Am I going back to hospital?"

"No, Oliver, I'm afraid not, but I spoke to the estate management office and they are going to repair your front door. They'll do a temporary repair first then fix a new one when they have the right one in stock."

"When?"

"By Friday."

Oliver said nothing. With a disconsolate look on his face, he stood up slowly, and, after barely one puff, stubbed out his carefully rolled cigarette in the ashtray, disposing of the butt in the container beneath it. As if in slow motion, he placed the half-eaten apple on the bench where Irving, Martin and Kathryn had been sitting, then gripped the zipper of his jump suit, and, after ceremoniously pulling the zip fastener all the way down, he peeled the sleeves from his arms, stepped out of the suit, picked up the uneaten half of his piece of fruit and walked naked as nature intended into the winter sunshine of Old Street nonchalantly eating what remained of his apple. The empty paper suit remained on the floor exactly where he disrobed looking as though the occupant had merely melted away.

———

After Oliver Pollard left, I gave Irving and Kathryn another appointment to see me and they left the court together, their friend Martin making up the unlikely trio. He was with them again when they attended their next appointment - right day, right time, sober and chatting merrily to one another.

A few days later I received a new request for a SER for Clerkenwell

Magistrates Court. The subject of the report was Oliver Pollard, arrested near Kings Cross Station about an hour after he left Old Street Magistrates Court for walking naked in the street. The stipendiary magistrate at Clerkenwell felt that the court should have more information about Oliver before deciding what to do. Because I had previously made the mistake of regaling my colleagues in the staff room with the tale of Oliver's disrobing in the court public area, the senior probation officer allocating reports knew I already had some background knowledge of him and sent the file to me. There was clearly good reason, I now realised, why it was frowned on to talk business in the staff room. I wrote to his home address offering two appointments. He kept the first. Fortunately, he was clothed, if you could describe the shreds he wore as clothes. Moreover, he smelt.

In retrospect, it is remarkable that more visitors to my office didn't have body odour. On the whole, people's living arrangements were less than satisfactory and even if they had a flat with proper plumbing, it cost so much to heat the water, either by gas or electricity, that hot baths or showers were regarded as a luxury. Yet for the most part, people managed to attend reasonably well to their personal hygiene needs. It was to be some time before I was able to develop a strategy for addressing those who didn't. Oliver's unprepossessing appearance, his repugnant smell and his extraordinary voice made interviewing him a real chore. He was resistant, even hostile, at first, though after a while he seemed to get the message that he had more to gain than to lose by being co-operative. His family, all residents of Hackney and the surrounding boroughs, had clearly had enough of him and though they may not have been actively ostracising him, they maintained a safe distance. He was extremely needy and, I guessed, wore everyone out.

Now it was my turn to be drained. Some of his answers to my questions were very astute. I began to understand what Dr.

Barnes had meant. He was not mad, not stupid, but some of his responses were nonetheless bizarre, as though he had no knowledge, or did not care, about normal social interaction. He did not seem to have a drugs habit and told me he had no time for alcohol or cigarettes, which interfered with his work, though I had seen him accept a roll-up from Irving Jensen in the court waiting area. But it has to be said that he smoked little of it before peeling off his protective onesie.

"I didn't realise you worked, Oliver," I said.

"Well you should have asked that first. I bet you just thought I was some kind of layabout, sponging off the state."

"People who receive state benefits are not spongers by definition." I countered. "In our system we can't employ everyone, so those who do work have to provide for those who don't. What work do you do?"

"I'm a musician."

"What sort?"

"Guitar. Jazz, blues, rock."

"Is that how you knew Irving?" he looked at me quizzically. "The guy who chatted to you after court at Old Street?"

"We didn't know each other. I've seen him busking. He's better than anyone I've ever seen. I'd give my front teeth to play like that, if I had any teeth, that is." He gave a belly laugh. A battle broke out in my office between body odour and mouth odour. The mouth odour seemed to be winning. (*I'm going to be sick. Would it be offensive to get up and open the window?*) I decided to persevere just a little longer.

"Where do you work, Oliver?"

"In Hackney High Street by the park. Look, I've got to go now. I've taken too much time off work already." (*There is a God!*) I walked down to the front door with him and bade him goodbye in the reception area.

"OK. We have another appointment on Monday. I'll see you then."

"Yeah, sure." Which I sooner or later learned meant "Never."

And, "yeah, sure" enough, Oliver didn't make it to the next appointment. Since I didn't have much on that was immediately pressing, I decided to make a home visit. When I got to his address in a really run-down block of flats, I could see that his front door had been badly battered and hastily but stoutly repaired, but there was no answer when I knocked on it. I realised it had been a stupid waste of time to rush out of the office in the hope of making an unscheduled house call.

His address was some way from the office and on the way back I passed Hackney High Street. I couldn't figure out what a musician would be doing working there so I parked my car and walked to the vicinity of "the park." The place they call 'the park' is a green area next to a restored ruin of a church tower which featured on Hackney's publicity material.

The High Street had been turned into a pedestrian precinct where motor vehicles other than small buses were prohibited. On the low wall separating the mown grass of 'the park' from the busy high street were four or five men of indeterminate ages bearing beer cans. I recognised some of them from court – the regular overnight charges – 'breach of the peace', 'begging' and occasionally 'threatening or abusive behaviour'. Almost next to the church was a fruit stall; the voluminous market trader, who resembled an inverted Incredible Hulk, calling his wares and exchanging cheerful banter with customers and passers-by.

There was a pervasive buzz about the place – Hackney residents of all shapes, sizes and colours going about their business – talking, walking, shopping, shoplifting. The scene was vibrant even though it was clearly a poor neighbourhood. I drank it in for a few minutes. Hackney was the borough in which I had chosen to work. Listed in some obscure socio-economic data source as the second most deprived municipality in the European Union, I found that, in a curious way, I liked it. There was a certain honesty about its unpretentious bustle. People seemed to be living their lives despite their problems – poverty, deprivation, racism, absence of facilities, lack of resources - and yet, to a large extent, remaining cheerful.

I was roused from this reverie by an extraordinary noise. Above the sound of greengrocers, drinkers, shoppers, buses and overground railway trains on the nearby viaduct, there was a sound, an almost, but not quite, rhythmic beat, a hint of music but no, it wasn't. A voice – or was it? Yes, a voice like I'd never heard before, a wailing, bellowing screeching pleading almost singing voice coming from the direction of McDonald's restaurant.

I moved towards it to get a better look. There, seated on the ground, was Oliver, playing (using the word in its most generous term) a decrepit guitar and singing (much more than generous) an unidentifiable song on the pavement outside McDonald's. I went over to him. His guitar case contained about eleven pence. He continued singing. I waited. He continued. Did he recognise me? I had to assume he did. Eventually he stopped.

"Oliver, you had an appointment with me this afternoon."

"And here we are."

"No Oliver, it was supposed to be in my office."

"I came to your office last time. This time you've come to my office. When I told you where I worked, I knew you'd come if you were okay. I guess you're okay."

"How long have you been here?"

"Since about eleven o'clock. After the talking to you gave me last time, I finally decided to go to the Benefits Agency first thing this morning to sign on. First time in my life."

"How much have you made?"

"There it is." I had been wrong: it was about thirty pence. "Have you eaten?"

"Not since yesterday."

"Would you like a burger?"

"Thanks, yes. Double cheeseburger, plenty of onions and lots of ketchup. Chips. Oh, and a diet coke." I queued up for it, paid and brought it to Oliver Pollard who stopped playing and thanked me. The relief from the music was worth the expense of the lunch. The noise had been awful. A few pedestrians now threw coins into his guitar case. *(Smart bloke, I thought, they reward him when he stops!)*

Oliver remained seated on the pavement while we chatted, he, leaning against the window of MacDonald's, munching ravenously, occasionally wiping his mouth with his ragged sleeve, while I stood next to him. We spoke cordially at length until I became aware of another person present, as if the sun were blotted out. Looking up I saw the large frame of the same greengrocer I had seen good-naturedly shouting his wares across the street.

"This man bothering you Olly?" It was a sinister tone, verging on the threatening side. This time he didn't seem so good- natured.

"No. I think it's gonna be OK. He's my probation officer."

"I'm right across the street if you need me Olly."

"Thanks. It's OK."

Then I realised. This is Oliver's world. It may not be the kind of world I've grown up to know and love. It might be completely alien to any world recognised by middle class probation officers, by social workers, by the courts, the police, mental health workers, but Oliver had built himself a kind of life, where those around him understood him, showed him some respect, gave him a little protection. This was his turf. We talked a little longer but when it became clear he'd had enough, he started to play again and I returned to the office.

Meanwhile, Irving and Kathryn patched up their differences and resumed their probation appointments. For a while all went smoothly.

16. Catastrophe

Sometimes things go right; sometimes they go wrong. Sometimes things go disastrously wrong.

Queenie Ravendale was in my office. She had been trying to reduce her drinking and was telling me that for the last week she had consumed only six large cans of extra strong lager per day instead of the usual eight or nine. At 9% alcohol, one large can of beer equated to approximately half a bottle of wine. Six cans! I couldn't manage that myself. She must be about half my body weight, perhaps even less. I imagined what damage she must be doing to her own body.

Our conversations to date had been minimal. She wore an air of mistrust like an overcoat tightly buttoned from throat to hem. I congratulated her on a considerable achievement but I was curious how she managed to pay for her alcohol. Living on Income Support didn't leave her enough to spend on anything but essentials. Her mother gave her the money, she said, adding that there had been a problem in her block of flats when she had knocked on neighbours' doors asking for money for some spurious purpose. Her mother didn't want any more trouble. When her mother refused money, Queenie told me, she would go 'up Stamford Hill'. Suspecting I knew what that meant, but not sure I was right, I asked her to explain.

"If I really need a drink," she said, "I turn a trick." I looked blankly at her. "You know, go on the game. I'm a prostitute."

"Is that the real reason your mother gives you the money, to stop you going out? Does she know?"

"Yes. I used to knock on doors of lone males in my block of flats offering various services, but then punters started coming to my house and pestering my mother. I wasn't going to tell you."

"Why did you?"

"Because I hate it. It makes me feel sick. And I'm afraid every time I get into a car. Some of the men are awful. They are dirty, they smell, they are, you know, rough, cruel, like when they speak, and what they make me do. Often, I am afraid to do what they want and afraid not to. But when you need a drink, you'll do anything." My own powers of empathy had not yet developed to the stage where I could imagine to what lengths I would go if I needed to get a drink as much as Queenie obviously did.

"Queenie, what is the most important thing?"

"My next drink."

"Even more important than that?"

"Nothing."

"Even if I accept that a drink is the most important thing for you there is something you have to ensure before you get that drink."

"Impossible."

"You have to ensure you live long enough to take that drink."

"Well of course, that's obvious isn't it?"

"But don't you see, you're putting your whole life in danger by everything you do?"

"I don't see it that way. I only see the drink at the end."

"But the drink will be your end as well. The most important thing is your survival, your health, your safety."

I handed Queenie a tissue from the box on the coffee table. She was trying to hold back tears. "You say that like you mean it?"

"Of course I do. I hate to see anyone suffer, especially someone in my care and especially when it can be avoided."

Queenie was openly crying now. "These men are worse than my stepfather when I was a kid," she sobbed. "My mum worked nights and he would come in my room. He did all kinds of awful things to me which I didn't understand and I was never able to tell anyone. When I tried to tell my mum what he made me do to him she said I was lying and she hit me..."

Queenie tailed off because the telephone was ringing. I let it ring. She stopped talking; the phone continued. I didn't want to answer it but knew it would continue if I didn't.

"Kathryn Lewis for you Wally."

"Does she have an appointment, June? I must have forgotten to write it down."

"She's not here, she's on the telephone."

"Thanks. Look, it's pretty difficult at the moment."

"She's insistent. Sounds like trouble." (Inward groan).

"OK. Put her through.... Hi Kathryn," and to Queenie, my hand over the mouthpiece, "Excuse me, Queenie, while I take this call. I'll be as brief as I can."

"Look, Irving is re-e-elly drunk and I've locked him out, isn't it? I'm afraid of him, bang-ging on the door and making a ter-rible row.

There's only the chain ho-o-ol-ding it. If he pushes the door in, I'm dead meat. I'm afraid of what the neighbours will say. They've had enough of him lately and I've had just about enough as well but I'm scared to kick him out, isn't it? He can be reelly, reelly vi-olent."

"What would you like me to do, Kathryn?"

"Well you could come round here and get him for a start. You're his probation officer."

"Kathryn, I'm sorry but I can't leave the office right now, I'm in the middle of something important and even if I could, I'm his probation officer not a child minder. If he's causing a problem you must call the police. Just dial 999 and they'll respond. If it helps, you can say your probation officer told you to call. Will you do that?"

"You're a fuc-king waste of time!" With that, she hung up.

I turned back to Queenie who had taken advantage of the break to compose herself. She was putting on makeup – I'd not seen her wearing it before – and stood up to leave. The moment to explore this latest revelation had passed, evaporated. Whatever personal traumas she might have been willing to share with me would stay with her until she again opened up. Queenie left.

I had been completely unprepared for Queenie's spontaneous disclosure and had no idea how to respond. I felt I had handled the situation clumsily and thought she felt the same way, which was why she left. I made a note to consult my boss, Jackie, later and meanwhile returned to a report I had started.

Sometime afterwards, maybe an hour, the phone rang again.

"Police on the line. I haven't told them you're in. Do you want to take it? They won't say what it's about."

"Thanks June, better take it I suppose."

"Are you Mr. Henry?"

"Yes, how can I help?"

"Probation officer of Irving Jensen?"

"Yes"

"Not any more you're not. He's dead."

"What do you mean?"

"I mean, sir, he's dead. He died trying to break into his girlfriend's flat. He was locked out, so he tried to break in by climbing out of the landing window and crawling along the top of the parapet from the lift lobby on the top floor to get in through an open window. He didn't make it. He fell off the wall from the eighth floor. He was dead when we arrived. We need someone to positively identify the body."

Even writing this now I still feel the guilt I felt then. Irving Jensen, a sensitive man and extraordinarily gifted musician, whose life was marred from the time he was conceived, had died because I made a wrong decision. I could have packed Queenie off, or asked her to wait for my return, and gone to persuade Irving to leave Kathryn alone. But I didn't. And now Irving was dead. Kathryn must be feeling dreadful. I phoned her but there was no reply. The police called back to say that Kathryn had agreed to make the positive identification and my presence was no longer required.

Before going home to my family, I went to see Jackie. I wanted to know if there were any formalities that probation officers had to follow when clients died. She was sympathetic and supportive, but no, there were no formalities. Just record the details, close the file and send it to headquarters to be destroyed. What did she say? Destroyed? That file is the last remnants of Irving's life: how could I send it to be destroyed? I did nothing for a while. I called Kathryn a few times but she must have been out. Just to make sure, I passed by her flat but there was no answer when I knocked at the door.

She didn't come back that evening. I called her from home but there was still no reply. Disheartened, I came to the sad conclusion that maybe this job was not for me.

Next morning I called Kathryn as soon as I got to work. The telephone rang for what seemed like hours before she answered.

"Hulloo?"

"Kathryn, it's Wally. I just want to see if you're OK or if I can do anything for you and to say how sorry I am about Irving."

"Are you mad? Are you completely fuc-king stupid? I haven't slept all night and the minute I doze off I'm woken by some murdering ignoramus who wants to know if I'm alright. Of course I'm not alright, you stupid bastard. If you'd helped me when I asked, my man would still be alive today. How can you say you're sorry when it was your selfish, lazy stupidity that caused Irving to die? Don't ever call me again. Don't write to me, don't speak to me, don't say hello, don't leave messages. I don't ever want to see or hear from you again. And if you breach my probation order I'll tell the court that I hold you responsible for the death of my husband. Now fuck off."

Over the next few days and weeks there were several bureaucratic letters and telephone calls about Irving Jensen. They all served to justify my inactivity over destroying the file. The Department of Social Security needed answers to some questions; Hackney

Social Services needed information; the Drug Dependency Unit phoned to sympathise. Interestingly, the post mortem was planned for a date beyond the funeral. My presence was not required. I felt somehow excluded, though it was of little consequence. Social Services organized (and paid for) the funeral which was to be held about a week hence.

Another phone call – probably more bureaucracy gone mad: "Martin Norland on the line for you Wally."

"Thanks June"

"Hi Martin."

"Kathryn asked me to call you to see if you would go to the funeral with her. I think she'd like your support."

"Martin, are you sure? When we last spoke, I got the slight impression she's gone off me.... In fact she told me she never wanted to see me again."

"You know how she is. She didn't mean it." *(I thought: 'Yeah, when she wants something...' but didn't say it.)*

"When is it?"

"Monday morning first thing."

"Are you going?"

"I'd like to, but it's a long way and I'm not sure how to get there. It's in Manor Park Crematorium. If you're going by car, perhaps we could come with you. It starts at nine o'clock. We could be at your office early. I'll pick Kathryn up and we'll come there together."

"Probably easier from me to collect you both at her flat. It's on the way."

"I'm sure she'd be very grateful for that. I know I am."

"Are you sure she wants this?"

"Totally."

"You're a good friend to them, Martin."

"Cuts both ways."

I wasn't looking forward to Monday morning but it arrived swiftly and I went up to call for Kathryn and Martin at her home. She said he hadn't arrived yet but when we reached downstairs in the lift, he was just coming up the path to the lobby. No-one spoke in the car going to the crematorium. At Hackney Wick we saw a hearse going in the same direction as our car. It could have been Irving; at first we had no way of knowing. But it drove sedately in the direction I was planning so we followed.

There were four mourners in the hearse. The stately old vehicle turned into the cemetery and stopped outside the crematorium. They carried the plain wooden coffin to the front of the public chamber. Kathryn, Martin and I were the only members of the congregation.

The service was brief, impersonal, and the official had a kind of Monday-morning-of-another-dull-week sound to his voice. There were mentions of God and what a wonderful person Irving had been before he was struck down in the prime of a fruitful life. Kathryn wept silently. She must have found this totally crass and deeply painful. I later learned that the official had never spoken to her before and knew nothing of Irving Jensen or his sad life. But this was a pauper's funeral. His ashes were to be scattered on the garden of remembrance, which on that winter morning looked neither an attractive nor dignified option.

Kathryn cried quietly throughout the ceremony, in the garden afterwards, and all the way home. I was tongue-tied and completely unable to help. Martin sat in the back of the car with Kathryn and put his arm round her in a gentle, caring way. When we reached her flat, Kathryn, still crying, invited me in for a cup of coffee but I hadn't the courage to accept. I declined as graciously as I could and went to work leaving Martin to escort Kathryn to her lonely flat.

—

17. Oliver Pollard's Interrupted Report

A few days later I was writing the report for Oliver Pollard. It was my turn to do office duty and, because of the excessive number of times I'd had to run downstairs to attend to my colleagues' clients, I decided to ensconce myself in an interview room on the ground floor which just happened to house the one spare word processor in the building. Partly because of recent history with Irving and Kathryn and partly because of my natural ability to allow myself to be easily distracted, I had left it dangerously close to the court date to actually sit down and compose the report.

But every time I sat at the keyboard there was another intrusion. I was only just becoming accustomed to word-processing and had difficulty remembering to save my work. The third time I was interrupted I had to go to reception to see a half-expected client whom I had agreed to see on behalf of an absent colleague 'if the client deigned to turn up' for his appointment. His probation officer had just been called away to court urgently and left the office hurriedly doing up his necktie and donning a smart jacket left conveniently in his office for such occasions.

It didn't take long to deal with his visitor, but when I returned, Laura was on the computer and my unsaved work had been completely lost. Of course, there were apologies all round, but it didn't really help. Not realising someone else was in the middle of a report, Laura just opened a new document and neglected to save the existing one on screen. When she finished fifteen minutes later, I returned to begin Oliver's report all over again and tried to remember what I'd written earlier. It occurred to me to ask June not to put any calls through, but I didn't. Sure enough, the telephone rang yet again.

"Kathryn Lewis on the phone Wally."

"Walter Henry, hello?"

"You bastard. You absolute bastard." She had clearly been drinking...

"What is it Kathryn?"

"Since you like causing deaths, I thought I'd give you another one to chalk up."

"What do you mean?"

"I'm going to commit suicide and I thought you'd like to know about it in advance. I won't tell you where I am so you won't be able to do anything about it. You took my man away from me and now I'm going to join him. I've got all my pills and another bottle of whisky and I'm going to do it as soon as I put the phone down. What's more I've already told everyone it was all down to you being a fuck-ing useless probation officer...."

I just wasn't prepared for this. In any case this wasn't in the training manual and I had no idea how to cope. I was completely tongue-tied. I listened; I didn't interrupt – but I didn't think of anything I could helpfully say. All the while her tirade grew in velocity, volume and vitriol. I wondered how much more I needed to apologise – or whether an apology meant I accepted it was all my fault that Irving fell off an eighth-floor parapet to his death.

"... and I don't even know why I'm bothering to say good-bye to you. When you read about my horrible death, you'll never forgive yourself and you'll always remember me." This was going nowhere: I had to interrupt.

"Kathryn, Kathryn, I'm sorry you're going to commit suicide."

"Oh, why?" *(Wally, don't engage. Stop. You're out of your depth here.)*

"Because, because.... Because you'll miss the canoeing tomorrow." *(Oh my God, Wally, what ARE you doing? Are you totally insensitive?)*

"What canoeing?"

"Don't you remember I told you about the Wednesday afternoon activities. Tomorrow we're going canoeing on the canal in the City Road basin."

"U-u-u-u-mm, I've never been canoe-ing."

"Oh, that's a pity. Looks like you've missed your chance now," I heard myself say. *(Oh my God, Wally, how crass. That's even worse! Say something else...)*

"Well why don't you come?"

"Me? What time?"

"Meet here at one thirty – no later. We've got a minibus to take us down there." There was a long pause. Not being able to find any words, I let it run on....

"You STUPID man..." she screamed, "You think I'd do it, don't you? Well, I would have liked to but I've got other plans. Just wait till they see all the things I've written about you. You won't stand a chance with all these allegations. They'll come straight to your office and arrest you. You'll be in jail before the week's out. See how you like it." And with that she hung up the phone.

Try writing a report after that...

Once the Social Enquiry Report goes off to court, it's anyone's guess as to what might happen. The magistrate might follow the author's recommendation, or disregard it altogether, with or without any explanation. On occasion the sentencer expresses an opinion on the calibre of the report, challenging the reasoning, the English or the wisdom of the recommendation. If this happens, the court duty probation officer present at the time of the sentence will write a note to the author, or, in cases where the judge is highly critical, the officer might telephone the author with a friendly warning that there may be problems coming down the road. While on court duty I have heard magistrates – and even a Crown Court Judge – openly criticise the standard of English in a probation report.

"How is one to conclude that a probation officer who cannot string two words together might be expected to control an offender in the community? One isn't looking for a work of literature, merely a coherent report with cogent arguments," said one.

Oliver Pollard 's report was mailed to Clerkenwell Magistrates' Court just about in time for the date set for sentencing. Sometimes, for any one of a variety of possible reasons, a case doesn't go ahead at the appointed time and is moved to a future date. The convicted person might fail to attend, for example, for valid medical reasons, lapse of memory, or sheer fright, or perhaps an appearance in another, superior, court which has taken precedence. The prosecution could have other offences to add and require time to assemble the case or conversely wish to move the case to another court to be married up with other matters. It's all too easy to forget about it once the report has been written, signed, checked and despatched from the author's office. New ones will be allocated without delay and the process begins all over again. I recall receiving results of court reports that I'd forgotten all about because so much time had elapsed between meeting the offender, writing the report and sentence being passed.

18. City Road Basin

Sylvester Mittee was an exhilarating person to work with. His sense of humour, his infectious laugh, his positive attitude all combined to produce this charismatic person with enormous energy and enthusiasm. But attractive as the idea of canoeing might be, even on a January day, I just couldn't work up any enthusiasm for it. I was afraid of Kathryn and what she might do.

It was a dull but mild day. I prayed for snow – or at least frost so the canal would freeze over. I'm clearly not big on prayers: the sun came out and it got warmer. By one-thirty there were seven people waiting for this afternoon's adventure. But Kathryn was not among them. *(Oh no, did I really expect her to come? Was I that easily fobbed off? She's dead and I did nothing about it. That's twice. Two people dead because of me.)*

Sylvester was rounding up the crew. Five men, two women. It was a good turnout. *(And you're just going to go off with them and not check? Callous swine.)* I went back into the general office and telephoned Kathryn's flat. It rang and rang. I imagined her lying there dead or comatose. Now what do I do? Sylvester came back into the staff room.

"Come on Wally."

"Sylv, I can't go. I think there's an emergency at Kathryn's flat. I have to check it out."

"Well I can't take responsibility for eight novices on my own. I need someone to help. Could you ask someone else to cover for you?"

"Canoeing or checking the emergency?"

"Either. Or, I've got an idea, why don't we drive to the place you've got to check? If it's a real emergency we'll be there to help."

"Sylvester, you're brilliant!" I said as we came back into reception and made our way to the minibus which by now was full of expectant adventurers.

"Headcount?"

"Ten including us."

"Ten? Wait a minute that's not right. I counted seven clients and us in the waiting room... that's ni...." I mounted the steps into the minibus and counted again.

"Kathryn! How did you get in here?"

"I followed everyone on, isn't it? I thought you were already in the bus." I was never so pleased to hear a Welsh accent.

The historic system of canals in Britain was, for nearly two hundred years, the main highway for freight such as coal, iron ore, clay, building materials and much else. Most of these cargoes were transported on the major canals, one of which, the Grand Union Canal, joined London and Birmingham in the Midlands, where it linked to Manchester in the north-west. Early in the nineteenth century, industrialists and entrepreneurs formed a plan to enable traffic to reach the London docks in Limehouse, East London by linking the end of the Grand Union to the River Thames. Designed by John Nash for the Prince Regent, the Regents Canal was constructed. The undulating terrain called for the construction of several tunnels, notably the Islington Canal Tunnel more than half a mile long under The Angel, Islington whose eastern end opened onto the City Road lock, aqueous gateway to Hackney.

Along the route, docks or 'basins' were created to encourage trade by facilitating loading and unloading of materials and merchandise to or from London Docks, or the North of England.

Trade is silent now, the Victorian warehouse buildings lining most of the basins hosting fancy apartments or new construction sites, but the City Road Basin retained a facility, part-funded by the municipality, for education, training and leisure.

Part of this was devoted to a canoeing centre, which is where Sylvester had arranged for our group to spend a cold winter morning. We were welcomed by two of the staff and all listened attentively to a water-safety session, then togged up with lifejackets. Men and women were supervised into their canoes. I was last on the jetty... with Kathryn.

"I'm not getting in that."

"Kathryn, it's perfectly safe - it's a canoe."

"It's not safe. Look how it wobbles in the water. I'm not getting in one of those. I'm going to walk home."

"Oh for God's sake, Kathryn, I give up. Look, why don't you share that big one with me?"

"Oh, alright then."

I got in at the stern in an ungainly manner. As the canoe adjusted to my not insubstantial weight, it sank dangerously low in the water. I was new to this but thought it a little late to 'fess up' now. I held the canoe as rigidly as I could against the wooden jetty while Kathryn clambered into the front and sat facing forward with her back to me. As we pushed off, she shouted over her shoulder:

"By the way, I can't swim. If I decide to do it now, you might find this a very mem-morable trip...."

And that was the last I heard from her for about an hour. We paddled with the others under the instruction of Sylvester and the canoeing club leader, a competent woman even smaller than Kathryn. I tried making conversation with my crewmate but if she replied, I didn't hear it. We canoed up and down the City Road basin for a while, first all together, then in twos, then singly, and when it looked as though most of us had got the hang of it, we were led off down the canal toward Hackney.

It was fascinating to see the streets of East London from the water. After a short distance, we passed the ruined war damaged buildings of the old carpet warehouse where film actor Charles Chaplin was employed as a youth before deciding to go to Hollywood to seek his fortune. The bombed-out buildings were now used as a film set for thrillers and horror movies. Later they were to be redeveloped as luxury apartments.

There was the usual banter among the men and boys in the canoes, cat-calling and wolf-whistling at young women on the towpath, shouting in tunnels to listen to the echoes, but an hour later I was relieved to arrive back at the boathouse. Thank God it had been an uneventful trip. Kathryn never spoke once.

As we handed back our lifejackets and warmed our hands on mugs of tea, Sylvester went over to Kathryn, "I could see you were enjoying yourself. In fact I thought your face had frozen into that broad grin. You're still glowing."

"I loved every minute of it, Sylvester, and I'm really glad I came. What's happening next week? Can I come to that as well?"

"Of course, that what it's for."

On the way back to the office we dropped some of the participants as we passed near their houses. Kathryn asked not to be dropped off because she wanted to talk to me. In truth, my heart sank. I was still anxious....

"I had a phone call from Irving's brother in America," she later told me. "He wants me to send all his things back there. If I pay for it, he'll reimburse me. I don't know anything about him and I don't even know if it's really his brother. I called the last number Irving had – which is about three years old – and spoke to someone who sounded sad, but detached, when I gave him the news. It was a few days before he rang back asking for Irving's things but the trouble is, I don't even know if it was the same person who rang back. You can imagine I've been in no fit state to remember things since it happened."

"What do you want to do with Irving's things?"

"He didn't have much. His guitar, his mother's ring, which he gave to me to wear," Kathryn held out her left hand to show me a simple gold band on her wedding finger, "his clothes and a rucksack. I'd rather leave them where they are for the time being."

"Then do just that. Why should you parcel everything up, mail it off at your expense to someone you don't know and never even met who has no greater claim on them than you, in the hope that you might be repaid? And if he's not Irving's brother, what if his real brother turns up?"

"So you don't think I should do anything?"

"Do you? It's what you think that's important."

"I can't focus on it at the moment."

"Then that's fine – you don't have to."

"Wally?"

"Yes?"

"I want to say something but it's very difficult."

130

"If it's too difficult Kathryn, don't say it, especially if you might regret it later."

"I want to. I want to say I'm sorry for being so horrible to you. I've felt so, so, well, so, oh, I don't know.... Irving said you were the first person in his life that ever reached out to him. He wished he'd had a father like you and now..." she began to sob.

"Kathryn, I think I know what you're trying to say. But don't get upset. You've come through a lot and it's understandable that I haven't been your favourite person."

"But you'll be wanting to hand me over to another probation officer?"

"Kathryn, you've been very hard on me but now you've apologised. That chapter is coming to an end. It's true I've been pretty exasperated – I miss Irving too: he was a very special person – but even if I wanted to give your file to another officer, which I don't yet, I don't think it would be allowed."

"I ought to go."

"Where are you off to? Do you have someone to be with you?"

"Martin said he'd come round. We're going to cook something. I haven't eaten properly for days. After that canoeing, I'm starving."

"That's a good sign, Kathryn. See you same time next week."

A couple of days later I received a notification from court in response to my report. Oliver Pollard was given a conditional discharge for his naked wanderings in the streets. There was a wry note at the foot of the form: "The magistrate commented on the very helpful report. He instructed Mr. Pollard to seek help from the probation service if he needed specific assistance. He should ask for Mr. Henry and if he wasn't available, he should go away and not trouble anyone else." *(Great, Wally,' I thought, 'You've just been sentenced to life with Oliver Pollard.)*

———

19. Office Duty

Probation work involves a certain amount of absence from the office. For a start, there's court duty – a day and a half each fortnight – then home visits. Throughcare clients – those in prison wanting to maintain contact with their home probation officer – are entitled to expect their nominated officers to visit them once in a while, then there are the inevitable training courses, both in the borough and at Head Office. Every few months there's a joint – borough-wide (or several boroughs) – team meeting at a different office each time; yet the work has to continue, and someone must always be available in the office to cover for absent colleagues. In addition, ill-health and sick leave, seemed to me to be rife among some colleagues and everyone gets annual leave.

The Office Duty Rota caters for these situations. Each officer takes a turn at covering the office for client visits, casual callers, phone calls, outside enquiries, in fact anything that crops up that cannot be otherwise handled. On my arrival at Englefield Road office, Jackie had suggested I wait six months to get the hang of things before going on the rota. Though I'd helped colleagues out a couple of times by covering their temporary absences, that time had now arrived and today was my first on solo office duty.

During Kathryn's diatribe the call waiting signal intruded on her attack. As I put the receiver down weakly, the phone rang again. It was June.

"Mr. Tudor in reception. He wants to see Richard. Richard's on leave. I've got you down as duty officer today. Can you see him?" I had to remind myself it was Wednesday and I'd agreed to do it; I felt wrung-out and ill-prepared, especially after that awful phone call. It turned out to be a baptism of fire: I had already dealt with a couple of minor interruptions from various probation caseloads, mine included, while writing Mr. Pollard's report on the spare office computer. Dealing with a manipulative and somewhat threatening client wanting money led to losing a part-written report, and I was already miffed before Kathryn's phone call. Now I was ragged – and frazzled – and it wasn't even lunchtime. *(Welcome to the office duty rota!)*

"I'll be right down, June," I heard myself say. My heart was no longer in this. I guess you can go off jobs just the same as you can go off people, I thought, as I went downstairs to the reception area.

"Mr. Tudor?"

"Yeah."

I stretched out my hand to greet him. The gesture went unreciprocated. "Hi. My name's Walter Henry and I'm doing office duty today while Richard is away."

"Fuck off."

"I beg your pardon?"

"I said fuck off. You're all a bunch of useless arseholes here. Probation officers are a complete waste of space, all except Mr. Richard. He's the only decent probation officer I've ever met and I want nothing to do with any of you."

"I'm sorry but he's not here. You'll have to wait until he comes back."

"Don't give me that crap. His car's outside and I want to see him. If he don't come down I'll have to go up, now fuck off out of the way." Funny how thoughts race through your head: *(Is this the*

reality my boss Jackie was trying to tell me about in supervision?
Do I need this? Why don't I just quit now?)

Mr. Tudor was much taller than I. He was powerfully built, agitated, and I was intimidated. We stood face to face for several moments during which I arrived at the wise conclusion it would be pointless even to try to stand in his way. Why don't I just show him Richard's deserted office and let him go on his way? I wondered. Nevertheless, I beckoned to him to sit down and backed off into June's reception office to look at the file she had thoughtfully taken from the records cabinet. I read Richard's meticulous notes.

"Shane Tudor was the victim of an attack in a pub. Unfortunately the assailants chose the wrong man to try to rob and he got the better of all four of them. When police arrived they were all laid out on the floor and taken to hospital where they had time to concoct their story. Poor Mr. Tudor got four years for his trouble. Since he steadfastly refused to admit his guilt and constantly maintained his innocence, he was refused parole and served the statutory time in full. Even when, after Shane's imprisonment, the same four men were themselves convicted for an identical robbery, in what he interpreted as a racist response, the court refused to entertain his appeal. What was worse, he seemed to have slipped through the net and was very bitter to have received no support at all from the probation service during his sentence." Richard's meticulous notes on the file were riveting. I read on. "He has no obligation to report at this probation office but now he's released after serving the statutory term without remission I will try to give him whatever support he needs...." What's good enough for Richard is good enough for me. I emerged from June's office trying not to show I was nervous.

"Mr. Tudor, Richard is away on holiday for two weeks. I'm going to make myself a cup of tea. If you'd like tea or coffee you are welcome to a cup but if you don't want me to try to help you, then please leave. How much sugar do you have in tea or coffee?"

"Three. Coffee" then, as a very late afterthought, "...Please."

While the kettle boiled, I composed myself and prepared to start again. Back in the reception area I handed Mr. Tudor his coffee. He still looked like a thundercloud.

"What did you want to see Mr. Richard about?"

"Is there an interview room or could we go to your office?."

"Oh, of course, I'm sorry. Come this way." We went to a dingy interview room.

"Since I've been out of prison, I haven't used any alcohol. I've got myself a small flat and I signed up for electricity but now the bill has come and I can't pay it. Now they're threatening to cut it off." He pulled out his crumpled energy bill. The form was printed entirely in red: in bold typeface at the top were the words "FINAL DEMAND".

"If they take it away, I won't get the support I need from A.A."

"A.A.?"

"Alcoholics Anonymous. Christ! Are you new or something? I've got a sponsor and when I'm feeling low, I phone him and he talks to me. If I lose my phone, it's all over."

"Have you spoken to the electricity company?"

"Whatever for? I owe them money." He clearly had little time for probation officers. The tone of his voice indicated he thought I qualified for the same contempt. He might just as well have added the word "idiot" to the end of each sentence.

"What did you want your probation officer to do, Mr. Tudor?"

"I dunno. He's usually so willing to help me. But I don't know what he could do."

"Would you like me to phone the electricity company?"

"And say what?"

"Let's suck it and see, shall we?" I was already dialling... "Thank you for calling LEB. This is Sheila how can I help?"

"Hello, my name's Walter Henry, I'm a probation officer and I'm calling on behalf of one of my clients. I need your advice over a delicate matter."

"Go on Mr. Henry, I'll see what I can do." This came from a warm northern voice of a woman aged, I would say, fifty. I already wanted to hug her. I gave her Mr. Tudor's account number and address.

"My client has been released from a prison sentence into the community. He's doing extremely well but the threat of losing his domestic electricity is causing considerable tension and I think that may hinder his rehabilitation. I can confirm that the probation service is providing all the support it can and is helping Mr. Tudor to get back into education and training. It would be a great shame if our efforts were hindered by a situation that could be managed in some way." I sounded like an automaton reading from a lame script but I continued.

"He has received an electricity cut-off notice and is worried that, without power in his flat he will not survive in the community and may re-offend. Mr. Tudor is clearly a responsible and principled person and I believe it would be enormously helpful if we could find a way to avoid cutting off his electricity."

"OK. Mr. Henry, I get the picture." said the Angel of Mercy. "Is Mr. Tudor working?"

"Are you working, Mr. Tudor?"

"No. I get income support." He was scowling.

"No, he's on income support."

"How much is the bill? – Oh, now I can see it on the screen. Well it's under forty pounds. How much a week could Mr.Tudor pay?"

"How much could you pay each week, Mr. Tudor?"

"Not much. I'm on benefit." Still scowling.

"I heard that. Ask him if he could afford five pounds a week."

"How about a fiver a week?"

"Ermmm.... Yeah, I think I could do that." Then, as if wishing he hadn't said it, "Maybe."

"Yes, he could do that, maybe." I felt like a moron repeating each person's words to the other. "Look, could he speak to you himself?" Hoping this Angel of Mercy might work a miracle, I handed Mr. Tudor the phone. With any luck her voice might cast the same spell on him as it had on me. He nodded as he listened and growled 'Thank you' two or three times. He listened a little more, then said "Yeah... errmmm yeah... OK." Then he said he would try to get the whole bill settled before the next one was due in about two months' time. I found this encouraging. People are much more likely to achieve what they actually say they will achieve, than they are to achieve goals which are no more than unspoken dreams.

But wait! Mr. Tudor was handing me the phone. As he did so, his face broke into a broad grin. It was as though the sun had come out in that dark and gloomy room. Before bidding me good-bye and thanking me, Sheila told me of the agreement she had reached with Mr. Tudor and said that if there were any more trouble, he or I should call the number on the bill and speak only to her.

As Mr. Tudor stood up to leave he looked at me sternly, then smiled: "I was wrong about you." he said, offering his hand which I grasped and shook proudly. Any thoughts of resigning evaporated.

---

20. Ulrich Verwood

In my tray next day was another new report request. I wrote to Mr. Verwood with offers of two appointments. This was an offence of 'theft from employer', a misdemeanour which the courts regard very seriously. To bite the hand that feeds you is, in the view of society, an unforgivable act. I always found it difficult, when reading the blunt facts on a request for a court report, not to form some kind of immediate response – usually of anger, disgust or dismay – exactly as any member of the public might when reading about it in the newspaper. Reading the file and interviewing the perpetrator often put the entire affair into context and it became easier to see how it all happened.

Mr. Verwood was a case in point. He arrived at the office a clean, casually dressed, small man in his forties with slight build but a big smile and large spectacles. He was open, no, talkative – garrulous even – but seemed to have not an ounce of malice in him. Yes, he stole the money from his employer, but far from trying to hide the fact, he meticulously recorded what he took in order to repay it, leaving a note in the till to remind himself and his employer how much he owed. He did not intend to 'permanently deprive' (a definition of theft) his employer of the money.

I asked him why he pleaded 'Guilty'. He told me that his solicitor had asked exactly the same question – even tried to persuade him not to do so, but he was adamant. In his view, borrowing without consent and stealing from the till both meant the same thing. Moreover, if he had tried to defend his position and lost, the court would be likely to be more punitive. He felt he needed to nail this problem once and for all and I began to gain the feeling that he was a man propelled by some inner plan, which only he really understood.

What problem did he want to nail? I wanted to try to understand it too. Mr. Verwood was a gambler. His habit appeared to be a sporadic one, comparable to some drinkers who binge, he said,

140

yet he could not say what the trigger was. He had several bouts of gambling to his credit, though none had led to theft or court action. His only previous offence was criminal damage as a juvenile – a boyish prank drawing moustaches onto advertisement hoardings – quite unrelated to the present incident.

Horses were his weakness, like his father's. He saw other similarities between himself and his father who was a painter and decorator and who left his wife and family when Mr. Verwood was about eleven. His own marriage broke up six years previously when his youngest daughter was nearly the same age. She was disabled by a genetic spinal disorder and, like a disproportionate number of marriages affected by a disability in the family, the marriage fell apart. He did not use that argument himself, but rather blamed his own incompetence as a father. I recalled once hearing a lecturer from the National Deaf Children's Society state that while, nationally, divorce had reached the level of one marriage in three, in families with a disabled child the rate was approximately twice that at two-thirds.

Mr. Verwood ("Oh for God's sake," he pleaded, "call me Rick. My dad named me after my German mum, Ulrika.") was a lively and convivial conversationalist. It was not difficult to see why he was successful as a relief pub manager. His engaging personality and his self-effacing humour would have made him popular behind any bar. During a spell when there was little painting and decorating work, a friend who managed a public house asked Mr. Verwood if he would be willing to stand in during a planned holiday. He waved aside Mr. Verwood' protestations that he had no experience and assured him he would learn it in no time. In fact he did, and the brewery offered to train him up as a regular relief manager. It was his fifth or sixth posting when he decided to 'borrow' the money.

"I had started gambling again" he said "though I don't know why. I have got used to living with my mum again and with regular well-paid work I found life quite easy."

"How long was it since your previous spate of gambling?"

"It was seven months. I remember because my daughter was in hospital. She had an operation on her spine."

"What about the time before that?"

"She was in hospital again, as it happens. She'd had some kind of relapse and was admitted in emer... gen....cy." His voice trailed off in the middle of the word, which he completed weakly after a few seconds.

"What's up?"

"She had been re-admitted when this offence happened. That's three episodes where I was gambling when she was in hospital. I'd never thought of it till this moment."

"But it was you who made the connection."

"Yes. I wonder how her mother copes with all that stress," he mumbled as if guiltily. "She's got two other daughters to look after and they're a handful. Teenage girls can't be easy." It was a strange moment. There were tears in his eyes, yet a look of quiet relief came over his face.

"I think I'll go and see them tonight."

"Do you want to phone from here?"

"Thanks, yes that would be a good idea. Can I let my mum know as well?"

"Fine." I realised the thread of our interview had now broken and decided to call it a day. "We need to meet once more. Can you make it same time on Tuesday?"

"Sure, same time. And thanks. Goodbye." I saw him out to the front reception office; we shook hands and he left. Mr. Verwood kept his appointment punctually the following week and furnished much more useful information for the report I was able to write in time for his appearance for sentencing a few days later.

I was on court duty on the day of sentencing. The ageing male stipendiary magistrate, not known for leniency, was regarded as one of the most severe, pompous, 'old school' judges on the local circuit. Mr. Verwood had clearly taken a good deal of trouble with his appearance, though he looked nervous in his slightly oversized suit, his thick spectacle lenses glinting with reflections from the harsh lights of the courtroom. I noticed he was carrying a blue synthetic leather overnight bag. Someone had primed him that he probably wasn't going home for a while. His solicitor, whom he admired, was unable to attend, having another commitment at a superior court. Instead Mr. Verwood's defence was conducted by a junior barrister who unashamedly behaved as though his client should be hung, drawn and quartered.

The magistrate read the report in an inappropriately short time appearing to toss it aside as if to demonstrate his disgust. Ulrich Verwood sat in the dock looking straight ahead while his counsel lamely mitigated on his behalf. If I was disappointed by the lack-lustre speech from the man whose job it was to defend his interests, Mr. Verwood must have been mortified. His advocate's trite mitigation could not disguise the notion that the defence barrister hoped his client would 'go down' for a long time. As the very young barrister sat down, the clerk bade Mr. Verwood to stand.

The magistrate looked harshly at him and said sternly, "Mr. Verwood .... One of the most serious crimes of dishonesty is theft from employer. You were placed in a position of considerable trust, which you abused. The only punishment for theft from employer is a custodial sentence, and this offence is not insignificant. As the loss is almost the maximum amount that can be tried in this court, it clearly merits the maximum sentence available to me which is a lengthy term of imprisonment. I have read the report by the probation officer and though I acknowledge that there are some significant problems in your life, that can be said of almost everybody, and most people don't go around stealing from their employers. The report writer makes no mention of that."

"You say you intended to repay the money but there is little evidence to support this." Ulrich Verwood looked down at his shoes. His head was only just visible above the rail of the dock. There was a long tense silence as the magistrate seemed to read the report again. This time he must have reached the end and seen that the signatory was the same person listed as his court duty probation officer. He glanced briefly, but coldly in my direction.

When the magistrate looked up, the barrister rose again.

"Ye-e-e-esss?" asked the magistrate impatiently, as if to say 'What do you want now?' but, rather than wait for the barrister's response, continued addressing the quivering wreck in the dock. "It seems from the report" the magistrate continued, "the brewery declined any offer of repayment for fear of prejudicing court proceedings. Nevertheless, you should be given the opportunity to do so." And to the defence counsel he said, accusingly "Why did you make no mention of this when you had the opportunity? How much has the defendant saved to this end?"

The brief walked over to the dock and spoke quietly to his client. Returning to his place he said to the magistrate "He is still in employment and has six hundred and fifty pounds with him to pay into court today." The magistrate was visibly impressed though clearly annoyed with the defence for not mentioning this in his mitigation. "The author of the report" the barrister continued, "is present this morning."

"Mr. Verwood." Ulrich stood up. "That, to me, is the kind of evidence I would have been looking for. It would have been much more helpful for the court to be told that at the outset." The magistrate leaned forward in his chair slightly, appearing to adopt a faintly more benign manner than that of his earlier irritated interaction with the defence counsel. "The author of the report" he added, "seems to think that he could help you deal with some of your problems. I am prepared to make a probation order if your probation officer will see to it that you continue to pay compensation to the loser. Do you agree?"

"Yes sir."

"Very well, a Probation Order of one year, compensation of one thousand nine hundred and fifty pounds to be paid within six months monitored under a Money Supervision Order."

I left the court momentarily to give Mr. Verwood his first appointment. Clutching his now redundant overnight bag he looked immensely relieved, as well he might.

"I just don't believe it," he said. "One minute I'm heading straight for jail, next I'm standing out here. Thanks Mr. Wally." Then he went straight to the court cash office to pay in the money he had saved and I gave him a date and time for his first appointment and returned to court duty.

Mr. Verwood turned out to be a model probationer. Over the next few weeks and months he maintained his appointments regularly and punctually; conversation was easy and he was clearly doing well in his job. His employer was a major force in the exhibition trade and he was promoted to foreman of an eight-man team. They would fit out and decorate trade-show booths and stands to their heart's content then dismantle and remove the whole outfit at the end of the exhibition. He was often required to travel to far-away cities throughout the country in which case he would routinely phone and re-arrange the appointment or leave a contact number at his digs or hotel where he could be reached.

He continued to pay off his compensation to the brewery and from time to time showed me his diminishing balance on the statement issued by the court office. As a way of reducing his alcohol consumption when travelling away he would choose modest commercial or B&B hotels which did not have a licensed bar.

21. Getting Busier...

There was a call waiting signal as I was on the phone to Wormwood Scrubs booking a prison visit for a court report interview. It was June reminding me I was duty officer again today.

"Martin Norland in reception for you, Wally. Sounds like an office duty visit but he asked for you by name."

"Really, June? I wonder what he wants." I recalled he was Irving Jensen's closest friend. As I came down the stairs to the reception area, I saw Martin Norland's large frame topped by a spectacular shock of hair, sitting in a corner of reception. He'd stopped by the office without appointment in the hope of seeing me. "It's slightly embarrassing," he told me quietly as we shook hands. "I've been arrested and I'm going to plead guilty. Will you do a report for me?" He seemed very open about this considering we were standing in the public reception area and others were waiting to be seen by their officers.

"You? Martin, I'm astonished. I can't pretend otherwise. Have you been to court yet?"

"No. I'm due in court tomorrow. When I told my solicitor that I knew you he suggested I come to see you today."

"I don't get to choose what reports I do – they're allocated on a cab-rank basis. Next one in goes to the next person available. But I can speak to my senior and see if she'll pass it over to me. What happened?"

"Shoplifting. Videos."

"Why?"

"I thought you knew."

"Knew what?"

"Heroin."

"WHAT??"

"I use heroin. I inject. Me – scared of needles, yet I inject."

This was all too much for me. "Wait a minute. You said you wouldn't let Irving Jensen stay with you because of the drugs."

"Of course, that's right. He may have been always drunk but he was drug-free. It was I who was using. I didn't want to do it while he was there in case it caused a relapse."

"Wally, call for you and another waiting." June called through the glass screen.

"Martin, I'll do whatever I can to help. Your solicitor will ask for a report?"

"Yes. I can see you're busy. Byee-e-e!"

"Put the call through to my room, June. I'm going straight back there." Then, out of breath,

"Hi, it's Walter Henry. Sorry to keep you waiting."

"Hello. It's Bernard Bryce, probation officer at HMP Camp Hill on the Isle of Wight. Barry Church is here doing four years and I understand you're his allocated home probation officer."

"That's right. I'm waiting for the file."

"He wants to see you and says it's urgent."

"Does he plan to write to me?"

"Maybe, but I just wanted to let you know that he worries a lot. He's also a pathological liar so you need to be warned."

"What do you mean?"

"He'll probably tell you he's being ill-treated."

"And is he?"

"Not a chance. This is Camp Hill."

"I'll arrange a visit. I probably need to OK it with my senior. Shall I look you up when I arrive?"

"No need. I work part-time. You can only visit on Thursdays but I'm not here then."

"Fine, we'll talk again."

Barry Church was serving a four-year sentence for wounding, grievous bodily harm, affray and criminal damage. He was sentenced about a year before I took over the case but the file had been mislaid. His folder in my filing cabinet contained only the latest couple of letters and forms. Of course, no-one had been to see him since he was sentenced – a serious mistake, but before my arrival at the office. A visit was well overdue. I made arrangements to go the following week and subsequently asked around in the office in case any colleagues wanted to share the ride to see their own clients. Only Richard was interested but he had just been so we agreed to confer next time.

Almost immediately the phone rang again - another insistent ring....

"Hello, Walter Henry."

"Jonathan Pettwood at HMP Highpoint here. Your client Wilfred Xanoffi is up for parole and needs a report. You saw him recently. He says he can stay with his parents. Could you check it out please?"

"Yes, I've been asked to do a pre-parole home circumstances report and have an appointment with them later this week. I should have the report by Friday."

"Fine, he's due before the parole board a week today." "No problem. Bye."

Meanwhile, it was a beautiful day, I was busy and I was enjoying it. There were two new report requests in my pigeonhole. Jackie Stuart, a shoplifter was in HMP Holloway women's prison awaiting sentence and Frank Grover, a burglar, in custody in Latchmere House. I made appointments to see them. Only after I put the phone down did I realise I'd just made an appointment to visit Frank Grover at Wormwood Scrubs. Were there two of them, or could Mr. Grover be in two places at once? A quick call to the Scrubs yielded the news that Mr. Grover had been transferred out after I'd booked the visit. No, they hadn't planned to tell me. The phone rang again.

"Yvonne Zeefort in reception asking for duty officer."

"Who is she, June?"

"The family's well-known to us though only her sister is on the books at present. She's Richard's client. Her brother's serving eight years but doesn't want probation contact. Yvonne's known at this office but not currently allocated to anyone. She has a baby with her." I went immediately downstairs to reception.

"Hello Yvonne, I'm on office duty today. My name's Walter Henry." Yvonne was in her early twenties, with striking features though I guessed she was currently not taking much care of herself.

"Yeah, hi." She ignored my outstretched hand. "Can I see you?"

"Yes. Down here?"

"No, in an office." We went upstairs to my room where, once seated, Yvonne took the blanket wrapping her infant, laid it out on the floor, then placed the baby on it.

"I've just come out of prison and I want to go to a rehab. How do I do it?"

"Drugs or alcohol?"

"Both."

"Are you registered at the Drug Dependency Unit?"

"No. It's a waste of time. There's a six-week waiting list. I could be dead before they see me."

"Have you tried?"

"No."

"Why do you want to go to a rehab."

"Because I've had it with all these drugs. And I want to stop drinking as well."

"How much do you use?" "About half a gram a day." "Chasing?"

"I'm injecting."

"What about alcohol?"

"About nine big cans of Extra Strong per day. More if I can't get the gear." (heroin)

"What have you done so far to find a rehab?"

"I've come to probation."

"How old is your baby."

"She's six weeks. I had her in prison."

"Do Social Services know about you or the baby?"

"No."

"Is that a good idea?"

"Why?"

"Because they would be the first port of call in getting the kind of help you say you want."

"All they do is take babies away from their mothers. I seen it happen in prison."

"That's not entirely true. In fact, it's not in their interest to do that. What a baby needs above all else is a mother. It makes most sense for Social Services to do all they can to help the mother to keep her child. It's usually the cheapest option as well."

"They have a funny way of doing it then."

"Do you know any rehabs you'd like to approach then?

"Yeah. The one in Islington. Milton, I think it's called"

"Why that one?"

"I've heard it's good, it's near and it's the only one I know." There was something very flat, deflating, about our conversation and I realised I was contributing to it by conducting the interview in the same detached tone as Yvonne's.

"Yvonne I really think your best bet is to ask the DDU to get you a place. I know you don't think they could help but I could phone them and ask them to see you right away."

"Why would they do that then? I've already had a knockback from them."

"When, recently?"

"No, before I went into prison."

"How long ago was that?"

"About four years."

"Have you been away that long?"

"Well, yes."

"What does that mean?" It couldn't be true if she has a six-week-old baby.

"I came out last May and went back in three months ago. Liah was born in Hollywood." (The inmates' term for HMP Holloway.)

"I'm going to call the DDU."

"Hi William, it's Walter Henry at Hackney Probation. I'm looking for your advice. I have someone here with a six-week-old baby wanting to go to rehab. I understood you were the best people to refer to rehab but I've heard you may have a long waiting list. What's my best course of action?"

"Is your client by any chance Yvonne Zeefort?"

"Yes, it might well be." I didn't want to appear to be disclosing too much information to him in front of her.

"We don't have that many patients with six-week-old babies," he continued. "Social Services notified us. We asked her to come in but she hasn't shown up."

"Should we look around for a rehab or is it better if you do it?"

"Best if we do it."

"How soon?"

"We could see her tomorrow morning or Friday. We prioritise mothers of young children."

"Hang on, I'll check." Yvonne said she could go in the morning. I told William.

"Fine. Tell her to ask for me."

"Thanks, goodbye William."

"Can you get to the DDU tomorrow about nine thirty? Ask for William."

"Yes"

"Where are you living, Yvonne?"

"Wiv me boyfriend."

"Where does he live?

"Wiv 'is mum. Opposite me mum's house. She'll look after Leanne for me tomorrow." As if in response, the baby threw up on the blanket. I handed Yvonne a bunch of tissues. She picked up her daughter, cleaned her face then cursorily wiped the blanket before picking it up and wrapping it round Leanne leaving the vomit filled tissues on my office floor.

"I'll come and see you again?" she said as we went downstairs.

"Best to see whoever is on duty, I think, Yvonne."

"OK. Bye."

A couple of days later there was a note in my pigeonhole. Jackie wanted to talk to me. I poked my head round her door to see if she was in her office.

"Come in Wally. I've got an interesting project for you. I'd like you to do a report on someone convicted of shoplifting."

"Why's it interesting?"

"It's interesting because the person concerned has specifically requested that you do the report."

"Ah yes, I meant to talk to you about that. I was approached by someone who was a close friend of Irving Jensen. I've got to know him pretty well and he's been charged with stealing videos and wants a report. He asked if I'd do it for him."

"Is it something you'd like to do?"

"Well, I already have considerable background about the bloke."

"OK what's the name? I'll make a note of it when it comes in."

" Martin Norland. Thanks." I made as if to leave.

"Where are you going Wally, I wanted to talk to you about a report, remember?"

"I thought you just did, Jackie. Wasn't that it?"

"No, I've got a special one here. Someone appeared at Old Street (magistrates' court) and has specifically asked for you to do the report. She said no-one else will do."

"Is it someone I know?"

"Apparently."

"Well who, then?"

" Yvonne Zeefort."

"Absolutely not."

"Why ever not?"

"Well... this isn't a supermarket you know. People can't go picking and choosing their report writers. Whatever next?"

"Like Martin Norland, you mean?"

"Well he's different. He already knew me."

"True of Yvonne as well. I understand she came and interviewed you for the job. The word is you did quite well, according to the court duty probation officer's note."

"Look, Jackie, I'm not keen on..."

"OK. Listen," Jackie didn't often cut me short, "I'll put both files in your tray. Take a look at them. If you won't do them both, put them both back in mine." I got the message.

---

22. Barry Church's Strange Behaviour

The drive to Portsmouth is quick and uneventful if you start at five on a dark February morning. Richard had told me that if I wanted to get to Camp Hill and back in a day, I should leave home really early, catch the 8 o'clock ferry to the Isle of Wight and complete the visit before lunch leaving the afternoon for a leisurely return with perhaps enough time to complete my report before close of business. I planned to arrive at the ferry terminal in time to have breakfast and made good time.

At the almost empty departure zone, I left my car where directed, bought a day return ticket and, before I could find where to buy some food - or at least some coffee - a port official beckoned me to hurry up as the ferry was waiting to sail. Thinking my car was blocking others from embarkation, and still worried about finding some breakfast, I moved it in the direction he indicated, only to find myself aboard. Only then did I realise it was only 7.15 a.m. and the ferry was pulling away from the quay. There were two other vehicles aboard and the refreshment bar declined to open for three passengers.

I had lived in Portsmouth for a while as a college student and had been looking forward to seeing the town again as the boat glided past Southsea and into the Solent. Disappointingly, it was still dark and a mist appeared as soon as we sailed so I saw nothing, not even the street lights. The sea was smooth as a mirror but there was no view. In the daylight at the other end I discovered, on disembarking, that it would be nearly two hours before I could gain entry to the prison, which I decided to find before stopping for food.

At this juncture, looking at my map, I realised I had come to the wrong ferry port. I should have departed from Southampton for Cowes. Instead, I had arrived at Ryde, much further to the east. When I eventually found Camp Hill - one of three of Her Majesty's Prisons in close proximity to each other - almost in the centre of the island - there was neither any sign of a café or restaurant for breakfast nor time to take it if there had been. Ringing the bell at the intercom beside the menacing iron gates, I was summoned into the gatehouse to complete the arrival formalities before being ushered upstairs to the 'legal visits' area. There was one other person visiting, a female whom I took to be a solicitor, judging from her smart appearance and expensive looking accessories, but no prisoners in sight. The room contained about a dozen small square tables, each with two or three steel stacking chairs. At one side was a larger table, presumably to be used as a desk by a prison officer whom I could hear outside the room calling names in a loud voice.

It would have been useful to spend the waiting time looking at the file, but though I had requested it from Central Records, nothing had arrived, so on this occasion I was 'flying blind'. Fifteen minutes or so later, an officer entered with two male prisoners and, after asking wryly which of us was Mr. Henry, pointed one of the men in my direction, the other to the seated woman visitor. Barry Church and I shook hands and he sat down across the table from my blank notepad.

He was - or had been - a handsome man, in his mid-thirties. Around six feet tall, he struck me as being of Caribbean origin and, indeed, spoke with what I took to be a Jamaican accent. His face bore a scar across one cheek which, though it could not be said to disfigure him, affected his speech, since I presumed the laceration had affected the muscles of his mouth. While talking, he steadfastly averted my eyes and kept looking around as if afraid of someone.

"I got a message from Bernard Bryce that you wanted a visit."

"Yeah, boy am I glad you've come. Thanks."

"Why, what's wrong?"

He lowered his voice. "They're out to get me."

"What do you mean?"

"I mean that I'm in danger here. Everywhere I go I'm being watched, there's people talking about me, people watching me - I can't stand it much longer."

"Who? Why would anyone want to do that?"

"I dunno why, but it's everyone - the screws, the probation officers, the other inmates, they're all after me." He was becoming very agitated and I wasn't quite sure how to respond.

"Has any harm come to you so far?"

"No, but it's only a matter of time, I can tell. I think they've tunnelled in next to my cell. I can hear them talking. I can't tell what they're saying, but I know it's about me."

"How long has this been happening?"

"Since I got here."

"Which is...?"

"Eight months."

"Why didn't you ask to see me sooner."

"I've been asking since I arrived but they haven't allowed me to speak to anyone."

I knew there had been no correspondence, since the old file of any previous correspondence was still archived and would not have been if it were a 'live' case. Nothing Bernard Bryce had said on the phone conveyed it had been a long-term problem. Every time I tried to change the subject to ask him about himself and his family, he brought the conversation back to his fears. He continued in this vein for several minutes. The other visitor in the room was talking in a low voice to a woman who sounded as though she may have been a solicitor. Meanwhile, Barry continued, his voice increasing in speed and volume. I had to interrupt without appearing to interrupt.

"Have you had any visits from anyone back home?" But he was still insisting that he was in danger. I remember wondering who could have been out to get him and why. ('Wait a minute, Wal, you're beginning to believe him.')

" Barry, do your family visit you?"

"No. I'm the oldest of six. They don't like me."

"Why do you say that?"

"Because it's true." I looked at him in that way that says 'Go on...' "When I was small, my dad left Jamaica to come here. My mum said it was to find work. I don't remember him going but I remember being with my mum. I didn't have brothers or sisters. When I was about four or five, she left to join him. I went to stay with my Gran. She brought me up after that." He seemed to be calming down a bit....

"When did you come here?"

"When I was nine. My Gran put me on the boat and someone took care of me until I got to Waterloo Station in London. I remember it was December. I was freezing cold and when the train pulled in to Waterloo Station my mum and dad were there to meet me. I didn't remember them at all. My mum vaguely, perhaps, but not my dad. The person who had been looking after me on the journey disappeared and left me with them."

I was reminded of a similar story Richard had told me back in the office staff room. One of his clients was frightened when he came as a child to London from Jamaica because the couple who met him at the station had smoke coming out of their mouths when they were breathing. They weren't smoking cigarettes and he thought they were dragons. He didn't notice that it was coming out of his own mouth as well. "It was so cold you could see their breath. I had never seen that before. I thought it was smoke," he told Richard. London was bleak in those days and must have been terrifying for Caribbean youngsters arriving to see parents they hardly knew. It was the age of steam and smoke. Those buildings still standing and not seriously bomb-damaged were mostly black from home-fire and industrial smoke, the air was so polluted and even as late as the mid-1950's frequent winter fog restricted visibility to a mere three to five metres.

Barry Church continued: "I didn't know my dad. He was a stranger to me, even though he spoke a bit like me. I remembered my mum a bit better, even though I hadn't seen her for five or six years. She didn't seem too pleased to see me though. I was frightened when we went on an underground train. When they told me they were taking me home, and we went down a moving staircase into the earth, I began to think they lived down there. Then a train came - I'd never seen such a thing before - and we got into it and it made such an awful noise I was even more scared and wondered what was going to happen to me."

"My parents didn't talk to me during the journey. Maybe they didn't talk because the noise was so loud on the train, but I thought it was because they didn't like me and didn't want me there. I wanted my Gran. She was a cool lady and I knew she loved me, which I was already certain my mum and dad didn't." At this last sentence there was a change of pitch in his voice. He had been talking increasingly loudly and then spoke almost tenderly of his grandmother. The prison officer, who earlier had stood up to come over to us, until I shook my head silently to indicate it was not necessary, looked up again as if awoken by the reduction in volume.

"When we got to their home - an old house with a lot of damage and a leaky roof - there were five other kids in our flat between the ages of one and seven. They didn't talk like me and had a funny accent. It was a London accent. They began to tease me and so did the kids at the school I went to because I talked funny. I hated them, I hated London and I hated my parents."

"There were about twenty-five people living in our house. Some of them worked nights and had to let other people sleep in their beds during the day while they were out at work. The landlord was a nasty man who my dad called a spiv and he came around on Fridays to collect rent according to how many people lived there. He tried getting more and more people into our house to get more rent. Everyone in the house complained, but no-one would do anything to stop him. My dad never stood up to him even though he used to bully and threaten other people in the house. He hit me a lot and my mum never protected me. He never hit my brothers and sisters. I used to comfort myself by saying 'When I leave school, I can go back to my Gran," or 'Perhaps my Gran will come and get me'."

"One day my teacher sent me to the head-teacher's office. This must have been in my next school. I must have been about fourteen. The headteacher said "Your Gran just died." and sent me back to the classroom. I was gutted. I felt empty. I think I'd been quite good at school up till that point. I remember I was always one of the best at school at home in Jamaica and in Hackney. From then on I just couldn't concentrate."

I remember being deeply moved by this story which was a common thread among many young black offenders whose lives had been turned upside down by economic forces acting on their vulnerable parents, many of whom had fought with the British forces in the Second World War. Once peace came, they had migrated to Europe in search of a better life for their loved ones and children. As war heroes, many of the early arrivals in the 1940's and early fifties had been invited by the British Government to make a life here to replace the large number of workers killed or maimed during the war. The unconscionable misery we offered them in return for helping to re-float our economy was a heinous and shameful way to repay them for their gallantry.

Barry's demeanour, meanwhile, had completely changed during this outburst. Though agitated at the outset, leaning forward in his chair, fists toward me on the table, he had become even angrier, his voice becoming louder, almost threatening. At one point he gripped the edge of the table with both hands as if he were going to up-end it in my direction. Then, gradually, as if divesting himself of anger as he told his story, he became calmer, almost submissive. Now he was composed.

I had a packet of peppermints in my pocket and idly took it out, offering one to Barry. As he reached for it the prison officer came over and said gruffly: "What's that? You're not allowed to give the inmates food." I offered him one, which he took. As the officer walked away from us, back to his desk sucking noisily, Barry took one for himself from the still outstretched tube. We each put a mint in our mouths at the same time and looked at each other trying not to laugh. It was the first time he had looked me in the eye. His teary eyes smiled at mine. I took it as a compliment. Nothing was said.

We talked quietly for a few minutes longer. Though he had had many offers of work, Barry had never been able to hold a job down for long. He'd worked as a cleaner, handyman, gardener, warehouseman, kitchen porter - a wide variety of unskilled jobs but never for long. I applauded his perseverance in always trying to get work. There were a few spells when he hadn't been working, he told me, but didn't expand on it. He felt that the fault was always on the employer's side but could not articulate the reasons.

Suddenly the officer banged the table as he said "Five minutes left." I jumped with surprise causing my steel chair to make a loud screeching sound on the concrete floor. It reverberated in the stark, almost empty bare-walled room. What important questions had I forgotten to ask? I wondered. I had better think of them before he called "Time!" Barry fell quiet. Suddenly, I felt stuck for words. I was reflecting on the fact that he hadn't asked me to do anything for him, I had arrived with no agenda and, frankly, I was out of my depth.

As the officer called time, Barry said "Will you talk to my mum?" and quickly told me her address. As he departed through the prisoners' door, he turned, waved and smiled faintly.

Back in the office later that day I went in to see Richard. "How come you're back so soon?"

"I took your advice and left at five."

"You did what? I said leave around seven and you'll be back by five. You never listen, Mr. Henry!"

"Can I ask your advice?" and I told him about Barry.

"Wally, the paranoia, hearing voices, permanent anxiety could be symptoms of mental disorder. He needs to be referred to the prison psychiatrist for some kind of assessment. Call Camp Hill and ask them to take care of him."

It was too late to do it then - prison staff tend to start early and finish at four or so. I made a note to call Bernard Bryce in the morning....

"Hi Bernard, I saw Barry yesterday. He seemed very frightened, possibly even paranoid."

"Oh really? I wouldn't know, he's not on my patch. I only phoned you in response to a phone message from the prison officer on his wing. There's no probation officer covering inmates in that part of the prison. We help out where we can but don't get involved much."

"I'm worried about him and would like to get him referred to a psychiatrist," I said.

"We don't have one in the prison."

"Well, a doctor, then."

"No, we don't have a doctor either. The doctor resigned a month or two ago and no new appointment has been made yet. Probably won't be for a while. We've got no Governor One either."

"Can a doctor be called from outside?" I heard a drawing of breath through clenched teeth. He clearly thought I was a pain.

"Not easily." He was becoming irritated with my call.

"What happens in emergencies?"

"Not a lot actually. We call an ambulance if it's serious, otherwise it waits for the nurse next day."

I could see I was not getting anywhere and pursued another line of enquiry....

―

"I'm going out on a home visit, June. Back in an hour" I gave June a piece of paper with the address Barry had given me for his mother.

"Hello, are you Mrs. Church?"

"No, I'm Mrs. Wilson. What's this about?"

"Do you know Mrs. Church?"

"She don't exist. Is this about Barry? I'm his mother."

"I'm Walter Henry. I went to see him yesterday." I produced my probation warrant card. She invited me in. The Victorian terraced house was tired-looking, with faded peeling wallpaper and bare floors, but the room was neat. I formed the view she lived alone. I explained who I was, why I'd come and told Mrs. Wilson why some of Barry 's conversation worried me. She seemed glad to have a visitor and was openly chatty. As if magically, she brought me tea, and sat chatting to me, nursing her own cup in both hands; it seemed to have been poured before my arrival.

"I had Barry in Jamaica just before his father left for London but when I came here to be with him, I found him with someone else so I lived with a different man, Len Church. Barry never knew my husband wasn't his father. Len gave me five children but never really took to Barry. He died ten years ago."

"I'm sorry to hear that."

"Are you? I wasn't. I always kept my own family name, Wilson."

" Barry talked fondly of you and asked me to come to see you. I think he wanted to send you his love."

"How is he?"

"I don't think he's well. He seemed very afraid of those around him and was worried that something was going to happen to him. Has he been like that before?"

"He was quite normal as a child but in his late teens and early twenties he was very difficult."

"In what way?"

"He acted strange. Had a temper. Didn't like to be around people."

"How was his health?"

"He was OK. Never had anything wrong with him."

"Did he have a doctor?"

"Yes, same as mine. Dr. James in Hoxton."

"Did Barry live with you?"

"No. I couldn't live with him when he became an adult. He frightened me. Sometimes he'd get a flat but he never kept them long and usually spent time staying with girlfriends or with other people I didn't like much. "

I went to see Jackie when I returned; she had said I could talk to her if I needed help. Without Barry Church's file I felt I was hampered. Jackie told me whom to phone in Head Office to chase it or see what had happened to my earlier request for it; when I did, as luck would have it, the file had now been found and would be delivered in the van tomorrow. There's a surprise, I thought.

Barry Church's file arrived next day. It was about five centimetres thick. The first thing I turned to was the notification of the most recent court case, the sentence and the sheet giving details of his previous offences. I was stunned by what I saw. Excluding the current offences for which he is serving four years. Barry had been convicted of no fewer than twenty-four previous offences, almost all of which were for violence.

The offences seemed to start around age nineteen when he was fined for threatening and abusive behaviour followed by a similar matter about six months later. Then there was a common assault with another fine and an assault causing actual bodily harm which earned him a short prison sentence when he was twenty-two. The seriousness of his offences escalated during his twenties, to grievous bodily harm, affray, wounding with intent to commit grievous bodily harm and so on, earning him more, and longer, prison sentences. At the time of the current offence he had been out of gaol for four months.

During the entire time Barry Church had been known to the justice system, not one person appeared to have given any thought to investigating the possibility of mental disorder. Over a total of twenty-five court appearances, each one an opportunity to diagnose an obviously serious behavioural problem, there was no evidence of any solicitor requesting a medical check for the defendant, nor the court, nor any probation officer. No prison staff had ever considered it, despite clear entries in the notes that his often violent conduct was highly suggestive of mental disorder.

I looked at the details of the latest offence. He was driving up Stoke Newington High Street when the driver of a BMW apparently cut in too close, or upset him in some other way. At the first opportunity, when the rush hour traffic came to a total standstill, Barry climbed out of his car, walked calmly to the rear, opened the boot of his own vehicle from which he removed an axe with which he approached the other vehicle. He then began demolishing it, starting with the headlights, the bonnet and the windscreen. As good fortune would have it, this incident took place directly in front of the new, glass-fronted Stoke Newington police station, from which poured several officers able to arrest him before he could inflict any serious personal injury. I picked up the phone and began to dial...

"Hello, Dr. James. My name's Walter Henry and I'm a probation officer in Englefield Road. I visited a client yesterday in Camp Hill Prison on the Isle of Wight. He is a patient of yours and I'm worried about him so I wanted to ask your advice. I realise that you can't talk about a specific patient so I'd like to frame some questions in purely general terms. If you can comment on that, I believe I'd find it very helpful." (As so many times before, I must have sounded like an automaton reading from a script.)

"I think I get the picture. Fire away."

"This man, aged thirty-one has been sentenced to four years for affray, criminal damage and grievous bodily harm. When I visited him, he was displaying bizarre symptoms which included agitated behaviour, and paranoia. He spoke of hearing voices and insisted he was in danger from the prison officers and from the other inmates. When I spoke to his mother, Mrs. Wilson, earlier today, she said that he had a serious temper but that she wasn't aware that he had experienced any mental health problems in the past. I have asked the prison to provide an assessment on his mental state but there is no psychiatrist in the prison, nor any other doctor. I am curious what you think I should do in these circumstances."

"Well thank you for calling me, Mr. Henry. I have several patients named Wilson, but is it possible that this young man has a different surname?"

"I assume, since we are talking about public safety here, that despite confidentiality protocols, I can mention his name. It's Barry Church."

"Thank you. Well, Mr. Henry, this one is fairly simple to deal with. It doesn't matter whether one is in prison or anywhere else. Every single person in Britain has the absolute right to proper health care. If it cannot be found in the prison in which he's located at present, the Home Secretary has a duty either to secure a suitably qualified doctor to examine him where he is, or to move him to where he can be properly assessed. However, in reality it is often not so easy to obtain what is available by right. If you are willing to act on his behalf, you should write to the welfare department of the prison, the chief medical officer, the governor, the member of parliament for this part of the borough and your line manager to cover your back. Oh, and perhaps you'd let me have a copy of the letter for the file? I assume he'll be released at some stage. I don't think I want him coming in here without some warning." It was Friday. The letter went off the same evening.

—

Monday morning arrived....

"Call for you Wally, Mr. Jones, Camp Hill Prison." "Thanks June... Hello, Walter Henry here."

"Mr. Henry, I've received your letter this morning, thank you. I'm acting Governor One at Camp Hill and take your note very seriously. We have no suitable personnel here to see Mr. Church but I've arranged to have him moved across the road to HMP Parkhurst this afternoon. With luck he should be seen tomorrow. You could call them on Wednesday and see what they say. Thanks for your concern. Good bye"....

"Good morning. HMP Parkhurst? May I speak to the prison psychiatrist please? My name's Walter Henry and I'm a probation officer calling about Barry Church, Prison No. ****."

"Just a minute, I'll put you through..." then same voice came back, "Sorry we don't have any Barry Church here."

"Did you have? He was due in from Camp Hill on Monday afternoon."

"One moment... Ah yes. Came in Monday and went out yesterday morning to... just a minute.... Ah, yes, HMP Wandsworth. Went there yesterday. OK? Bye."

"Good morning Wandsworth. May I speak to the prison psychiatrist please? My name's Walter Henry and I'm a probation officer calling about Barry Church." A pause, then the call went straight through...

"Medical unit. Donaldson."

"Good morning. May I speak to the prison psychiatrist please? My name's Walter Henry and I'm a probation officer calling about Barry Church."

"Which office are you from?"

"Englefield Road"

"What's your phone number and postcode?" I told him. "And your connection with him?"

"I'm his home probation officer - case was allocated to me last week."

"Ah yes, got your letter here. Jeez, you really put the cat among the pigeons. Never seen any response as quick as that before. I'm going to put you through to the Hospital Governor, Dr. Harriman." Dr. Harriman was a cordial man with a gift for communication. I introduced myself and we chatted briefly about Barry and his case history.

"Why has Mr. Church come to you?"

"Good question. When he had an initial examination at Parkhurst, they thought he was so seriously ill that he should be examined by a senior staff member or a consultant psychiatrist outside the prison system. They didn't have that facility on the Isle of Wight so they sent him to us. Our transport was already there and about to leave, apparently. Our Governor One's none too pleased - he's trying to get rid of inmates, not collect difficult customers from around the country. Someone pointed out the local MP was interested in this one so he had no choice."

"So what's going to happen?"

"Well, he's been examined under Section 47 of the Mental Health Act and is to be moved out of the prison system into a National Health Hospital right away. It's likely he'll have to stay there for an indeterminate period. That could mean life. Does he have family ties?"

"His mother's concerned, though not especially close. She may have been telling me less than she knew."

"What about the girlfriend, what's her name, ah yes, Sheila?"

"I'd no idea about a girlfriend. He never mentioned her, neither did his mother."

173

"Well look, if you can find out, all well and good. You can invite both of them to call me if they wish. I think I ought to explain the situation fully to them."

"Thanks. Where are you going to send him?"

"We don't know yet - depends where we can find a place in a secure hospital. Of course, Hackney Hospital would be ideal but at this stage there's no guarantee they can help. We'll try to let you know in a couple of days - we want him out of here as soon as... Someone will call you, though it might not be me."

"Thanks so much for your help, Dr Harriman."

"Not at all, it's a change to have something buttoned up so quickly when it comes to light in this way. Thanks for your part in it. Good piece of work: well done. Goodbye."

'Nice of him' I thought '– people don't often say nice things.' And that, for the time being, was that.

There was a girlfriend who had been supportive all along and who had visited Barry once a month at Camp Hill though he'd mentioned nothing to me. She had not told anyone about his bizarre conduct as she thought the prison staff would notice and do something about it if it merited any action. Once Sheila found that Barry was nearby in hospital, she lost interest in him. Mrs. Wilson was able to visit her son and later phoned to thank me for my help.

23. Trying New ideas

Supervision with Jackie was usually pretty straightforward. After less than a year in the job, I was still regarded as the new boy, despite the fact that only one other person in the office, Richard, was older than I. We would discuss my caseload in general terms, then one or two individual cases in detail. Rounding off after one such session Jackie asked:

"On another subject, how's the Wednesday activities group doing? I mentioned it at a Borough Seniors' meeting and several colleagues thought it was a great idea."

"Well, it's going very well. Some of the more stable clients of other officers get to comply with the attendance conditions of their order in an enjoyable way, I get some quality time with some of my own clients, and the amazing Sylvester Mittee makes sure we all keep fit. It's a win, win, win option. But I'm glad you brought it up. It reminded me that I wanted to ask you something. Some of the members have been asking what kind of work they could train for other than the building trade. I've been thinking. Now the numbers are increasing, it might be a good idea to introduce some kind of lessons. Nothing formal, of course, but something they'd enjoy, want to come back here for, something that could make them interesting to an employer."

"Walleeee? You've got that look in your eye again. Where is this going?"

"Well, you asked me to accommodate a spare table in my room so it didn't get sent back to head office. It's a nice table but..."

"Yes, yes, but that was only to be temporary..." she interjected, assuming, wrongly, the direction of my argument, then...

"Unfortunately, there's a problem with it. Not only does no-one have any demand for a large table, but there's nowhere else it would fit. The conference room already has two and won't accommodate another, and all the other offices are too small, so if it's in your way, it'd be a pity to lose it but I'll arrange to have it sent back to HQ storage if you like."

"No, no, no, it's not in my way - I have a use for it. If we could get a computer and monitor, and maybe a colour printer as well, I could show interested clients the rudiments. Anyone who took to it could get more instruction elsewhere, but it would boost their confidence to begin with and eventually make them more employable. I've costed it – it doesn't come to much."

"I'm afraid it's out of the question, Wally. Any computers here have to be part of the probation network and it wouldn't do to have clients working on a system that might give them access to confidential data. And even we don't have colour printers. There'd be no chance of getting you one." Jackie had slipped back into a rare moment of bureaucratic mode.

"Do I get right of reply?"

"Sorry..." Jackie just smiled benignly and shook her head slowly.

Some days later there was a borough seniors' meeting in the large space, grandiosely called the conference room, at our office. There were three probation offices in Hackney at that time and they had monthly meetings for the management from all the offices to meet and do things that managers do. They were presided over by Robin, the borough boss, Assistant Chief Probation Officer

I first met Robin five years previously. I had already been involved for a few years as a volunteer with the probation service. At that time he was responsible for the organisation of a charity-funded adventure holiday for families of long-term prison inmates. When a married man with children receives a long custodial sentence, it is usually the family members who suffer most. The probation service was instrumental in organising events to help some of the worst affected families and the holiday in the countryside was the biggest of these ventures. I had taken time off from my business to attend as a helper on the trip. I have never forgotten the first words Robin ever said to me in his educated Scottish accent on the first day of a memorable week when we all arrived at a youth hostel in South Wales:

"Wally, you look like a man who might have packed a spare towel." Such insight! I was proud to prove him right. And now, in Hackney, I ran into Robin in the corridor after the Borough Meeting had ended.

"Hallo-o-o-o Wally" he said. "I've just been hearing about you. What's this about a computer?" I told him. "I think it's an interesting idea. It would need to be one that was not compatible with the probation system. How much would one cost?" I had prepared figures to discuss with Jackie before she squashed my idea flat as a pancake.

"Computer and colour printer, about three hundred and eighty pounds plus software starting at forty-five or so. The whole project could be up and running within a week for about four hundred- and-fifty-pounds top whack."

"Well, Jackie spoke very enthusiastically about it. She thought it was a great idea and asked me to consider it as a suitable item for our special projects fund. Write me a note, get Jackie to countersign it and keep me informed as to how you get on with the project."

Three weeks later I unveiled the computer at the busy Tuesday morning group. I listened to their banter as the clients in our weekly group got acquainted with the idea.

"What's that?"

"It's a computer, stupid."

"What does it do?"

"It'll do lots of things."

"Yeah? What then?

"You can play games on computers."

"Oh great, what else, clever dick?"

"Erm, errrrr......"

"Computers are crap. They take jobs away from people. That's why we ain't got jobs."

"It's not true, there's lots of jobs in computers, I nicked enough of 'em. Keeps me in a job!"

I thought it time to intervene before losing control completely.

"OK. OK. You already know that computers are becoming very important. I thought that before we let them take control over our lives it might be a good idea for us to learn a bit about them so we can take control of them first. Anyone got any suggestions what we might aim to do with it while we learn how to use it?" The room went quiet.

"Erm, can it write letters and things?"

"Yes, if you tell it what to say."

"How do you do that?"

"Any ideas anyone?"

"Do you type on the keyboard?" asked Diane.

"What's this?" said Craig, pointing to the mouse.

"Anyone know?" Complete silence. Well I thought I'd ask.

"Erm, does it move a thing on the screen if you wiggle it around?"

"That's great, Mike. You want to have a go?" He took it in his left hand with the lead at the front as he sat down at the table. When I showed him how to hold it the right way round in his other hand, he wiggled it a bit. After a few seconds of awkward movement he seemed to have got the idea.

"This is weird. I'm usually left-handed. Now what do I do?"

"Move it so the pointer lands on one of those pictures – they're called icons – and press your index finger to make a click. No, only once will do. Good. Can you see a tiny picture of a pencil drawing on a pad? Try one click on that. Good, that's right." A drawing programme appeared. "Great, now, while still holding down your index finger move that thing – it's called a mouse – so you get a line appearing on the screen. Great, you've got the hang of it. Now see if you can draw something...."

"Wassat?"

"It's a cat, dummy. A cat drawn by a mouse."

"It's fat. Looks more like Wally."

"Hey... This is better than wanderin' the streets. How do I get this onto a piece of paper?"

"Can I have a go?"

"No, I'm next..."

"OK, OK, take it in turns. You'll all get a chance to do something today, and when you come for Tuesday group in future, those of you who are interested can get a lesson on what it can do, and how to get the best out of it. Eventually, when you go down the Job Centre, you'll be able to say you have elementary computer skills." As the animated banter died down, the members of the group became more and more absorbed in what they were doing, accompanied by a few scornful comments among the shouts of admiration and encouragement. Everyone had a turn, and after they'd been introduced to the writing programme each member produced something to print and proudly take home. They were as pleased as Punch. When I'd seen the last of them off the premises, I went into the reception office.

There were two new report requests in my tray. On first glance they both seemed simple jobs. New names, new files, no previous and nothing in the way of correspondence. 'Should be easy ones' I told myself. Frank Grover, a 24-year-old burglar, was in custody in Wormwood Scrubs. Jackie Stuart, a female shoplifter was in HMP Holloway awaiting sentence. I made appointments to see each of them.

24. Brown Powder

Up till now I'd only had one court report to prepare at a time. Now, more than six months in the job, I was starting to get two at a time and the temperature began to hot up. When I called Wormwood Scrubs to make an appointment to interview Frank Grover the following week they said it would have to be two weeks because of building works on the visits facility. A few days later I received a prisoner's letter from him asking me to visit him. The letter came from Latchmere House, not Wormwood Scrubs. No official word was ever received from either institution telling me that he had been moved.

A few days later I was on my way to HMP Latchmere House to visit Frank Grover. The once stately Early Victorian home overlooking Ham Common had been requisitioned by the War Office at the onset of the Second World War and subsequently passed to the Home Office for use as a Detention Centre for young offenders as well as adult offenders in preparation for release. Now, like many Home Office assets, it has transformed its identity into elegant housing for the well-heeled.

The person who arrived at my cubicle was a handsome young man in his early-twenties, of Caribbean origin, with striking good looks and a soft voice. He explained that he was arrested for burglary and also charged with criminal damage. Police were called when he and his accomplice were seen to break into a derelict warehouse building in Homerton. As police were coming up the stairs, he could see that the only way out was through the second-floor window onto the roof of a large white van parked in the goods entrance below the window.

The two men jumped together. Had they jumped singly, Frank said, they might just have got away with it. Unfortunately, the van wasn't built to take the weight of two bodies simultaneously from twenty feet up. As the roof buckled inwards, they crumpled into a human heap and the two were easily captured by the police before they could recover their composure. It just happened to be the police van – and three officers were still inside when the pair landed on their roof. It was hard to say who was more shocked, the hunters or the hunted.

Although it had been clear the two would plead guilty from the start, they had been in custody awaiting their Crown Court appearance for seven months. Jeffrey Kenton, Frank's co- defendant, was in custody at another prison and they had not seen or been in touch with each other since their arrest.

But the purpose of the interview was not to find out the facts of the case but to establish Frank's personal history, the circumstances surrounding the offence and to explore options for sentence. His father disappeared when Frank was around four or five, he told me, leaving his mother to bring up her son and three daughters in poverty. The need to earn a living took precedence over controlling the children and they were, he told me, left to occupy themselves on the Hackney housing estate where they lived. One day, when he was playing on the roof of some garages in a neighbouring estate, a woman came over to tell them to get down because she thought it was dangerous.

"She stared at me in a funny way," he told me, so he said

"What you lookin' at?"

"Is your surname Grover?" He had never seen the woman before. Taken aback, he acknowledged it was. How did she know?

"Because that's my husband's name and you look exactly like him. He never told me he had kids."

He asked her where she lived and though she wasn't specific, she gestured in the direction she had come, towards a typical block of council flats with long open balconies that gave access to all the flats on each floor. Later Frank returned to that building and when, after a long wait, he saw which flat she came out of, he returned often, sometimes waiting for hours in the hope of seeing the man who might be his father. Eventually he saw a man leave. Sure enough it had to be his father. There could have been no doubt about it. Frank stood at the foot of the staircase until his father came down. When the man looked at the child who blocked his path, their eyes met. Frank hoped there would be some recognition, or even warmth, but no, he walked straight past without a word. He tried again and again: same result.

Frank saw that incident as pivotal in his life. He didn't describe it as rejection. The word he used was 'gutted'. It conveyed his feelings admirably. He fell in with a gang of tough kids on his estate and as he grew older assumed leadership. When he outgrew that group, he graduated to another. He remembered one particular day when the older ones were smoking something unusual, cigarettes, but these smelt funny.

"Here, Frank, you try."

"Nooo-o-o-o!"

"Wassamatter, you scared?"

"No-o-o-o-o!"

At fifteen he already smoked.

"Well, go on then. You can't be with us if you don't."

"...and that was how I came to use drugs. After the first reefer I was hooked. I thought it was just draw" (marijuana, cannabis) "but then I learned it was cut with heroin. Heroin became my drug. I began to steal to make enough money to buy it then a few years ago I was caught taking a man's wallet. It was my first conviction and I got three years in prison. Three years of my life lost because of brown powder. It doesn't make sense."

"What do you plan to do about it?"

"What can I do? I'll get another prison sentence and as soon as I get out, I'll be bang on it again."

"Is that what you want?"

"Of course it's not, but that's the future for me. It's the same as all me mates in Hoxton. The black ones anyway. They do drugs, they get nicked, they serve time, they come out, they do drugs, they get nicked, they serve time and it goes on like that till they die. Sometimes, if they're lucky, they die first."

"Is there any alternative?"

"Nope. I'm finished." I was looking for an opening, some spark of optimism, but Frank was so vehement in his pessimism that it was hard to know where to start.

"What if the judge didn't send you down? What would you like to do then?"

"No chance. I'm black. Caribbean. You know what that means. As soon as he sees I've done time before, he'll send me back." This was an all-too-accurate perception.

"No, tell me. What if....?"

"I've been to a couple of NA meetings here. At first, I only went to get out of my cell. It was better than being banged up for twenty-three hours a day."

"And...?"

"Well some of the guys are good. They seem to have made it – but they're still back in here."

"So...?"

"I would start going to NA on the out. There are meetings morning, afternoon and night-time."

"What else?"

"Dunno."

"Would you spend your whole time going to meetings?"

"Don't you understand? I don't know anything else. I left school at fourteen. I can't read or write, I never learned anything, I never worked, I just blagged to feed my habit. I have to find out what life is all about. I got no dad to ask. My mum has had enough of me. There's no-one out there for me. I want to stay in prison."

"Wassamatter, you scared?"

"No-o-o-o, well, no, but, but wouldn't you be?" *(Hang on, you're supposed to be asking the questions, Wally.)*

"If you got probation, where would you live?"

He laughed. "You're having a joke, aren't you?"

"Would your mum take you in."

"Only until I went back on the gear."

"So try it."

"OK. When I get my jam roll."

"Jam roll?"

His eyes rolled to the ceiling... "Paro-o-o-le."

"Look, Frank, I'm not supposed to be selling you this idea, I just think it would work and you'd be a fool not to jump at it." The prison officer outside the glazed door silently held up five fingers to indicate time was nearly up.

"What? What are you talking about?"

"Probation."

"Are you nuts? I'll never get probation."

"Well you'd better start thinking about it now, because time's up and I've got to go and write a report to tell the judge what to do with you. I happen to think you'd be great on probation and I'd like to propose it if you'll agree to put your back into it. I think you're an able man with loads of talent. You're quick, you've got a lot of personality and, if you can get rid of that chip on your shoulder, you'd be a terrific example to others."

"You said that like it was true."

"I believe it is, OK? And something else is true. If you spoil things or make a monkey out of me, I'll take you back to court. Now, do we have a deal?"

Suddenly it seemed as though the sun came out. His grin truly sparkled. "Do you really believe I could do it? Would you help me?"

"Here's my hand on it." He shook my hand for all he was worth.

This was more than a challenge but I hoped it could turn out to be worth the effort.

Frank Grover's case file had been delivered from head office and was in my tray when I got back to the office. He had been convicted before but had received only custodial sentences, hence the file was fairly thin – no officer had ever visited him before and there had been little or no probation service involvement. While I was reading the file and my notes, June rang.

25. Ulrich Verwood's Pitfall

"Mr. Verwood for his appointment Wally."

"Sit him down, June, I'll be right there." I always enjoyed Rick's visits. He was consistently cheerful and seemed to be making great progress. He stayed away from bookmakers, worked enormously hard, his compensation was almost completely paid off and, though he and his wife were still apart, his family life was reasonably stable. It was one of the more gratifying aspects of the job.

But when, a few moments later, I held out my hand to greet him, he didn't look the same. As we mounted the stairs, I wondered what could be wrong. It was with difficulty I observed my self-imposed code of not discussing anything on the staircase or in corridors, but I was impatient to find out what was going on.

Once seated in my office he began to tell me why, in what seemed a flat, alien tone, he had completely lost his sparkle.

"I've lost my job, Wal."

"What happened?" (Meaning, what did you do wrong?)

"Nothing happened. In the exhibition trade it's all or nothing. You don't take on a job for just one exhibition stand – you do four or five, or twenty. My boss started losing jobs and now has nothing on the books for the foreseeable future and he's had to let me go. I'm the last one. For three weeks there's been only the two of us – there were more than a dozen when I joined, with plenty of overtime and I was making enough money to keep everyone happy. Now I can't even feed myself."

"Rick, I'm sure something will turn up soon. You'll sign on, keep an eye open at the job centre, and as soon as an employer sees you, he'll snap you up."

"I've never signed on in my life. I've always managed to get jobs on the books, and I don't believe in taking handouts from the government."

"Why not? Whenever you're employed 'on the books' as you call it, you pay tax and national insurance. Insurance means that if the risk you've been paying towards turns out to be a reality, you make a claim. You have a car, don't you? What happens when you have a knock? Would you be too proud to ask the insurance company to pay for the repair? What's more, we all pay tax and insurance so that you, and others, can eat and live when there's not enough work to go around."

"You make it all sound so simple."

"Well isn't it?"

"Not quite. I haven't told you half of it. I'd saved up some money for my wife and my mother, for people I owe, and for the last bit of the court payment. I gambled again and lost the lot. Mum's thrown me out, my wife won't talk to me and won't let me see the kids, and even my friends are turning their backs on me..." He talked without jokes or quips for almost an hour and a half. I listened intently, believing it better not to interrupt.

"What would you like me to do, Rick?"

"I've come to you for help." He said in a flat voice, not pleadingly but in a way, which said 'I know you'll come up with something.'

"E-e-e-erm."

"Rick, I'm Rick." He looked at me almost disdainfully. "Fuck it, even my probation officer's forgotten who I am."

"No, no, I'm thinking."

"Oh, sorry."

"I'm going to telephone the Department of Social Security and get their advice. Do you have a P45?"

"Of course I do." I was already dialling. Talk about gambling. This was really a lottery – would I get a reply? Would I get a helpful person? Would it be someone like that dreadful telephone receptionist at the housing office?

"Hello, DSS Good morning." The rapid-fire greeting didn't inspire confidence. I explained the problem in garbled terms, tripping over the words and saying things I felt I should have held back, holding back on things I should have said.

"Hold on I'll put you through to new claims."

"New claims."

"Good morning. My name's Walter Henry. I'm a probation officer and I'm phoning for some advice for a client who's sitting with me right now. He's 44 years old, never claimed benefit before and is a little reluctant to sign on, though I can confirm that he has no visible means of support. He has a P45 from his last employer"

"No problem. We'll invite him down here and see what we can do. Get him to pick up a B1 on the way down. I could talk to him myself if you like?"

"I think that would be a very good idea." I handed Rick the phone. After first holding up two hands to say 'no way' he reluctantly reached out his hand for the telephone.

"Yeah, hello." He was not enjoying this. He listened. "Yeah? where do I get that then? No, of course I've got nothing on today. Yeah, well.... I could come right now.... You would? That would be great... Do I ask for you? What's your name then? Damian.... OK. I could? Yeah, I'd like you to, yeah. OK, great. Thanks. Yeah, I know where that is.... OK, yep, right.... Thanks. Do you want to speak to my probation officer again? OK, goodbye."

"Is that what I was afraid of?" he asked me, astonished, as he handed me back the receiver. "That's amazing."

"It might not go so smoothly once you get down there. There's a lot of waiting around. And you won't come away with any money today but you'll set the process in motion. You OK with forms?"

"Not very good but I think I'll be able to manage. Damian asked the same question and said he'd help me. I'll go there now. He explained where to get the B1 on the way."

"Right. I'll come downstairs with you - there's someone waiting. Come and see me next week at the same time, but drop in or call if you get a problem."

"I'm feeling better already. Thanks for the tea. And thanks for the help."

26. Change of Plea

When people fail to turn up for interviews on which a court report is to be based, they are usually offered another chance if there's time before the sentencing date. The SER, later called the Pre-sentence Report (PSR), is the convicted person's best chance of putting across any ameliorating factors that might affect the outcome. Some people either don't realise that it's their chance to have their say, or don't care. Either way, it's a mistake to miss out on the opportunity. After finding two new files in my tray I had two reports to prepare, but unusually, neither person turned up for either of the two interviews offered.

Always ready to maximise efficiency, Jackie asked me if I'd be willing to do a simple report for the local Youth Court. Accordingly, I sent out the normal appointment letter inviting Hameed Iqbal to attend for a chat. At the appointed time, a very fresh-faced adolescent boy came to see me to talk about his part in a car theft. I had all the documentation I needed from the Crown Prosecution Service. Hameed, a seventeen-year-old juvenile (though that term has now fallen out of use), had no previous convictions and was a passenger in a car stopped by police officers who found the car to have been reported stolen in the last hour.

Both boys were convicted of car theft after pleading guilty. The two were classmates, though, apparently, not friends. Hameed asserted in his statement that he had left his home on an errand for his mother. The driver of the car had spotted him leaving his home, told him he was driving his new car and, learning of Hameed's errand, offered him a lift. When later arrested, the driver, co-defendant in the case, assured police that Hameed had made him do it. Hameed, on the other hand, felt the police had threatened him by saying 'Admit it now or it will be worse for you,' so Hameed was easily persuaded by the solicitor whom his parents instructed privately (not one of those on the court duty rota) to plead guilty, having been led to fear a worse outcome if he denied the offence.

I had been designated to tell the Youth Court something about Hameed's background, hence the reason for calling him in to the office for a Pre-sentence Report interview. The officer to whom the report was originally allocated was, again, on sick leave so as the court date approached, Jackie asked me if, in view of my two no-show interviews, I could fit another in, and I agreed to oblige.

When Hameed arrived, I discovered he didn't talk. I tried all I could, but nothing worked. Open questions (questions requiring more than a yes or no answer) just didn't seem to work and had no useful effect at all. In response to questions about his identity, he would merely nod or shake his head as appropriate, but to other questions, he would give only monosyllabic replies, if indeed he even answered. He later said he was too scared and he still thought I was a police officer. We had booked a one-hour appointment, but after thirty-five minutes I was exhausted and anyway, had a home visit to make and needed to leave the office as soon as possible so I cut the interview short.

I didn't have a clue how I could possibly compose a report on what little information I had gleaned from Hameed. Then I noticed Hameed's home was between the office and my destination, so I offered him a lift in my car - the irony was lost on me – and on him. He accepted gratefully. As we pulled out of the car park, Hameed began to speak.

"Mr. Probation Officer, I didn't do it," he said, almost crying. "I had to wait in with my little brothers and sisters for my mum to come back from the doctor's. She's disabled, you see? She had a prescription which she asked me to get from the chemist. That's why I went out when I did."

"What time was that, Hameed?"

"About four o'clock."

"How long had your mum been at the doctor's?"

"About an hour and a bit."

"But they said in court that the car was reported stolen at three p.m. - that's at least an hour before your arrest."

"Yeah, but I couldn't convince them I wasn't with Tyrone when he took the car. Anyway, he told me it was his – or at least, his dad's. Then, when they got it out of him that he'd taken it, he told them I made him do it."

"Did the police see the prescription you were carrying?"

"Yes, that was the only reason they didn't keep me in custody. They gave me bail."

"It's a pity they didn't read it properly. Some prescriptions state the time they were written. If they'd seen that they'd have known you were telling the truth. But either way, if your mother will confirm you were in the house when she left and when she got back that should be helpful." We chatted on and on about his family, his school, and many different things. By the time we reached his home, where he invited me in to briefly meet his mother, I had enough to write a full report. This time I did share my findings with my supervisor, and Jackie helped me with her suggested wording. As custom demanded, the report began with the sources of the information contained in it....

"This report is based on one office interview with Mr. Hameed, and one home visit where I met (Hameed's) mother and siblings. I have read the prosecution bundle and would wish

to draw the court's attention to a possible oversight in the evidence. Mr. Hameed continues to assert his innocence and I have discovered incontrovertible evidence which supports this. Accordingly, I would urge the court to accept a change of plea. My reasons for this are given in the body of the report."

After showing my report to the prosecution, who agreed with my observation, the magistrate accepted the request for a revised plea and, in view of the new evidence, struck out the previous record and allowed a new plea of 'Not Guilty'.

Having arranged care for her children, and despite her apparent disability, Hameed's mother was in court and agreed to be helped to the witness box where she confirmed that her son was in the house with his four younger brothers and sisters when she got home from the doctor's. In other words he was still at home at the time the car was stolen. Since the arrest came within minutes of the mother's return to the home, Hameed could have been in the car for only a very short time and was clearly an innocent passenger. The defence solicitor asked the court to accept that since the prescription had been seen and recorded as "prisoner's property" by the police it should be accepted as evidence along with his mother's statement from the witness box. The bench decided that a new trial even for a substitute charge of 'Allow to be carried' would not be in the public interest and a 'Not Guilty' verdict was entered. Hameed walked free, still with no convictions to his name. I never saw him again.

In the meantime my caseload was flourishing. In supervision Jackie asked if I was concerned about this exponential growth. Somewhat taken aback, I explained that I had now been in the job ten months and assumed this organic growth was par for the course.

"Well, Wally, in a way you're right, but it's unusual for so many recommendations for probation to be followed by the courts. If it gets too much, let's agree that you can hand some of them over to colleagues if you need to."

"Thanks Jackie, it's good to know I may do that but it seems OK at the moment. The weekly client group is removing some of the strain. I've reached the stage where I think it's OK to invite even new probationers to join the group if there are no immediate delicate or confidential issues that demand one-to-one contact."

"Fine, but the offer's still there." And so the groups progressed and attendance increased.

---

27. Progress? Whose?

Frank Grover was very lucky: he received a probation order from Crown Court. He showed up at my office with his co-defendant, Jeffrey Kenton, whom I had never met before. They had appeared in court together but there had been no report prepared for Mr. Kenton.

My probation colleague at Crown Court phoned me with an account of the proceedings after the case. The gruff judge took a long time, she told me, to eventually agree with the extremely tenacious and persuasive defence counsel that both his clients should be dealt with equally, despite the fact that Frank Grover had more 'previous' than his accomplice.

The barrister was quick to argue, contrary to the judge's stated opinion in favour of custody, that the two men were being sentenced for the current matter, not what they had done before and alerted the bench to the fact that both men had already spent seven and a half months in custody while on remand.

Both men had the same barrister who had to work extremely hard to convince the bench. There followed some animated exchanges until the judge was finally persuaded, although he commented that he had previously made up his mind that custody was the right solution. It was Mr. Kenton's relative lack of previous offences that enabled Mr. Grover to avoid a further prison sentence.

Nevertheless, the judge cautioned the two young men that if there were any failure in their performance of the probation order, they would be returned in custody to Crown Court for re-sentencing.

"Be in no doubt," he said sternly, "I will not be persuaded a second time." The judge then pointedly reserved the case to himself, which needs little explanation. Both men were instructed to report immediately to the probation office on release from custody at the court building.

Frank Grover's friend and co-defendant sat mute during our first meeting. He nodded and smiled weakly when we were introduced but took no further part in the proceedings. I explained that when his papers turned up from court, a file would be created for him and a probation officer allocated, but until he heard from that officer, he had to maintain contact, so I suggested he attend the Tuesday group. That meant that Frank Grover would have to attend as well. True, it was against the guideline I had originally set myself: I rationalised it by telling myself that the two had already been in custody for seven months and, with their guilty plea, had accepted responsibility for their crimes. Moreover, they were still, so far as I could tell, drug free.

This was a turning point in Mr. Grover 's life, he told me later – and indeed it was, at least for the time I knew him. Having spent a long time in custody awaiting trial and sentence, he was confirmed by the Drug Dependency Unit as being drug-free when he left court so needed no pharmacological help from them. He did, however, ask if I would make a referral for him to get specialist advice and counselling. I asked him if he would consent to DDU staff notifying me of drugs test results.

While Mr. Kenton also nodded approvingly, Frank Grover replied for the pair of them:

"Of course we will," Frank said, "It's our best insurance. We know that if we slip up you will get to know about it, and that's our best deterrent against using drugs in the first place." He exuded energy and enthusiasm.

I wrote a brief note to Jackie explaining that Jeffrey Kenton had reported and I would provide temporary cover until the case was properly allocated. Twenty-four hours later, his file was in my pigeon hole with the relevant case papers. The file had been allocated to Joanie to write the court report in between her spells of sick leave, but no action had been taken so now the case was transferred to me.

They were an unusual pair, Frank Grover and Jeffrey Kenton: Frank was talkative, Jamaican, very dark skinned and handsome with a stunning smile, while Jeffrey was Scottish, white, gentle and extremely shy. He looked down at the carpet most of the time and signified agreement or approval merely by looking out from under his large eyebrows without moving his head or by nodding, or in rare circumstances, smiling bashfully, lips together.

Cross-cultural friendships were not the norm at that time. Groups of friends rarely mixed across racial or ethnic barriers. But Frank Grover and Jeffrey Kenton were inseparable: they lived close to each other, they went to NA meetings together, went to the unemployment office together, the DDU together and reported to probation together. Frank described this strategy as his safety mechanism. He felt responsible for Jeffrey and wouldn't do anything to risk their relapse, failure or friendship.

What I didn't expect, and this highlighted a flaw in my brilliant plan, was that they would attend the Tuesday group meeting for my own clients, the Wednesday afternoon activities, and also want to come for individual time (albeit together) as well. However, at this stage I wasn't overburdened and calculated it wouldn't last long. The truth was, and I have to admit it now, that a certain amount of vanity came into play here – I was understandably flattered by their attention!

Meanwhile the Tuesday groups were thriving. It often happened that people who vaguely knew each other met in my office and there would be a mix of embarrassment and laughter as they related to each other how they came to be here. Tea, coffee and fresh fruit turned out to be key ingredients and I looked forward to these weekly sessions. It was encouraging to see people, who at first seemed to think they had very little reason to feel good about themselves, finding some positive ground where, for once, they could build their own self esteem without hurt or harm to others.

What astonished me was the depth of insight of some of the participants from whom I might not have anticipated such wisdom.

One week, with everyone talking about religion and the use of the word 'love' all over the place, Micky came into the debate with:

"It's all crap.... All this 'love everybody' nonsense. I don't love any of you, but I enjoy seeing you every week and I have a lot of respect for everyone here, even Mr. Wally!" (Embarrassed laughter all round.) "But if you don't use the word 'love' and use 'kindness' instead it's much easier to understand. If people were kinder to each other, like understanding their differences or race and that, there'd be a lot less friction. Last time I was arrested I got a really nice custody sergeant in the nick an' I thought 'I bet you're a really nice bloke. I bet you've got a nice family.' An' after I was put on probation, he recognised me in Ridley Road Market when he was with his wife an' 'e nodded, smiled an' said "Good result Mickey – good luck." Now, what's that got to do with love? Nothing. What's it got to do with kindness? Everything. That's what the world needs: kindness. That's how we got here today – and that's what we have to learn."

The weekly client groups were definitely beginning to show positive results. My original objective of enabling pooling of information and sharing experiences came to pass and the added bonus for me was my own training on the job. Though I had now worked for almost a year without a break, I couldn't help having some regrets that my summer holiday was fast approaching. Would we be able to pick up where we left off if the meetings were to be discontinued for a few weeks? There would be only one way to find out. I shared my apprehension with Jackie.

"Just go with it, Wally. If it resumes when you get back, it will say an enormous amount about the group and the motives behind it."

"Oh, right, so what you're saying, Jackie, is if it doesn't, it tells you all you need to know about my ability as a probation officer?

She laughed. "I think we've already got a pretty good idea."

That afternoon was my last supervision session before my annual leave. Jackie asked me to present brief details on my current caseload which had now swelled from the original eight to a total of twenty-nine. She asked how I felt about increasing my workload to the projected forty or so and wondered whether I would be able to manage eight reports a month increasing to ten over the next six months. I assured her that I was eager to become a fully-fledged member of the team and to shed the mantle of 'new-boy' so I'd be delighted. Jackie reminded me that I myself had been 'on probation' since joining the team as a newly qualified officer last September.

"It's normal for a new officer's probation period to last the full twelve months" she explained, "but I've spoken to Robin (her boss - ACPO) who agrees that we should confirm you as a full main-grade probation officer now. We're not going to witness any spectacular displays of performance while you're away so we're happy to remove any apprehension you might suffer while sunbathing and now I'd like to congratulate you and welcome you as an established member of our team."

28. While I Was Away...

One of the appealing benefits of working in the public sector was the provision of holidays with pay. In my previous incarnation, working in my own family business, the mere idea of prolonged time off was a myth. Now I was able to enjoy my first ever holiday with my wife and children during their school summer break. My wife, Ellen, worked in the field of university education so our opportunities for a family holiday were governed by the academic as well as the school calendar. We travelled abroad and had a wonderful time exploring rivers and valleys, mountains and beaches, castles and playgrounds. We met people of different backgrounds from many walks of life, who seemed, like us, to be without a care in the world. It was a far cry from Hackney and I was astonished how soon the problems of the office faded from my thoughts. But all good things, as they say, have to come to an end and our exciting holiday surely did........ with a resounding thump!

I had been away for three whole weeks, the longest holiday in my adult life. During that time my office had been diligently tidied; my desktop was totally clear. I had never seen it like that before: even on my first day there were welcoming leaflets, instructions, files all arranged to make me feel important. I sat down.

"I've forgotten what I do!" I said out loud with a chuckle.

(Try your in-tray, I told myself.) I went down to the reception office to find my in-tray full to overflowing. While speaking to a client on the phone, June waved and smiled broadly in greeting. As I gingerly made for the door with an armful of papers and files June, now off the phone, said:

"Welcome back, Wally. We couldn't get any more in your

pigeonhole, so the rest is on the table." She waved at the table by the window, normally the home of telephone directories, hostel guides and other reference sources. There was an untidy heap of files, letters, sheets, envelopes, journals, and a carton or two.

"Yes, it's all yours." she grinned. It took two more journeys to get it all to my office. Cartons? I like gifts. These were a new dictating machine with a supply of mini-cassettes and a pocket Dictaphone - invaluable for dictating letters and records while 'on the run'. (The trouble with that was, when I used it, I forgot to enter the notes in my trusty notebook-cum-journal.) The professional magazines and journals I set aside for later reading, likewise the circulars from the Home Office and probation headquarters.

Much of the correspondence was mundane but most of the files that were piled up had a form or a letter clipped to the front cover. Each form reported the outcome of a case involving one of my clients, or of a hearing for which I had written a report, while each letter reported some disaster or demanded some urgent action. Some of these results I had been waiting for, though the actual sentences were sometimes unexpected. One or two were from people already on probation who had re-offended or had appeared for earlier matters not yet dealt with when the probation order was made.

There was clearly a mountain of work and I suddenly realised that I was no longer a new boy and that I no longer had a protected caseload. There were six new files to prove it, cases of people whose probation officers had moved to another location, retired or seemingly permanently extended their sick leave. This was, at last, the real thing so I set to....

It took almost the first week even to make a dent in the mountain on my desk. Ayesha, my secretary, had moved on and Josie was now appointed to keep me under control. She set about organising my appointments in order of urgency. I had seen some clients in the meantime and Josie sent out appointment letters to the rest. The Tuesday group meetings would start again the following week. Josie sent reminder letters to all the regular members of the group. Memories of my holiday were fading, helped in no small measure by some of the disasters in my in-tray. Some reports I had written before my holiday, in which I'd recommended community sentences like probation or community service, had resulted in custodial sentences, some of them swingeing.

Several of the unexpected results left me stunned. One in particular knocked me sideways. One of my star clients, a West African mother of three, performing brilliantly on her probation order, with completely clear blood and urine tests at the DDU and, so far as I knew, no outstanding cases, received a four- year prison sentence. I knocked on Jackie's door.

"Can I talk to you about something?" Jackie quickly warmly quelled any doubts I had about my appropriateness in the job, but reminded me that nothing is ever as it seems in this field. She suggested I make a prison visit to the client concerned to see what she had to say. She also told me it frequently happened that more cases would be added once a defendant arrives in court, perhaps transferred from other courts, or even dredged up from the past once the Crown Prosecution Service was able to connect all the dots. Sometimes the defendant would ask for other offences to be taken into consideration. These 'TIC's' as they were often referred to, could often tip the balance in favour of custody when a community sentence might have been indicated without them. It was Monday; in the meantime I had to concentrate on clearing the backlog of work from my holiday.

"Nothing is ever as it seems in this job..." This prescient comment was both comforting and daunting. At this point I could not have known that this one particular case would fill a book of its own.....

But I digress.

It should be made clear at some stage – maybe now is as good an opportunity as any – that the salary of a probation officer is not very large. Low paid they may be, but at the time of the events in this book, teachers and nurses got more than probation officers. Prison officers received significantly more but not as much as police officers.

It's true that there is a certain amount of job satisfaction working in the probation service, as there must be in teaching or nursing, but, as with those professions, there is also considerable responsibility and always an additional element of risk when dealing with potentially dangerous or violent people – though it is not argued that all people are 'potentially' dangerous or violent, merely that some definitely are and others may be! Like all jobs concerned with the behaviour of human beings, the ever-present feeling of frustration is never far away.

Something that never became apparent during probation training was the amount of time it would take to spend on extraneous but loosely related matters.

As trainees, we had all learned that the main objective of probation was to reduce offending. That meant encouraging and enabling offenders to change their behaviour for the better. It also meant performing court duty, writing reports for court to recommend appropriate sentences for guilty offenders, supervising those serving sentences in the community in a way that would deliver a change in their behaviour, remaining in touch with those in prison to facilitate their productive return to liberty and attending ongoing professional training. At the same time probation officers must keep abreast of changes in law, procedure, treatment protocols for drugs, alcohol, mental disorder as well as local community provisions affecting us and people in our care and, worst of all, write down everything they do, step by step. Simple enough, I suppose.... But the reality was even more complex than I expected and I found it difficult. Only when I began to keep a notebook did I realise how much more there was to this job than met the eye.

My first paid employment was a holiday job as an assistant warehouseman in a non-ferrous metals warehouse. During the long hot summer holiday after leaving school at sixteen, it was a lucky opportunity to earn enough money to buy my first suit and a season ticket for the real job that was to begin in September.

The unskilled work was, essentially, that of a labourer, but I did come away with two very satisfying gems. The first was that I learned how to drive a fork-lift truck. This, for a sixteen-year-old was a thrilling way to pass even part of the day. (Health and Safety regulations were not merely non-existent – they were completely unheard of!) The second was heeding the advice of the ageing, and very popular foreman, Ernie:

"Wally, if you ever have to walk around where you work, always carry a clipboard or a big notebook. It will encourage people to think that you're doing something important and will deter them from giving you trivial jobs they don't want to do themselves."

Things were very different in those days not long after the war, but not only was the advice sound then, and much later when I became a probation officer, but, according to my now adult children, it is still valid today.

I mention this merely because, many years after benefiting from Ernie's advice, moving around the corridors of the Hackney probation office on various errands, or between tasks, as a newcomer to probation with a low caseload I would encounter colleagues who from time to time might ask something like:

"Oh, Wally, have you got a moment? I'm supposed to be in a meeting/ on court duty/ at Holloway Prison/ Drug Dependency Unit" or any of a number of tempting, impressive or even spurious sounding excuses. "I wonder if you could do me a favour: I have a client due in shortly – could you see him for me?" One problem I've always had in life is saying 'No'. I do like to help people. I don't like to see others in difficulty. It drives my wife crazy – especially when she has plans for me! It's also got me into a lot of trouble, but we needn't dwell on that here.

For the first few months I did allow myself to get bogged down in tasks that were time-consuming but not necessarily productive or educational. But recalling and heeding Ernie's advice did, I discovered, reduce the number of presumptuous or just plain stupid requests I had to deal with. Exercise-style notebooks were readily available from Jean, our esteemed administration manager, who supervised the secretaries, reception staff and stationery supplies.

But what was the point of carrying a notebook which, if someone should examine it would be found to be completely blank? So I began to make entries in it, keeping the notebook like a diary, the collection of which I have to this day, the notes in which form the basis of this book.

29. No Time for Tedium:

A Random Week

There is no such thing as a typical week in the probation service. As in life, nothing is predictable and nothing goes exactly to plan – at least, not for long. On the face of it, working days might be regarded as routine enough though, just as in the retail business I left to become a probation officer, you can never, ever, predict who or what might come through the door next.

So, to illustrate an ostensibly fairly normal working week, here are some extracts put together from my notebooks during one week early in my second year.

Monday

For those who arrived before nine-o'clock, every working day began with coffee in the staff-room; not just instant – this was real coffee from a French press with ground coffee and supplies paid for from the monthly coffee fund, contributions ably managed by June, our wonderful receptionist. At nine o'clock, June would excuse herself from the jollity of the coffee room and take her place in the reception office, protected from the waiting area by a safety glass window from behind which she welcomed callers on the telephone and personal visitors of all shades and stripes. Filled with mirth and mischief, the morning staff-room chit-chat was an indispensable start to the day which set us all up for the battles to come.

I couldn't stay long; I had to go down to Old Street Magistrates' Court - today was my all-day court duty day, with help from a colleague on the half-day duty rota just for the morning. In the small windowless office above the courtrooms, reports for submission to sentencers had to be read and checked before being personally delivered to the chief clerk or magistrate. Court case lists have to be inspected to see if any defendants are already known to a probation officer who will need to be informed about the matter. The court duty probation officer has to interview the overnight cases in the police cells beneath the court building - people arrested in the previous twenty-four hours who may need to tell someone – whether family or probation officer – of their whereabouts. Those people need to be contacted by phone or letter. All this before ten a.m.

Any other cases involving defendants already known to the probation service must be recorded on notification forms with details and case progress noted, before sending the completed form to the supervising probation officer (PO). So as each new accused person enters the dock the duty PO needs to be alert to identify what is relevant. I was never a good note-taker. At first, I would become so absorbed by the facts of the case, people's behaviour - not just the accused but also the judge and the court officials - that I would forget to write anything down. By the time I pulled myself together, the next defendant had already appeared and the fascinating details of the new case blotted out any memory of the previous case.

Court adjourns for lunch, usually from one until two. During this time the duty PO catches up on paperwork and prepares for the afternoon list if there is one. After lunch, court might finish any time between three and five, allowing time to complete any more documentation or telephone calls before the building closes around six. On that particular Monday, I finished in time to rush back to the office to see a probationer reporting at four o'clock. There were messages and items of correspondence in my pigeonhole which I glanced at.

One of the messages was from my four-o'clock date asking to

re-arrange to late-reporting night on Thursday, since he had now found a job and didn't get home until seven. That gave me time to return some phone calls. A psychiatrist at Hackney hospital had called to say one of my court report clients, just interviewed, had declined the psychiatric help he so clearly required. The doctor wanted to know what I would like him to do. I phoned him back and asked him to write a letter to the court to that effect, stating his own preferred course of action, preferably in time for the man's next court appearance.

I had invited a client, Ian, to see me at five so we could work on housing applications together. Ian had difficulty writing, though he was clearly very bright. I enjoyed our interaction and he was grateful for the help. I went home about six o'clock.

Tuesday

Next morning was the day of the weekly Tuesday client group. I was able to complete a small amount of correspondence before seven people arrived in time for the start. Four more arrived at different stages, while one or two had to leave for different reasons at different times. A total of eleven was good. Three hours of intense client contact without a break is probably too much at one go, but there was lots of stimulation, some laughter, a bit of hand-holding for someone down-in-the-dumps, some local resource discussion and some more mirth.

Prompted by my observation that many of my clients appeared to be innately intelligent but had difficulty reading, writing and organising, I had prepared a session on literacy but didn't present it; there was plenty of constructive material to fill the time. One incident was revealing: Diane, a professional shoplifter on probation mentioned drug dealers in Sandringham Road in a way that made me think she knew more about the topic than most people. Diane was neither a drinker nor a drug-user; I said nothing but made a mental note to speak to her about it later.

After the meeting, while bidding goodbye to my clients in the reception area, I invited her to drop by for an informal chat on Thursday morning and made a note in my diary.

After lunch in the staff-room I had booked two interviews for SERs (precursors of Pre-Sentence Reports). The first, a late middle-aged man from Mauritius had pleaded guilty to a minor offence of theft. It was unusual for a person's first offence to occur after the age of fifty and the magistrate wanted to know more about him. He did not exhibit any evidence of alcohol or drug misuse. He did not gamble, had a steady job and there were no indicators of mental disorder. He said he really did not know why he stole the frivolous item and had no understandable need for it. After describing his family as happy and normal with one married daughter expecting her first baby, he paused for a while. Tempted to break the silence with a question, I noticed his eyes watering and I held back.

"My wife was killed a month ago," he blurted out. "She was standing at a bus stop talking to friends and the car ran off the road and hit her." The tears were by now rolling down his cheeks and he struggled to find his handkerchief. I handed him a box of tissues expecting him to continue but he just sat there sobbing, silently, eventually breaking the agonised quiet with a whispered "Thirty-nine years.... thirty-nine years! Our parents arranged our marriage and it was love at first sight. We were sixteen. We were so lucky." (After a home visit disclosing no evidence of unexplained wealth, my report proposed an absolute or conditional discharge, the first of which the court followed.)

I needed a cup of tea before the second interview. Luckily, it was with Martin, stalwart friend of the late lamented Irving. He'd been arrested for theft of videos and pleaded guilty at first opportunity. Such a move is likely to please the court. It saves money. He reminded me about his drug use and asked me if I could help him just as I'd tried to help Irving and Kathryn. After a lengthy chat, I told Martin I thought probation would probably be the best outcome and agreed to propose it to the court. It's not normal for a convicted person to choose his sentence, but in this case it did seem the most appropriate. He seemed pretty motivated. It was way after six when Martin left. I looked in my pigeon hole in reception: it was full again. I decided to leave it until next day.

Wednesday

Our team meeting was due to begin at ten-thirty. There would be just enough time to attend to some of the correspondence I neglected yesterday. I found I was spending too long on interviews with the result I was getting behind with letter writing. So, I spent an hour and a half with Josie to help me.

There was a formal letter and application form from Cranstoun, a drugs rehabilitation organisation known for excellent work with drug and alcohol dependent adults. The letter asked for background, offending history and other personal information on one of my clients serving a long-ish custodial sentence. I dictated a reply saying the client on whose behalf they were writing was at present in custody and I would need permission before sharing any personal information but I would contact them as soon as I had the person's consent.

A couple of letters later, a phone call from June told me a probation client without appointment wanted to see me urgently. I didn't welcome the interruption but went downstairs to speak to her in the lobby only to find out she wanted money – a considerable sum with which I was unable to help her. She pressed me for time to talk, clearly hoping to persuade me, but colleagues kept hurrying me along as they passed through the public area on their way to the team meeting. When I offered her an hour tomorrow, she turned around in a huff and departed. We'll see if she keeps the appointment.... I rushed back upstairs to Josie and more correspondence.

Then the phone rang. During what developed into a long conversation, Josie excused herself to get on with the mounting pile of work. "We could continue later," she mouthed from the door as she left. I finished the phone call as quickly as I could and hurried downstairs again for the team meeting. But, waving through her security window, June beckoned me into her office just as I was about to join the meeting. Another brief interruption regarding the family of one of my clients in custody – I delayed action until after the team meeting.

My late arrival at the meeting drew glances of disapproval and my attention to the proceedings frequently wandered, trying to figure out what the problem was all about and what I was expected to do. The team meeting over-ran and we disbanded into the coffee room to discuss the morning's business for half an hour until Josie cornered me for a while to finish the morning's post and letter writing, then cordially dismissed me for my regular Wednesday date.

By now it was two o'clock, time for the Sports Activities Group with Sylvester Mittee and I hadn't even started on the rest of the jobs set aside for today. Eight people turned up – quite a good turnout on a cold day – but only two of the clients were from my own caseload.

When I got back from the group activities, there was more work in my pigeonhole and on the top of it was a message to phone social services urgently, about...... Mrs. Bingham's children.

Thursday

First job was to call Hackney Social Services about last night's message. The social worker had called in sick – again – and someone would get back to me.

Diane, my client from the Tuesday group, arrived in the cold early mist wearing her large cape. Warming her hands on a cup of tea in my office she complained, with a twinkle in her eye, about the chilly weather. Pointing at her warm voluminous cape I looked her in the eye and raised one eyebrow. "Yeah, I know," she smiled, "I always used to wear this to go 'shopping' when I was shoplifting to order. Spring, summer, autumn – I'd wear the same thing. Same as most women pick up their shopping bag when they go out. I could get anything! You wanna chicken, a coffee table or a carpet? I could get 'em all. I used to steal to order. They'd pay me half the price on the label. But since I was last in court, I've managed without. This is the first time I've worn it just to keep warm in cold weather. It's great - an' it's so much warmer without a frozen turkey down me pants!"

Diane was what one might call a 'character' and managed to make most things funny. She was a great catalyst in group meetings, but never 'hogged the floor'. Deciding not to pursue this present line of conversation for the time being, I asked her to expand on her heavily whispered aside at the group meeting about Sandringham Road, an infamous street known locally as 'The Strip'. In such a chatty mood, Diane needed little encouragement. She knew, as everyone did, she said, that some bent coppers were involved in drugs trafficking. There were beatings, too, where junkies (drug users) had their gear (drugs) seized by the police, but no charges were made, only bruises and broken bones. Of course, no-one made any formal complaint to the nick.

"How could anyone? Just imagine it," she said with a giggle, "You go down the nick to make a complaint.... 'Oi officer, there I was, mindin' me own business quietly tryin' to chase the dragon when one of your officers comes over, beats me up and nicks me gear'."

She mentioned the name of a police officer who was a regular 'privileged' visitor to her husband's shebeen (a shebeen is an unlicensed drinking establishment) in a basement flat. The name meant nothing to me. He visited often, drank little, she said, but was friendly and used his friends there as sources of information on what was happening on the strip. Diane's husband regarded his free drinks not so much as rent, more as protection money. The officer was never seen to be involved in the drugs goings-on, but everyone assumed that he was part of it all and that being friendly to him would exempt them from any of the regular brutality in the street. I thanked Diane for her visit and for the local 'lowdown'.

The young woman to whom I offered an emergency appointment yesterday did turn up, nearly on time. She had obviously taken an unusual amount of trouble with her normally hungry and homeless appearance and today looked practically glamorous. Her heroin and crack habit had caused her to lose weight – and teeth - to an almost dangerous degree. Sustenance and hygiene are normally unimportant to a person gripped by addiction. I greeted her in reception. "I don't really need to see you after all," she said. "I got the money another way. Look, I can't stop now I gotta be somewhere. Since I seen you twice this week can I have the week off next week, I think I got an important client."

"No, it doesn't work like that," I said as I handed her a card showing her next three appointments. Putting the clues together (her appearance, 'Gotta be somewhere' and 'client') I deduced with a slight sense of sadness and a feeling of failure that she was back on the game – and on the 'gear'. I was about to invite her to discuss the matter in my office but she had already turned and left without saying goodbye.

Phone calls peppered the day. A priest from HMP Belmarsh called to tell me one of his flock asked him to call me to say he had been banged up. When I learned the name, I was surprised; I didn't even know he'd been arrested. This might explain his last three missed appointments and got me off the onerous hook of preparing a breach of probation case for court. My lucky day!

Social Services phoned twice and left messages about Mrs. Bingham, whose name I still didn't recognise. I thought I was being smart by checking on the computer to see if we had any clients registered under the name of Bingham, but there was no record of such a person. The calls were from yet another social worker, Marge Wills, with whose name I was unacquainted. I wondered what this was all about. When I called back, I learned she had the wrong probation officer's name and borough so it was all a ghastly mistake.

"What's a Diary Meeting, Josie?" My secretary tells me she likes to know what appointments I've made without telling anyone else and explains that if I need to leave the office, say, to court, or a borough meeting, a home visit or anywhere else and take my diary with me, she has no way of making appointments that might crop up in my absence if she doesn't know my plans. Duly chastised I agree to regular diary meetings during which she updates her own. The meetings are generally brief.

And it was only lunchtime. The afternoon was spent in client interview appointments. Kathryn was the only one who didn't show up. She had been pretty good at keeping up attendance and was gradually managing to recover from the tragic loss of Irving. Although still drinking, she was almost methadone free now, which was progress. She came to occasional group meetings. I dashed off a reminder letter with her next appointment.

It was almost time to go home when the dreaded telephone rang again.

"Hello Wally, it's Derek." Derek was a senior probation officer in Camden, a man for whom I had immense respect. He had known me since I worked as a probation voluntary associate in the days when my wife and I still had a thriving business. Whenever our paths crossed, Derek always showed genuine interest in my career development– or the lack of it! I greeted him warmly, managing just in time to refrain from telling him I was just about to go home.

"There's a meeting coming up about sports activities and someone just told me of your involvement in a scheme in Hackney. Would you like to come?"

"Certainly, Derek, thank you. When and where is it?"

"It's here at my office. Er-r-r-rm, it's tomorrow afternoon. I know it's short notice, but I already spoke to Jackie and she told me she'd like you to be involved on behalf of Hackney Probation." Guessing, accurately, that I didn't have a lot of choice in the matter, I agreed and put it in my diary. We chatted for only a few moments longer and I went home to my family realising later I'd forgotten to tell Josie.

Friday

A couple of days ago I'd offered to cover office duty for a colleague called away for this morning. Mentioning it in the crowded coffee room, I was rebuked by Richard.

"You fathead, Wally! Look, I know you always want to help your team mates but I bet you didn't arrange a swap?"

"What do you mean, Richard?"

"When anyone asks you to cover court or office duty, if you want to say yes, make sure you BOTH have your diaries. The correct response to the question is 'When can you pay it back?' otherwise, word will quickly get around that you're a sucker and you'll be covering court or office duty five days a week." I had to admit I hadn't booked a return date. It was also Richard's gentle way of reminding everyone else the rules of business.

There were only two or three calls on my time for office duty tasks which took me away from my work during the morning. An early phone call from a psychiatrist about a colleague's client in prison; message taken and passed on in writing, no action required. A newly released parolee was fulfilling his obligatory duty to report at once to his supervising probation office on his way home having left prison that morning. Another person (client of the same absent officer) had been residing at a probation hostel as a condition of residence, but had been expelled for persistent drunkenness and failure to observe the curfew. Now homeless and in breach of his order, he needed some concentrated emergency housing input. Unfortunately, he arrived around lunchtime on our doorstep with his bags and with his hand out for money. As luck would have it, I was able to persuade him to wait for an hour until his own supervising officer arrived back and took back his office duty as well as looking after his own needy clients.

After lunch I attended the inaugural meeting of the new so-called 'North of Thames Activities Group.' It seems someone had the great idea of getting probationers involved in something constructive.... I didn't ask the convenor why I had been invited only as an afterthought. Like most probation or training department gatherings (I was to learn) they would usually start with 'introductions round the room'. Nice as this may be, it usually becomes a time-wasting exercise since almost by definition, people who put themselves forward are often those who want to be heard the most. I merely said "My name's Wally. I work in

Hackney and when I grow up, I want to be a probation officer. We have a weekly sports activities group for any clients in our borough." There were few smiles from the earnest gathering.

Apart from various politically very correct objectives, no specific ideas came to fruition. My own group was not thought to be relevant. At that time no other borough in the group had any probation activities planned or in progress. The meeting of around seven probation officers took just under three hours and, apart from each agreeing to be the activities representative for his or her borough, resulted only in deciding a date for the next meeting. I was never invited to participate. My main contribution had been to suggest as a starting point enlisting help from each local authority for ideas and available resources within each borough.

"No we prefer to keep this as a purely probation initiative," said the self-appointed chairperson without consulting the meeting. I wasn't asked for any further contribution. It was already late so I went straight home afterwards. Sitting in rush-hour traffic I had time to reflect that today was the first day this week I hadn't been involved with the peripheral family matters of one of my clients in custody. Strange how someone can be so demanding when not even present! But the out-of-borough meeting had been a revelation of a different kind: how did they expect to accomplish anything at that glacial rate?

It was a natural progression to realise how lucky I was to have been posted in Hackney: it was hard to imagine another location where I might have a conversation like:

"Jackie...? I have an Idea..."

"OK, Wally, sounds interesting. Have a go. Don't spend any money but get on with it and tell us all in the team meeting how you get on."

Any week in probation is unlike any other, so the idea of a "typical week' is unrealistic. What is accurate is the notion that every week is crammed with activity whether scheduled or unexpected and most of it gives rise to a high level of personal tension.

———

30. Improvised Activities

The following Wednesday at work was hectic, as I remember, because I was covering a colleague's office duty in the morning in parallel with the team meeting and, as well as catching up with other pressing matters, I had the clients' activities group in the afternoon. Nine people turned up.

Sylvester Mittee was not his usual effervescent self. "What's up Sylv?"

"I haven't been able to book any sports facilities. All the courts are full, the swimming pools don't have spare capacity. I just don't know what we're going to do this week. I suppose we could go to the park and play football, but there's no real sense of occasion in that. I've still got the van, though."

"How about going to Epping Forest?"

"Wow, that's a great idea – do you know the way?"

"Sure." So we left Hackney and drove to High Beech where eleven of us took an invigorating walk in the forest. Sylvester and I were astonished that the men and women in our group enjoyed it so much. No longer strangers to each other, they ran around like excited children, kicking a ball, throwing sticks, climbing trees, sliding down banks and some of them behaving so differently from the macho males they portrayed on their home turf. Seven men and two women made a varied group of people of different ages, races, backgrounds, offences, some on parole, some on probation, they behaved as though they were suddenly released from captivity. Sylvester's field is fitness; he was a former Commonwealth Welterweight Champion boxer. It's no wonder he wasn't going to let us pussy-foot around so he led us at a pretty smart pace. As the 'Old Man' I didn't want to look as though I was the one holding everyone back so I tried to keep up, though with difficulty, but I found it a tiring walk uphill and down dale, jumping streams and climbing gates.

At the end of the walk after ninety minutes or so, we returned to the minibus which Sylvester had parked close to another vehicle, a large van. By the time we got back it had turned into a mobile cafe with a lift-up side panel and was open for business. We all enjoyed cups of tea, amid banter and chatter you might expect from a football or rugby club, each poking fun at the others, laughing, giggling, joking about Sylvester and me, but all in good fun and completely lacking in malice. Some of these men had crimes of violence to their credit, others were drug or alcohol dependent. One or two clearly had mental disorders, but out here in Epping Forest, on neutral turf, where no-one was a threat, everyone was equal. In the van home we discussed this very topic.

Without exception they all thought this had been a lesson they were glad to learn. There was no need for violence or threats, macho conduct or looking big. But they couldn't articulate why things changed on their own doorstep or in their own neighbourhoods. Some useful discussion developed, but as ill-luck would have it, there were no congested streets on the way back and all the traffic signals were green, so we made it back in record time and our debate was curtailed. Few accepted an invitation to continue the discussion over a cup of tea in my office and the moment passed. But nine radiant clients left the office that afternoon, exhausted but cheerful.

All the same, throughout the adventure I spent the entire time wondering what I was doing there, when there were other such important things to attend to. Later, much later, looking back I reflected that this enforced break from the tension of what I was experiencing was probably as therapeutic to me as it was to the probation clients for whom it was intended. Either way, the day passed and I felt better that I had reached a decision to be pro-active about some problematic events back in the office.

31. Tiny Tracy Oakley

There was another new file in my pigeon hole: Tracy Oakley. She was in custody at HMP Holloway. She had just reached her eighteenth birthday and had pleaded guilty to possession of Class A drugs with intent to supply. The file gave the appearance of being complete and contained, besides the court information documents relating to the current offence, police interview transcript, witness statements and a list of previous offences: possession of cannabis, theft x 2 (shoplifting), deception, and three counts of threatening and abusive behaviour. That seemed quite a lot for an eighteen-year-old but there were no other records nor correspondence relating to earlier matters. I made an appointment to visit.

Her account of the offence when I eventually interviewed this diminutive woman at Holloway prison, coincided largely with the prosecution's version but theirs was extremely one-sided. There was no other information about her, her offences prior to this one, nor any explanatory correspondence. I had reached the stage in my job where I began to look for clues in even the minimum amount of documentation in the file. For example, convictions for threatening and abusive behaviour could be indicators for use of stimulants, alcohol or the presence of mental illness. Without making any pre-judgments, I decided to explore that aspect.

"I see from the file this all happened over a year ago. Do you know why it's taken so long to come to court?" I asked her. She was tiny, and looked frail. In her delightful Birmingham accent, she explained...

"I was brought up in care in Beermingham. Me moother moved to Glasgow with her boyfriend. She left him and was later murdered by the fella she was living with, then he was killed as well. They were drinkers, serious drinkers. I think my sister went to Glasgow to look for our mum. Dunno why. She was no good to us. She rented us out as sex toys to awful old men who paid her money for drink. We 'ated 'er and what she did to us. I lost me virginity at six. I must 'a been about nine when I was already in a children's home. I think they found me difficult. I was farmed out to various foster parents, but none of them wanted me so I was always sent back to the children's home where I learned things no child should ever know about. I was forced to do things that even the girls on the street at Kings Cross didn't believe. Soon as me periods started I got pregnant. I was twelve. I don't ever wanna tell you about the things that went on in children's homes or some of the foster homes."

"So you must have a social worker? Whom can I get in touch with?" Tracy gave me a name and department. I would look it up and contact her later.

"How did you end up in London?"

"By the time I was fifteen I was unmanageable, they said, and they were planning to try setting me up in a flat-share with some other people, young adults, who'd been raised in care but who were, they said, 'more responsible' and would be a good influence. There'd be resident key-workers too. But the key-workers who got the job were the people who had been sexually abusing me and the so-called responsible flatmates were all victims too. We were hand-picked - and we were all scared."

"So what happened?"

"I used to bunk off a lot – sometimes stay out all night or two or three nights at a time. So I thought I'd have some real fun and jump on a train. I thought I was on a train going to Glasgow but I was on the wrong platform. The train I got on was going to London, but I didn't know it at the time. I didn't have a ticket but didn't get caught. I thought they'd come looking for me. A blowk in a uniform on the train asked me for my ticket an I dodged into the lavatory.'E caught my arm and said 'You 'aven't got one, 'ave you? Get your clothes off or I'll turn you in to the inspector. I let 'im give me one an' 'e went away laughin'. "

"And...?"

"After I got off the train and discovered where I was I never 'eard from social services again."

"But you were not yet an adult – technically you were still a child – even when the offence happened. Even now you should be in a Young Offenders' Institution."

"I had always lied about my name and my age. They only found out who I am when they linked up the old shoplifting offences. Dunno how they did it. That may be why it took so long to get to Crown." Almost in the same breath, she continued...

"So when I arrooved at Euston Stytion thees blowk picked me oop. We 'ad a coffee, then a drink at a poob an' 'e said he could get me somewhere to live. I spent a couple o' nights with 'im and he took me to this flat and introduced me to cocaine. I'd used that stuff once or twice before but only a few times. After a couple of weeks of usin' it every day 'e gave me some like I never saw before. Yellow kind of crumbs - 'rocks' he called them. I asked him how'm I supposed to snort those up me nose an' 'e said 'You down't, you smoke 'em.' I'd only used Charlie before."

"Charlie?"

"Cocaine in a white powder. When I smoked 'is rock, I 'ad the mowst extreme experience of my life. I corn't descroibe it. An' 'e got me more after that. I thought it was great – for a coopl'a weeks or so. After a while, though, 'e said I'd 'ave to get some money, like, because he couldn't buy any more. I 'adn't any money meself, an' no job so 'e suggested I think about ways of makin' some money. I 'ad no idea what 'e meant at the time."

"The bloke said 'is name was Philip an' in a couple of weeks 'e got me a flat of my own an' moved in wi' me. 'E didn't 'ave much stuff, so I guessed 'e still 'ad the other place (but I never knew where it was) but what little 'e did 'ave included a case with some instruments in, like laboratory things. When I asked 'im about it 'e told me to mind me own business but said it was 'is profession. He said 'e often 'ad to go away on business and would stay away a few days then come back."

"One day 'e told me 'e was in a load of trouble and couldn't pay for some stuff 'e 'ad to buy. 'E said the man was coming round to get 'im but if 'e was out I should ask 'im in to wait. I was to give 'im a drink, Philip said, an' if 'e got', you know, sexy like, I should let him 'ave it wi' me for a long time. Then I 'ad to make out that 'e'd be in danger if Philip found us so he'd get worried that Philip would find us together and split before 'e got back. I was worried at first, 'cause I didn't know this bloke but eventually I agreed to do it, just for Philip. The bloke arrived and 'e was OK akcherly, and we 'ad some fun, like, for a long time, but after I started to make out I was afraid if Philip walked in, e' did get a bit nervous an' e' gave me an 'undred pounds an' left. I waited for Philip to come back and then got the shock of me life. 'E was there all the time – in the big wardrobe in the bedroom, an' 'e could see everything. 'E took the money off me right away an' said I could 'ave it to spend on cocaine, but if I wanted any more I'd 'ave to do the same thing an' I could go out on the street and use this flat. That's 'ow I became a prostitute."

"That's a terrible story, Tracy, I'm so sorry to hear about it."

"Well, that's not all. I soon learned 'is business was getting ordinary coke and cooking it into rocks of crack by mixing it with something, but 'e didn't do it in 'is flat, 'e did it in mine. An' eventually instead of paying for his coke, he'd get his supplier to come an' 'ave sex wi' me to pay him for Philip's cocaine. Now I was powerless, 'cos I needed crack all the time an' ordinary Charlie was no good to me any more. Philip never used it 'imself. I never saw 'im use at all. When 'e was mykin' the rocks 'e would do it on the kitchen tyble an' use those little gold weighing scales to measure it out and put tiny little bits in kitchen foil or in those little poly bags that zip up. I hated the whole scene, but it never occurred to me that I was part of a gang."

"Is Philip in custody too?"

"You must be 'avin' a joke, aren't you? 'E disappeared. Took the Charlie and the crack and left the things. Drugs paraphernalia, the police called it. Police never found 'im. An' I never knew where the first flat was cause we only went there in the dark in 'is car. I never been anywhere in London. They said I 'ad a good story, but I was lying an' I was clearly the drugs baron. They serious? In my state of poverty? Jus' look at me. I'm so broke I can't even afford tits."

Even in custody it was easy to see that Tracy was a pitiful victim. She was pale and underweight, maybe six and a half stone – perhaps forty kilos. To me she looked perilously anorexic. Her thin lank yellow blonde hair needed attention. In a women's prison, inmates spend a great deal of time locked up in their shared cells and customarily pass time tending to each other's hairdressing needs. This activity had clearly passed Tracy by.

"What do you think is going to happen to you, Tracy?"

"In a way, I hope I go to jail. When social workers or foster parents tried to show me how to survive, I never listened and always wanted to do my own thing. It's obviously never worked. I'm no good at judgin' character and as soon as someone offers me something that sounds good I'm hooked. I'm a failure on the out. Prison would be good for me. I can get drugs in here. Some of the screws know I do sex – women officers as well as men and they'll confiscate something off someone else and give it to me for sexy favours. It's 'cos I still look like a little girl, see? I've got tiny tits and no hair, you know, down there. They love it. Anyway, I'm pregnant." Oh... my... God... I had absolutely no idea how to respond to this...

"But you've been in custody for a year."

"Yeah, it was one of the prison officers. I 'aven't seen 'im for a while. They move around a lot y'know. He was nice to me when I lost my baby and I was in the prison medical wing. Then 'e was always friendly when I went back on the remand wing. `E knew I'd give 'im oral sex if 'e was nice to me. After a few months it just 'appened. E' fooked me. I 'aven't done a test yet, but I know it's right. It'll be my third pregnancy. Poor little boogger will be born in jail. Around February or March I think."

"Tracy, this is terrible." In truth, I just didn't really know what to say. "You've had an awful time and it's about time somebody treated you as a human being. I have to write a report for the court to read before they pass sentence. I'd like to ask the court to help you. Do you think that would be a good idea?"

"They wouldn't do that. They think I'm just a worthless prostitute who's been caught dealing drugs. Why would they want to do that?"

"Because judges are human beings just like everyone else. They will be able to see from my report that you are the one who's been used and that you should have a chance. Aren't you interested in getting off the drugs?"

"Of course I am, but I don't see how."

"If I propose a probation order I could put you in touch with some people who could help. And if you're willing, we could sign you up with a doctor, look at options for being a successful mother and later get some training for a job that won't involve you in humiliation and cruelty. Could you agree to that?"

"I'm sorry, sir, I don't remember your name, but I don't think it'll work. The social workers always had high hopes, but it never came to anything." Visiting time ended. I didn't know whether to be relieved or sorry. After the bell I thought of so many questions I had planned to ask but it was too late. The prisoners were escorted out of the legal visits area and body-searched in the adjacent lobby. I saw Tracy outside my interview room being lingeringly patted down for contraband. Was that one of the officers she mentioned? I wondered....

I was upset: how could I not have been? I'd been in the job for just over a year. Should that have been enough time for me to have learned how to deal with situations like this. I felt awful. Yet I tried never to let my work affect my family life. As usual, when I got home that evening, I put the key in the door and as I opened it, I called out 'Hallo-o-o-o-oh'.The boys called out from doing their homework upstairs, "Hi da- a-a-ad." "Yo dad!"

Ellen, on the other hand, called from the kitchen: "What's wrong darling?" It seemed at that moment, that was the support I needed; in fact, the best support anyone could ask for. My children, my wife, solid. I didn't need to explain to Ellen what an awful day it had been, and she was smart enough not to ask, but of course it all came out later when I was less upset.

Next day, I found the phone number of social services in the area of Birmingham where Tracy had lived and called the duty social worker. Tracy 's former social worker had taken early retirement for reasons of ill-health and there was no-one at the office who remembered her case. There were, apparently, no easily accessible records, so I was asked to write.

While doing so, I also wrote to West Midlands Probation Service seeking any records they might have. In true 'jobsworth' style they replied to say I would need to write to the Youth Offending Service at the address given. Records for this service, it turned out, were at the same address as the probation service. It was clearly too much trouble to merely forward my original letter to the correct department one floor up in the same building. Time was running out. A note in my pigeonhole told me the case had been brought forward to a date ten days hence, so I needed to get a move on.

A few days later I received a rather thin file from the Youth Offending Team with few official records, sparse notes and a sheet stating "Case Closed" without explanation.

On closer inspection, however, the file did contain some information which confirmed much of what Tracy had told me – particularly about her earlier life, her mother's murder and her troubled career in care. There was even an oblique reference to reported child sex abuse in one of the children's homes – followed by a suggestion that it was all a fabrication. The file was closed shortly after her mother's death when Tracy disappeared and cursory searches failed to find her. The date did not align with my own calculations of when Tracy must have come to London but I blamed my sloppy arithmetic.

"How am I going to get all of this in a report?" I wondered aloud in my next supervision session. In fact, when I raised it, Jackie told me there might not be any need to go into that much detail. The court is likely to recognise that Tracy is an extremely vulnerable person and, though I shouldn't rule out custody, a probation order would probably make the most sense. One thing we did discuss was a concern I was beginning to have about my caseload. No, I wasn't worried that it was growing faster than Jackie had planned for me, but I had noticed that out of fifteen or so clients, five were female – and I was aware that the prevailing gender ratio among offenders was about 8 males to 1 female.

Was I doing something wrong? Jackie assured me that the situation would regress to the mean eventually – by which she meant that the numbers would gradually balance out – but was I, she wondered, worried about working with women? I sensed that this was a loaded question but replied that I had no difficulties with those issues. I assured her that if there were something I did not feel confident in handling, I would gladly seek her help as my supervisor or that of another female colleague. So far I'd managed – and had already discussed some things with Jackie or other women officers as they'd arisen, or later in supervision.

I recall from my training that, contrary to many people's expectations, the incidence of male officers entering liaisons with female clients was far, far less than that of female officers having relationships with male clients. The reason put forward is that females caught up in the justice system are often vulnerable people with multiple problems who would not be the obvious target of attention from a probation officer seeking a relationship. Male clients, on the other hand, are frequently attractive, confident, macho personalities who use their charm to win favours or concessions from anyone, even female probation officers. This view may be open to criticism now, but at that time it was fairly prevalent. In fact, during my entire career I learned of no cases of male officers behaving unprofessionally and of only one female officer having a relationship with a client, though that has no statistical validity. Anyway, I showed Jackie the report, just to cover my back before I sent it off to court. All I had to do now was wait for the notification of sentence.

I was not required to attend court, though later I developed a habit of attending Crown Court sentencing to present my reports if I were seeking a contentious probation order, if for no other reason than to give the judge an opportunity to ask questions. This practice, I learned from my colleagues, was usually appreciated by the court and, they assured me, stood me in good stead with the client when a probation order was made seemingly as a result of the probation officer's attendance. My views were frequently challenged, but I soon learned that by delivering my responses confidently, I was often able to persuade the judge to accept my view. Of course, the court had the trump card; if a probation order or other community sentence made at my suggestion were to fail, the probationer would be brought before the court under breach proceedings and re-sentenced – often with a term of custody.

But in Tracy's case, the court made a probation order without much persuasion. There was, however, a condition of residence at an approved probation hostel and Tracy was instructed after court to report immediately to the hostel in Camden. She arrived and was signed in by staff who told her the rules and the routine of the hostel. She was required to sign to indicate her acceptance of the terms, which she did. However, she then left and did not come back that night.

When she appeared the following day, she was immediately told, once again, by the Senior Probation Officer at the hostel that she had broken the rules and, if it happened again, would be returned to court in custody. The following night she again did not return, and hostel duty staff telephoned me to say they were sending her back to court. If she preferred not to be remanded in custody, she was warned, she should remain living at the hostel and obey the rules. Tracy later appeared and told the deputy warden that she was trying to contact her grandmother to go to live with her – without stating where her grandmother lived, or even her name.

She removed most of her belongings from her room, leaving just one or two items as if to demonstrate her intended return. Tracy was not seen again at the hostel. With no contact address it was not possible to give her an appointment at my office. I called Old Street Magistrates Court for advice on how to commence breach proceedings on a missing person. It was with great relief that I learned that breach proceedings could not commence before the actual court order had been received by the supervising officer, and since it had not yet been issued by the Inner London Crown Court that made the order, I had a few days leeway to find her.

Had I been smart, I would have waited, then commenced breach proceedings immediately upon receipt of the order.

Some days later, seeing me passing her window in reception on my return to the office, June called out "I have a message for you, Wally." She passed me a note through the gap under the protective security glass. Tracy had called giving a new home address. I wrote giving a new list of appointments. Two weeks, three letters and an unsuccessful home visit later I felt slightly relieved when Tracy came to the office, though not at any appointed time. I saw her in reception. She was dressed in what I might have described as school uniform: a grey skirt with white shirt open almost to the navel, flat shoes and knee-length socks. She had a shoulder-bag, like a school satchel, and a dark blue cardigan clumsily draped over the bag so it dragged on the floor.

"I'm pleased to see you at last, Tracy, but where have you been?"

"Because I was discharged from court after a year in jail and I wasn't given any money, I had to turn a trick, didn't I?"

"But that was over two weeks ago."

"I've come to tell you me new address. I live on me own now." She gave me the details which I didn't immediately recognise. It certainly wasn't the address on June's note from a fortnight ago. I reminded her that she was required to live in the hostel nominated by the court.

"It's no use," she replied, "I can't hack it. That's me address now."

"Tracy, you don't have a choice. It's going to be either that or custody. You were lucky to get a probation order."

However, I allowed myself to be distracted by the notion that, since the address was outside the Hackney boundary, and since it was no longer in my borough, I would not be expected to hold the order as supervising officer. It could be transferred to Tottenham where she was now living. Another feeling of relief came over me, though I stopped short at telling her right away.

I remembered that I had now received more information from West Midlands, including an alternative list of previous offences (the Form 609). This had made it patently obvious that some of her story, related during my report interview in Holloway, didn't ring true so I arranged a home visit – just to check whether she really did have a new address. After all, she claimed that she always gave a wrong name, date of birth and address. I could be another sucker, for all I knew.

So, I arranged to go to see her at the new address and was relieved when she opened the door. The brick building was constructed to look like a terraced house, but had two flats on the ground floor and two on the first floor, all sharing the same front door. It was in a street of terraced houses on a development of council owned properties, probably erected just after the war in the 1950s.

The flat itself was small – one bedroom and a living room with a kitchen in the corner. A cramped bathroom adjoined the bedroom. It had been sparsely furnished thanks to Social Services. On the floor next to a bare mattress on a bed-frame with no legs, her suitcase lay open with a few clothes spilling out.

There was neither hanging space nor drawer space. A cooker, a tiny refrigerator, two old chairs and a non-matching kitchen table were the only items in the other room. We sat and talked for a while and I acquainted her with the requirements of her probation order – to maintain contact at least weekly, let me know of any change of address or circumstances, attend the DDU for treatment as required and stay out of trouble. I reminded her of the obligation to live in a hostel as soon as a place became available. We also talked about the requirement to go for drugs and alcohol treatment. I said I would help her find a GP and an ante-natal clinic. I would even accompany her if she wished, or could get a female assistant probation officer to go with her.

"I can't do all that, it's all too difficult." she said, "It's easier being in the nick."

"We'll take it slowly shall we? One thing at a time. You did tell me in Holloway you wanted help getting off drugs. We could start there."

"Well I changed my mind about that. I learned a few new tricks in Hollywood." Hollywood was the inmates' name for HM Prison, Holloway. "Anyway, it's workin' out OK. So I don't need no hostel." *('Don't go there, I told myself – not just yet, anyway....')*

"Right, well you do at least have to come to see me every week. That's a condition set by the court, not by me. Here are your next two dates." I gave her an appointment card with my office phone number and the dates of our planned meetings. As I left, she asked for money which I declined to give her. "If you come to the office, I'm permitted to refund your fares if you bring the bus tickets." On the way back to the office I made a mental note to ask Jackie to tell me the procedure for transferring the case to Tottenham.

"It's simple enough, Wally. Just get the file in apple pie order, show that she's keeping appointments and that your records are up-to-date. Apply to Old Street Magistrates Court to transfer the order on account of her new address, notify the Senior Probation Officer at the new office and when they accept it, send the file in the internal mail. Job done." It sounded simple. I had a nagging feeling it wouldn't be.

Tracy failed to attend her next two appointments and by the time I had written two warning letters, of escalating firmness, she had missed the next one as well. Another home visit was unsuccessful and I noticed that one of her windows was broken.

But other matters at the office were also demanding my time. Reluctantly, I made a note to start transfer proceedings. I telephoned Tottenham office.

"No, I'm sorry Mr. Henry, we can't accept the case. It doesn't work like that, not in Tottenham anyway. If you've proposed a probation order and it's unsuccessful from the start, it probably means it wasn't a good idea in the first place. It's no surprise that no-one else is going to want to tidy up a mess they didn't create, is it?"

A couple of months went by; Tracy still didn't report despite more letters from me. On one occasion, I was driving home with Ellen and the boys after a thrilling evening at the supermarket. Much of the entire route, the main road from Stamford Hill towards our home was, at that time, a haven for prostitutes – to the great annoyance of the local residents who constantly did battle with the local authority and the police to try to deter it.

We pulled up at traffic lights where a car two or three vehicles ahead of us was already stationary at a red signal. A woman pedestrian was leaning on the car, bent over as if accosting the driver through the open passenger window. All that was visible from our position was a bottom sticking in the air, a short skirt and two thin legs. As the lights changed, the hapless driver must have declined her proposition and screeched away, leaving the woman screaming abuse and making an obscene gesture with her middle finger. The other cars hurried through the green light and as we passed the woman, I got the shock of my life; it was Tracy. My heart sank and though I needed to speak to her, now was clearly not the time, with my wife and children in the car. Anyway, I consoled myself, it's way out of hours. At least she doesn't look so thin now.

So next day I resolved to go to find her on the same street. It wasn't that far from the office so I could pop out to see if she was around. But that would be inefficient – I could miss her by seconds or days – and I did have other pressing work to attend to. Anyway, what if police came along and arrested her for soliciting and me for kerb-crawling? Or worse, it's not that far from my own street... What if neighbours, came along and saw me? Come to think of it, supposing someone from the boys' school spotted me? I could see the headline in the local paper "Primary School Parent Governor Seen With Prostitute".

"Jack-ie-e-e-ee? ? ?"

"Come in Wally." So I explained everything to my supervisor.

"This is where you need to step back from being too involved with your clients, Wally. I know you put a lot into this, and you think she has a lot of problems and if only you could help, her life would change for the better. But don't forget, probation was not her idea. She told you she feels inadequate on the outside and hoped for a custodial sentence. Give her some credit for knowing herself. You can't save everyone, Wally. Just complete the forms for breach proceedings and send everything off to the court. They'll issue a warrant without bail and she'll be back inside before you can say 'knife'. It's not your failure – but it will be if you let it get out of hand. Just protect your back by following the right procedures. It's quite easy." I thanked her, though with some misgivings, and left.

As I reached her office door, she added, "...and if you do feel you need to speak to her in the street, keep a clipboard and pad in the car and hold it up to look as though you're making official notes while you're talking to her. Keep me updated on this one. Like most cases of this nature, it may get worse before it gets better."

I tried to put Tracy out of my mind. Indeed it was several weeks before the file was ready for court. I had corresponded fruitlessly with Birmingham Social Services requesting chapter and verse on the case but they were tardy in responding. There was still at least one reply outstanding. Jackie said that didn't reflect negatively on my performance. Eventually, returning in my car from a prison visit, I saw Tracy on the same street, though happily in a quieter location. I parked a distance away and strode toward her protected by my trusty clipboard.

"Tracy! Where have you been?"

"Philip's back. 'E don't live wi' me but 'e knows where I am. I'm back on crack in a big way an' it's 'opeless now."

"Why didn't you come to see me? I could have helped. All you had to do was ask. Now I have to take you back to court if you don't comply with the order."

"Oh fuck the probation order, fuck the court and fuck all the social workers. They're the ones who started all this. None of 'em ever did me any good. The ones who didn't fuck me ignored me or told me I was lying when I tried to tell them what was happening to me and the other children."

"Tracy, this isn't a good place to have this conversation. Why not come to the office? I know there are people who can do much more to help you than I can. I've had to start breach proceedings to take you back to court. It's not too late to stop that if you'll only keep your appointments with me."

"Look, it's not you, Mr. Probation Officer, it's the whole fuckin' system. Just do what you have to do, I don't fuckin' care no more." In an attempt to end on a positive note, I gave a friendly parting shot.

"At least you're looking better than last time I saw you, Tracy. Have you put on a little weight? It suits you."

I was unprepared for her vituperative reply. "You stupid, stupid old man," she screamed, "That's 'cause I'm fuckin' pregnant you ignorant bastard, an' it's beginning to show. Now, do you want business or not? If not, fuck off, I've got a living to make. I could'a made forty quid while you been talkin' to me – sixty if I swallowed it."

I reeled back to the car, dazed, speechless. At the office I sought solace in the staff room, but it was empty. My closest colleagues were all out – court duty, prison visits, training courses. Jackie was busy all afternoon. So I just went and stewed in my office......

.

32. Another Active Interlude

Work, of course, had to continue as normal. Reports, client supervision, meetings, client groups, activities. We had news that Jackie had a car accident in France and would be away from the office for an "indeterminate period." Chris was to take over management of both teams. He gave no clue as to how burdensome this must have been; the office continued to run like clockwork.

I remember one day very well. It was Wednesday; the afternoon activities had gone particularly well. Eleven people had turned up for weights, swim and sauna. Weightlifting was always popular with the macho crowd, but this time some of the women, eager not to be left behind, began to get interested. Sylvester was on hand with his solid, cheerful support. I enjoyed the swimming. Water makes everyone equal; it is like a friend, can be fun, could be dangerous and needs to be treated with respect. And I had yet to meet a non-swimmer who couldn't learn a few strokes in one afternoon session.

This week was no exception. Two people, one male, one female and neither of them my own clients, had expressed dismay when we told them the programme. He, a pale, scrawny youth of about nineteen, she a bold Caribbean woman in her mid-twenties. When I explained they would swim a width of the pool by four o'clock they both looked petrified. But to give them credit, the pair got as far as changing into their swimming kit like everyone else once we moved from the weights room to the pool. The others entered the water with Sylvester organising an activity, while the three of us sat down near the water to chat.

"Jade, Max, tell me why you want to learn to swim."

"If I ever have kids, I want to be able to go in the water with them." Jade said nervously. I remember feeling moved by her sudden tenderness when talking about the idea of having children. Jade was one of the tough women who had attempted weightlifting for the first time.

"I was always left out by me mates when they swam in the canal." was Max's response.

"OK, good." I lowered my voice slightly as shrieks from the nearby pool made it harder to carry on a conversation. "Now, just between us, what's stopping you?"

They both leaned forward and said, "I've always been scared of the water" - then laughed because they both said exactly the same thing at once.

"Perfectly natural. OK, I want you to go back to the changing rooms and wash your faces."

They looked puzzled, but did as I asked, taking their towels with them. Moments later they returned with dry faces.

"Oh, sorry, I didn't mean you to take your towels; I meant to tell you to leave them behind. Now, this time I want you to leave your towels here, wash your faces again with lots of water, splash it all over the place, get very wet and come back here soaking."

Max came back first and had clearly washed his face very energetically, his normally tousled long hair now soaked almost completely flat. Jade obviously took a shower and emerged from the females' changing rooms with a big grin, water streaming down her face from her thick black Afro hair.

"Excellent. Now let's get in the water." They followed meekly as we went gingerly down the wide easy steps into the teaching pool

– often called the children's pool because it was very shallow. There was no ladder – the teaching pool wasn't nearly deep enough, but the wide steps that took up all of one side of the pool were easy for parents and children, teachers and pupils, to sit on, chat, change their minds, or gently enter the water.

"To start with, just sit in the water on the steps. Now move down, one by one, and sit on the bottom of the pool. The water will come to just below your chest. You both seem OK with that so far?" They nodded cautiously, clearly worried about what might be coming next. "OK. Now your faces are already wet, try splashing yourselves gently at first, then more and more." They did so with increasing vigour.

"Right, now come and sit on the top step again and go down the steps on your backsides, one by one. Good... Now you're sitting on the bottom step, just lean backwards and try to lie down on the steps. What happens?"

"My legs come up," said Max.

"I can't keep my bum on the floor!" added Jade.

"Good. Time to go to the main pool."

We entered the adult pool via the ladder at the shallow end. The water was about just over waist high. Jade and Max splashed themselves and each other gently, laughing shyly while awaiting instructions. They looked nervously towards all the noise and excitement coming from Sylvester and his team who were having fun several metres away. Jade and Max seemed reassured that no-one was watching us.

"This time, let's try to kneel on the floor of the pool," I said. "Hold on to the rail at the side of the pool while you're doing it." They managed that with no difficulty, but we were crowding the steps and other people wanted to enter or leave the water so I asked them both to follow me a little way toward the deep end where the water was, of course, not as shallow as where we had entered.

"Right, where were we?"

"Kneeling" replied Jade.

"Good, let's do it again."

"Oo-er, I can't do it," said Jade

"Why not?" I asked.

"Because when my chin touches the water my knees won't stay on the floor."

"Great. That's exactly right."

"It's my shoulders," shouted Max above the noise of a nearby group of children. "They won't stay down!"

"Terrific, now we're really getting somewhere. Come down here a little further and, holding on to the rail, try to lower your shoulders under the water. Don't let go of the rail. What happens?"

"My legs float," Jade said excitedly.

"I'm floating!" yelled Max grinning widely.

"Good, now kick your feet up and down and make a lot of splashing." We all did it together.

"What's happening now?"

"It's pushing me into the rail."

"Good. Do that a bit more.... then stop."

By now, it has to be said, Jade and Max were beaming. Whatever their problems in the outside world, and I had no knowledge of their offences or circumstances, they had forgotten them all. And at the moment they seemed to have forgotten they were afraid of water. They also seemed to be enjoying themselves.

"OK, you're both doing great. Are you ready for the hard bit?" With an apprehensive glance at each other they both nodded.

"Right, look at me, take a deep breath and hold it......now breathe out slowly through your mouth. Good. Again... Again... Excellent. And now we're going to do the same but breathe out through your nose... That's great. Luckily for me you're both terrific students."

"Right, now I want you to wet your faces again..." They splashed their faces, "but this time I want you to put your faces in the water – no, wait a moment – but first take that big breath and breathe out through your mouth making big bubbles in the water. Just do it a little – and don't breathe in while you're down there!" They both did as I had said and came up, with surprised looks on their faces as if to say "Wow, I survived that!"

"Can you do it again, several times? Try breathing out through your nose. This time, when you breathe in, do it by turning your head to the side until your mouth is clear of the water. Do it alternately, once through the mouth, once through the nose and so on." They tried that for a while, looking proud when I stopped them.

"OK, next, face the wall, stand with your feet wide apart and hold the rail with one hand. The wider apart your feet are, the easier the next bit will be." They immediately settled so they were chest deep in the water. This time you'll take a deep breath, put your face in the water and paddle with your spare arm as if you're doing half a front crawl."

"How can you do half a front crawl?" asked Max.

"He's joking, dummy."

"Wait, wait.... When your arm goes in the water, put your face in the water, when it comes out, turn your head to the side, so your mouth is out of the water, and breathe in." I showed them. "Try it." They both managed it. There was a bit of spluttering, but not enough to deter either of them and they soon got the hang of it. They tried it with the other arm. I showed them how they could use their arms to paddle more efficiently, as if spearing fish with the hand in a pointed shape as it went into the water.

"OK, we're nearly there. Turn around and lean on the side of the pool, feet apart as before, shoulders below water level. Now, while still leaning with your backsides flat against the wall, try the exercise again but this time with both arms alternately. Each time one arm comes out of the water, turn your head to the side and grab a breath, remembering to close your mouth before you put it back in the water."

"I can see where this is going," grinned Jade. In order to get their backs against the wall they needed to position their legs to wedge themselves.

"That's great. Now do exactly the same thing but this time only touch the wall with your backside. Go." And off they went. After just a few strokes, they realised they were swimming, then stopped in astonished delight. "Oi, where're you going?" I called.

"I swam!"

"Look I can swim!"

They laughed and splashed and giggled like a couple of kids. They did it again, starting from the side of the pool as before.

246

"Look, I can really swim!" Max said again, "Can you teach me to dive now?"

"No, Max, you need a proper teacher for that. But first you've got to be able to swim at least to the other side." Max and Jade needed no greater encouragement. By this time, Sylvester and his protégés had stopped to watch. When Jade and Max came up after a second, this time successful, attempt to swim a width, the group all shouted, clapped, cheered and generally made whoopee in encouragement. Jade and Max grinned from one ear to the other and splashed each other again in embarrassed pride.

After that, the sauna was a glowing climax. Naturally people remained suitably attired in swimsuits or shorts for the occasion and for most of them it was their first time in a sauna. Everyone was chatting and there were congratulations for Jade and Max from all the others. People exchanged stories of how they learned to swim, how they felt much more confident in themselves, and how they enjoyed the esteem of others when they were no longer restricted to watching or paddling. Gradually the numbers thinned out as the temperature in the cabin was slowly raised and, of course, it was the same macho crowd of weightlifters who stayed to endure the highest temperature, but this time the group included Jade and Max. The drive back to the probation office was a real buzz and Sylvester was full of praise for the two new swimmers. Today had been a real milestone for their own self-esteem.

It had been an enormously successful afternoon for the activities group. Eleven people had enjoyed weights, swim and sauna, and for many of them it was the first experience of one, two or even all three sporting activities. Sylvester dropped us off but this week didn't stay for our customary staff-room cup of tea and wind-down chat. I was by now the last person in the building.

Should I do some more work or might I go home on time for once?

My reverie was interrupted by the phone......

---

33. Tiny Tracy's SOS

"Mr. Probation Officer, I need 'elp." Only one person addresses me this way. It sounded as though Tracy had been drinking. I had discovered, over the first year or so in the job, just as my experienced colleagues had warned me, the word 'help' in this context was a synonym for 'money'. My conscience was alert even if I wasn't, telling me to stay away and stop the call now. *(Remember what Jackie said about not getting too involved with your clients... Just follow the rules.)*

"Tracy, I'm sorry but there's nothing I can do. The file has already gone to court for breach proceedings and a warrant will be issued soon. As far as I'm concerned, you're no longer on probation."

"But Mr. Probation Officer you always said you'd 'elp me."

"It's too late, Tracy. I urged you to come to the office but you didn't come."

"You're just like all the others. Fuckin' great.... Just when I need you, you turn your back."

(Oh, my God! What am I to do?) I decided to hang up, but hesitated.

"But what's wrong, Tracy, why now? It's after six in the evening?" *(No, No. No, idiot, don't engage! Just stick to the rules.)*

"I wanted to stop all this, the sex, the drugs, the alcohol so I refused to give sex to Philip 's supplier," she sobbed, "Philip didn't get 'is stuff and now 'e's comin' to kill me. Oh please come here, please..." she was crying now. She sounded like a child in deep distress. *(OK big shot,' I thought, 'get out of that!)*

249

"Tracy, I have to go now." Slowly, I moved the telephone receiver away from my ear, but I could still hear her.

"Oh, no, Pleeeeease...., Pleeeeease...." Louder now, much louder, it was more of a wail, a howl, as if in terror of pain to come. As I put down the phone, I could still hear it, ...and I can still hear it today.

"Hi Da-a-a-ad."

"Yo, Dad!"

"You're early darling." Of course, Ellen with her extraordinary antennae knew something was wrong and she didn't have to wait long before I told her about the call. Over supper I told her I felt I had a job to finish. Mulling over the risks of making an out-of-hours home visit to a client known to be engaging in prostitution I turned to Ellen:

"I want to ask you something. You can say no, and I'll understand, but I'd really like you to come with me." And, because she's Ellen, she agreed. Fortunately, we had friends staying with us who were willing to stay with the boys.

It was dark when we arrived at Tracy's flat. There was a police car parked outside. As we climbed the stairs, we saw a uniformed police officer barring the entrance.

"We've come to see Tracy." I said to the officer standing astride, arms folded.

"And who might you be?"

250

"I'm Walter Henry, Tracy Oakley's probation officer and this is my wife. I produced my probation warrant card. What's going on here? What's happened?"

"Ah, we've heard all about you. We were hoping you might show up, she's waiting for you now. My colleague is with her. Go on in," he said without explanation. Ellen followed me into the flat.

Tracy appeared, followed by a uniformed female police officer. Tracy was in an awful state. She had clearly been subjected to terrible violence. Her flimsy and blood-stained shortie nightgown, stretched tighter by her just noticeably swelling pregnant belly, could not conceal her injuries. She had been bleeding from the nose and the side of her head, one eye was so swollen it was closed, both arms and torso were bruised with long wheals as if she'd been beaten with something like a baseball bat. One thigh had a right-angled cut, still oozing after first aid administered, presumably, by the police. The blood on the bedroom wall and floor was smeared as if her head had been banged against the wall and rubbed in it, caused her to fall, then been dragged across the floor. When she saw us she burst into tears. "Oh, Mr. Probation Officer......"

"Who did this, Tracy?"

"Philip Quick."

The other officer came in and closed the front door. Tracy sat down. There was more furniture than I had seen on my first visit. A chair had been smashed. I could now see a bloodstained chair leg which lay discarded by the front door. I introduced Ellen.

"Your husband's wonderful," Tracy said tearfully.

"Try living with him!" was her usual response to a positive comment about me, but this time she had the savvy to just say,

"Thank you, I know." *(Can I have that in writing? I remember thinking.)* And in response to my asking what happened, Tracy offered the following explanation. "Philip came here. He'd heard what happened, like I told you on the phone, and he beat me up. He threatened to kill me if it happened again."

"Will you tell the officer everything you told me?"

"Everything?"

"Yes, Tracy, it's safe to do it." So she told the officer about the drugs, the sex, the prostitution, the procuring and the blackmail. There was enough to put him away for a very long time.

"Have you called an ambulance?" I asked the police.

"She refused an ambulance."

"Tracy, did you tell the police you're pregnant?"

"No."

"Tracy, I think an ambulance should be called right away." She nodded through her tears.

"I'll go and take care of it now," said the male officer. Ellen spoke gently and comfortingly to Tracy in a way that only women can and she stopped crying. She sat beside Tracy as the policewoman managed to get Tracy to talk about Philip while taking down copious notes about him. Tracy was obviously in a great deal of pain and spoke with difficulty. All the while, I couldn't get out of my head the idea that decisive action on my part could have avoided this terrible situation. Bugger the rules; the one time in my life I follow the rules it goes pear-shaped.

After what seemed like ages, eventually the ambulance

arrived and the paramedics helped Tracy into it, making her as comfortable as possible before they drove away. I ascertained the hospital and phone number as well as contact details for the police officers present that night. They had been impressive; their conduct with Tracy had been gentle, sensitive, persuasive and re-assuring. They were from the local domestic violence team but said that this evening's incident was much more serious than most of their cases. Their arrival was prompted by distraught calls from neighbours reporting screams of terror from Tracy 's flat. By the time they arrived, of course, Philip was nowhere to be seen but they had enough to go on. He was already known to the police.

Ellen and I went home in silence. I think she was beginning to get a different view of my work. I had to be up early next day and after my morning swim, went straight to Old Street Magistrates Court where I had an all-day slot on the court duty rota.

Court duty is never boring, and fortunately some days are less pressured than others. The last case of the morning concluded a little early with a defendant being given an order for community service – unpaid work - and I had to leave the court momentarily to give him reporting instructions. When I returned to pick up my files to take them back to the office, another case was beginning. I remember being puzzled since the court was virtually empty a moment ago. There was a man seated in the dock. Minutes earlier the clerk and prosecution had been planning to leave for lunch, now they were in a huddle with a gaoler from the custody area who was handing over some papers. Another gaoler stood beside the closed gate of the dock and addressed the magistrate.

"One late charge in custody, sir."

"Can it wait till this afternoon?"

"The prison van is leaving shortly, sir." This was code for "It's a serious custody case."

"Very well, I'll hear it." And to the defendant, "Stand up." He stood up. He was a tall, well-built black man of about thirty to thirty-five, perhaps Caribbean, very smartly dressed in a suit and tie - almost distinguished, exceedingly handsome with a benign face.

"Will you please give the court your full name?" asked the court clerk. His reply caught me off guard:

"Philip Quick."

"Do you live at....?" he gave Tracy 's address, the flat where I had been with my wife the evening before.

"Yes."

"Mr. Quick, you are charged with assault occasioning actual bodily harm, but I understand there are other charges pending and I have been advised by the prosecution that today's matter should be adjourned to a later date. Will you please sit down?" I was stunned. The prosecutor was on his feet.

"At approximately seven p.m. last night" (he gave the date) "police were called to the defendant's address where they found the defendant's partner, Tracy Oakley, in a state of extreme distress having suffered several serious injuries. She is pregnant and is still undergoing examination in hospital concerning the well-being of her unborn child. Other injuries include a broken arm, a broken nose, a black eye, hair pulled out, cuts to the face, fractured rib, cuts to the legs and multiple bruising. The victim alleged the attack was by her partner, the man in the dock, who was no longer present by the time the police arrived but who was arrested this morning. There are other matters of a serious nature currently being investigated which in due course will be added to the current charge."

"Thank you. Is there any defence solicitor?"

"Yes sir, thank you." A solicitor rose to his feet. "I've no knowledge of the case since I received my instructions as duty solicitor moments before Mr. Quick was brought into court. I would ask for a remand on bail so that I can interview my client and obtain advance information from the prosecution."

"Very well, thank you," and to the prosecution "Is there any objection to bail?"

"None sir, there's nothing here."

(Luckily, my subconscious was alert even if I wasn't: 'Wally, Wally wake up! You can't let this happen. He'll KILL her!' But, I argued with myself, I can't play a part in the prosecution or the defence... 'This is neither, this is public safety you idiot. Stand up! DO SOMETHING!' I stood up lamely but noisily from my squeaky tilting seat, not knowing what I was going to say next. All eyes were on me and I was paralysed.)

"Er, sir, erm, I wonder if I might have a word with the prosecution before a decision is made?"

"What do you want to say?"

"I need to consult the CPS about this matter."

"Anything you have to say must be said in open court, you should know that. Will you please come to the witness box?"

I walked self-consciously to the witness box.

"Please give your name."

"My name is Walter Henry. I am a probation officer serving this court. The alleged victim in this case is on probation and I am her supervising officer. My wife and I attended the scene of the alleged offence last evening and we were admitted to the premises by the police. We saw the victim who had serious injuries. She was transported to hospital by blue light ambulance.

Ms. Oakley is in fear of her life from the accused man who, she told me, has made threats to kill which she takes seriously. Moreover, in accordance with probation procedure I have made two home visits to the property and at no time have I seen any evidence of a male living at this address or in fact, anyone other than the victim living there. I have serious concerns for the safety of the victim and her unborn child if bail is granted, especially if there is a condition of residence at this address."

"Thank you, Mr. Henry. Does the defence have any response to that?"

"Perhaps, sir, bail with a condition of residence, maybe even in a bail hostel, with a condition not to contact the victim or go within one mile of her address?"

"Mr. Henry?"

"Well, sir, it's now well after one o'clock and since most court morning sessions will have ended, there are unlikely to be spaces available, though I am willing to try. Perhaps more importantly, sir, in my view a bail hostel would be unlikely to offer Mr. Quick a place in view of the violent nature of the charge against him."

"Thank you for your contribution, Mr. Henry, please return to your seat." and to the defendant: "Mr. Quick, I am remanding this case for two weeks for you to see your solicitor and get advanced information from the prosecution. You will remain in custody."

While the magistrate was saying this, I had crossed the court walking behind the dock and the solicitors to return to the probation desk. The clerk droned "The court will rise." Everyone stood while the magistrate left. The gaoler opened the gate to the dock and as Philip Quick turned to leave it, he looked in my direction narrowing his eyes, jutting his jaw, and clenching his left fist raising it threateningly to about waist height. For some reason I thought immediately of an incident at my junior school, when a disgruntled class rival made the same malevolent gesture to me across the room during a class. I was scared then – as I was now.

The afternoon court session was uneventful. The main court had a trial scheduled but the matter was withdrawn at the last moment. Court two was hearing traffic matters and other cases regarding non-payment of council tax. The Magistrates' Courts Act requires a probation officer to be present, or at least available, at all times while the court is hearing criminal matters but for these hearings my presence wasn't required so I was able to return to my office.

Since I had not been expecting to be back in the office, this free afternoon was a good opportunity to catch up on correspondence necessitated by the morning's court activity, record keeping, report writing, staff-room chit-chat and other important matters. Next day – which was the day I had planned to do the now completed reports, I proudly took the "Non-Reports" in to show Chris who was still filling in for Jackie.

"Well done, Wally. Look, I know you're up to your limit this month, but could I ask you to take on another? Joanie was supposed to do it but she's off sick again. The client is due in later this morning. It'll have to be a quickie, because it's due in court on Tuesday. He handed me the file of Samir Patel. Thanks, Wally."

"Sucker!" said Richard, laughing, in the coffee room later. "That'll teach you not to boast!" he said as he picked up the phone, which he handed to me.

"Very dishy man come to see you, Wally."

"Now, now, June!" and, still clutching the Patel file, to Richard, "Gotta go and see Joanie's client."

The staff room is adjacent to, but not visible from, the reception area or the entrance hall which is always under June's watchful eye. I walked into reception, deserted except for one male with his back to me, talking through the security glass window to June. As he turned, my heart sank: I wanted to run. It wasn't Mr. Patel; it was Philip Quick.

"Mr. Henry, I wanted to talk to you."

"Fine, sit down. How come you're here?"

"Because you wanted me banged up, you mean?" He spoke gently in a soft Jamaican accent, with no suggestion of threat or anger. "My barrister appealed the custodial remand decision to a judge in chambers at Crown Court. I'm not to go within two miles of Tracy 's place and not to see her or make contact."

"So why have you come to see me?"

"First to assure you I didn't beat up Tracy an' I'll be acquitted. I'm not a violent person or a rapist or a murderer. Then I think you should know that there are a lot of things about Tracy dat you don't know. She lie all de time; in fact she never tell de troot."

"Is there something you can tell me?"

"No, dat for you to find out. I not on probation, I don't have to talk to anyone. I can see why you did what you did, but I'm out now so that's OK."

"But I have to remind you that you're in breach of your bail conditions and I have to notify the court."

"How so? You lie."

"Because Tracy lives less than two miles from here so by definition you've gone into the forbidden area. Now, if you think you need to talk to me again, just phone me. Here's my number. Otherwise, stay away from me and from her." Placing my card in his jacket pocket he went about his business and I went about mine. In Jackie's absence, I thought it a good idea to tell Chris about these developments. Though I felt I had a lot to answer for, he was good enough not to lay the blame at my feet.

34. Tracy's Case Conference

I don't know how long Tracy Oakley remained in hospital. She did not come back to see me after she was allowed to go home to her little flat in Tottenham. When Philip Quick re-appeared at court, the case was discontinued and he was discharged. I tried to find out why from the probation officer on court duty that day.

"The victim withdrew the allegation and refused to press charges. Without the key witness, the case falls apart," came the all-too-frequent explanation.

"And the other matters?"

"Same story. She declined to testify"

Some weeks later I was invited to a social services case conference. Such meetings are held when a person receiving social services care is known to other agencies – healthcare, housing, schools, police, probation service, drugs agencies and so on. Tracy had been invited but didn't arrive. The social worker tried to arrange for a colleague to find her but to no avail.

The meeting went ahead anyway, but it was clear from the lacklustre discussion that all the other agencies were as disheartened as I was. The two officers from the Metropolitan Police Service, Pamela and Andy, were from the local vice squad and domestic violence team respectively, and described how they had befriended Tracy – with far more success than I had managed – and told of their efforts to impress on her the steps she could take to ameliorate the risks of her profession as well as giving her health and drugs awareness education.

Being a prostitute, they told the meeting, was not in itself illegal, though it was a crime to solicit on the street and to be a pimp or to force another person into the sex trade by force or by threats. It was clear they knew that Philip Quick was behind all this. He was thought to be similarly linked to other women but none was willing to testify. Whatever the adversity and suffering endured by those forced into lining his pockets with money, he had an extraordinary hold over them. Not one would come forward as a witness.

I was asked to give an account of probation service involvement and described how Tracy came to be under my supervision and how it had been a failure from the start. Though probably the oldest person in the room, I sensed that I was the least experienced in this particular area and my account must have conveyed a certain degree of self-blame. Interestingly, the male police officer came immediately to my rescue and his female colleague assured me - and those present at the case conference - that there would have been nothing I, or anyone else present, could have done to improve Tracy's situation. The social worker added that she was in some ways relieved that her client was Tracy's unborn child and that Tracy was legally in my charge, so to speak.

Social services had tried to get Tracy into a programme for new mothers, but she had resisted – or just failed to attend – and they raised their hands in despair. But they had to be pro-active for the baby's sake and it was widely felt that though Tracy was uncontrollable it was clear that the baby, when born, would instantly be a child at risk and would need to be taken into care immediately for its own safety.

Though Tracy had registered with the Drug Dependency Unit, they never got to meet her so were unable to add much to the discussion. They were able to say, however, that if, as was thought, Tracy was still using drugs and alcohol at the same levels as previously, the foetus was almost certainly already addicted and would need to be admitted to intensive care at birth for treatment. The senior social worker added that if another case conference were called, the relevant neonatologist from the local hospital should be invited.

Housing department staff added that since it was now known that Tracy was working as a prostitute, she therefore had income and no longer qualified for housing benefit. Technically, her rent was thus in arrears and once the baby was taken into care she would be evicted from her present address and become homeless. Criminal proceedings would follow automatically and measures to recover housing benefit would be initiated.

The committee member from the benefits agency then added that in that situation, Tracy would be prosecuted for claiming benefit while working. In addition to any financial penalty she might be given by the courts, she would have to repay any benefit she had received over the last five months, plus of course, the rent paid in housing benefit. This last contribution to proceedings led to the most animated discussion of the meeting with, to my astonishment, the police speaking in defence of Tracy trying to urge the housing department and the benefits agency to adopt a more sympathetic approach to enable the police and other agencies to help Tracy find some practical solutions.

But it was all to no avail. By this time, the baby was due within just over one month and plans had to be made for the unborn child to be admitted to the Intensive Care Unit for drugs detoxification and later to be taken into foster care. Other arrangements were required to recover Tracy's rented accommodation, the wrongly paid housing benefit and the wrongly paid Income Support payments as well as plans to prosecute for deception caused by earning while claiming benefits. In short, it was necessary to show that each government agency was working efficiently and according to the regulations, but there were no plans to help Tracy.

Some days later the minutes of the meeting arrived on my desk to be added to the now bulging file of papers all created by professionals like me, all powerless and impotent, all watching their backs, all terrified lest an inspector might find one poor officer, worker or agent, responsible for any imminent disaster.

In supervision, Chris consoled me. "Wally, can't you now see that it's not your fault. Give yourself a break, can't you? If all the other agencies are as helpless as we are, surely you have to accept that none of us is individually at fault?"

"Thank you, Chris, you may be right, but it doesn't make me feel any better and it doesn't stop me wanting to do something to alleviate the situation."

35. Hospital Visiting

"Whittington Hospital for you Wally."

"Thanks June. Please put them through.... Hello, Walter Henry."

"Mr. Henry, this is Staff Nurse Boxall in the Maternity Unit. I understand you're Tracy Oakley's probation officer? She's asked me to phone you to say she's just had a baby girl three weeks premature. The baby weighs 2.1 kilos and is now in intensive care being treated for alcohol and cocaine withdrawal. Ms. Oakley is very poorly and will remain in hospital for the time being. Her doctor is Dr. Schmidthoff. If you should come to visit her, please speak to him while you're here."

Ellen and I had a friend who had been admitted to the Whittington for minor surgery just a few days prior to this so we decided to pop in to see Tracy after our planned visit to John (who was doing fine when we visited him, in case you should wonder!) Wearing a faded hospital issue dressing gown, Tracy, on the other hand, looked terribly unwell. The baby was brought to her in a sterile incubator while we were there. Tracy wasn't allowed to pick up her frail daughter – or even to touch her, encased as the tiny baby was, in her protective perspex pod. It was a tragic, heart-breaking sight.

There was little conversation. As soon as she saw us, Tracy burst into tears, with enormous sobs, just like a child herself, in fact. "Look what I've done," she wailed, "what chance does this poor little fucker have? I should have listened to you. I'm a failure. I wanna die. I wanna DIE!!!"

With a lump in my throat and on the brink of guilt-ridden tears myself I was unable to respond. Luckily Ellen came to the rescue with words of solace, encouragement and hope. Before long a nurse came to return the baby to intensive care. She asked us to identify ourselves, then asked if we would speak to the doctor or the nurse before we left. When the baby was removed, Tracy, still sobbing, covered her head with her bedclothes, turned her back to us and, from her cocoon of blankets, still in the foetal position, screamed at the top of her voice, "OK, you've had your fun, now FUCK OFF!"

I was always surprised by what I now realised was Tracy's 'normal' behaviour. Whether a result of drug misuse, alcohol or personality disorder, her mood-swings always caught me off-guard. This time I did exactly as I was told. Only Ellen demurred long enough to say a quiet farewell and a promise of our return. I knew she was as upset as I, yet I admired her for sharing the burden of my role (for which I felt totally unprepared, completely ill-equipped and, it still pains me to admit, solely responsible) and for offering to visit Tracy again. We returned to the nurses' station to enquire for Dr. Schmidthoff, the consultant.

"Dr. Schmidthoff isn't on duty tonight, but there's a note here that he wanted to talk to you." She checked that the phone number on file was indeed the correct one. "Ms Oakley is extremely weak and is likely to stay here for two weeks or more," the nurse continued, "She is of very slight stature and doesn't seem to have the physical stamina of a woman her age. We can't find anything wrong with her but we're mystified by her lack of physical development."

"Could this be related to drug or alcohol use? I imagine you've spoken to Dr Lindbergh at Hackney DDU?"

"No, I don't think we have. That's helpful. It may explain

everything, thank you. We'll stay in touch. Do come to chat if you visit again." She wrote details of Dr. Lindbergh's involvement in Tracy's notes. I thanked her, gave her my card and left the ward with Ellen. It was two days before we came back. We were greeted by the same nurse as before.

"Oh, Mr. Henry, Ms. Oakley has been moved. We thought it better for her and the other patients if we put her in a single room. It's number 5 on the right down the corridor. She's eating her supper now. She seems better since your last visit. She said some very nice things about you both. I know she'll be pleased to see you again."

The Whittington Hospital was at that time an enormous Victorian edifice, undergoing modernisation for the healthcare of a large slice of North London's population. The spartan Victorian corridors echoed with the sound of our footsteps as we walked in the direction of the nurse's gesture. Room number 5 was empty when we arrived, though it was clear someone was in residence. A half-eaten meal remained on a plate on the bedside table. After several minutes' wait, I went back to ask the nurse if Tracy might be elsewhere in the hospital.

"No, the shop and cafe are closed now, but I'll check the bathrooms." Moments later Ellen and I could tell from the look on the nurse's face that she wasn't there – or anywhere else. She hurriedly left to check the intensive care nursery where premature babies were cared for. We waited a while and when the nurse returned, clearly relieved that the baby was safe, waited a little longer while she checked the public areas in case Tracy was looking for somewhere to smoke an illicit cigarette, but didn't see her anywhere.

Recalling with horror Tracy's parting words to us on our last visit, I thought immediately of the local suicide bridge, not three hundred metres from where we stood. Whittington Hospital stands on Highgate Hill, a very short distance from the Archway, an ornate Victorian bridge enabling Hornsey Lane to cross the Great North Road more than a hundred feet below. I alerted the nurse to my fears, and Ellen and I left the hospital to return to our car which we hurriedly pointed in the direction of Hornsey Lane. We thought she had not been missing long enough to have reached the bridge and we would surely have seen her. We searched, but found nothing.

Crossing the narrow bridge, I stopped the car midway and leapt out, leaving the engine running, driver's door wide open, while I tried to peer over the parapet to look down at the busy main road below. In my panic I completely ignored the anger of other drivers obstructed by my stationary vehicle. To my horror, all I could see were the flashing blue lights of an emergency vehicle with traffic backed up behind it. Back in the car I quickly continued across the bridge.

By the time we got there, traffic was moving again and I stopped to speak to the police officer directing traffic. It was clear that there was no disaster; a motorist had been stopped for a minor traffic infraction and the officer was uninterested in my over-detailed enquiry.

Ellen and I were both speechless. We drove home in silence hoping that Tiny Tracy was somewhere in the hospital and would return to her room and cold, half-eaten supper.

Next day I called the hospital to learn that Tracy had not returned to her room. The baby remained in ICU and social services had been informed of this latest development. Tracy seemed to have left the hospital wearing only her own night-clothes, a hospital dressing gown and slippers.

After updating Chris, he wisely advised that I should ask the duty probation officer to see my next two clients and make an urgent home visit. I drove to the flat where I had seen Tracy twice before. It was unoccupied and boarded up. Housing department had already taken possession again while she was in hospital. This was not one of the enjoyable aspects of the job and nor did I feel I was excelling in professional practice under these challenging circumstances.

Nothing was heard of Tracy Oakley for four or five weeks. Work resumed its normal pace with occasional rises and falls in excitement. From time to time I worried about Tracy but with no way of contacting her there was little I could do but wait. Then, one day June called me saying the vice squad were on the phone.

"Wally, it's Pam." I recognised the voice but couldn't imagine why she would call me. "I have some sad news, I'm afraid."

"Has something happened to the baby?" I asked

"No, I'm afraid it's worse than that. Tracy's dead. She was murdered."

"When, how, by whom?"

"It may have been over two weeks ago. She was using a one-roomed flat near the strip," (That was how the police and social workers referred to the street where the women plied their trade.) "The landlord of the property was called by neighbours to investigate a smell and he found her severed limbs and mutilated torso in a wardrobe in an advanced state of decomposition. It has been very difficult identifying the body but now there's no doubt it was Tracy. Andy and I are very upset because we thought we were getting somewhere with Tracy, and we know you will be because she always told us you were the only person she trusted. She said you were the first person in her life to show her respect."

I had no idea how to respond. At times like this I was always stuck for words. I thanked her for calling me. She told me the baby was doing well and would be placed with a loving family. Fortunately, she said, she need never know about her mother or her problems. A murder enquiry was initiated and I might be called upon to make a statement in due course. In any case, Tracy's file in my office would be at their disposal if needed.

I was neglectful in completing the final entries to Tracy's file. Though Chris didn't exactly chastise me in supervision, he did gently allude to the need to keep records up-to-date especially in cases that might for some reason, be the object of later scrutiny. He told me that, while he hadn't been acquainted with the whole story as it unfolded, he recognised that the entire experience had been a painful one for me. So, bit by bit, I completed the various stages in closing down the file. Re-reading it, I noticed that at least three letters seeking information on Tracy Oakley from Birmingham Social Services remained unanswered. Unfortunately, pressure of work caused me to neglect completion of closing the file.

It was an unexpected jolt then, one morning two or three months later, to find a letter in my pigeon-hole from Birmingham Social Services....

Birmingham

Department of Social Services, New Street, Birmingham

Telephone: 021654142309   Fax: 061423289049098

Mr. W. Henry, Probation Officer
Hackney, London

Date xxxxxxxxx
Our ref. xxxxxx

Dear Mr. Henry

Tracy Oakley d.o.b. 15.8.1972

Thank you for your letters requesting confirmation of facts relating to Ms. Oakley. We apologise for the delay in ascertaining her whereabouts. Though she was known to this office between 1981 and 1987, she left this area at the age of eighteen. She was reported as a missing person and at first the search was concentrated on London where she had been known to travel and where she had several court appearances.

It was not discovered she had moved to Scotland until much later. Then, in January 1991, we were notified that she was arrested, charged and later convicted for the murder in 1988 of her mother and, separately, her mother's previous partner in Glasgow. Ms Tracy Oakley is now serving two life sentences in a Scottish prison and can be contacted through the relevant Scottish prison authorities.

Regarding the person in your care purporting to be Tracy Oakley, we cannot say with certainty whom she might be, but we do know that the retired social worker whose name you mentioned in your letter, now sadly deceased, worked for many years with Tracy's younger sister, Brenda, d.o.b. 9.2.77. who disappeared from care in a Birmingham children's home in 1990 aged thirteen. All attempts to find her failed; police were notified and she was listed as a missing person.

It was always suspected that because she idolised her older sister she may have moved to Scotland to be with her, but we were never successful in finding her. So far as we are aware, she never knew that her sister had murdered her mother whose partner was alleged to have committed serious sexual offences against the two children.

The two Forms 609 you referred to in your letters were indeed, we have ascertained, the list of convictions of Brenda's older sister, Tracy Oakley, now serving a life sentence and so far as we can tell, Brenda herself had no convictions and was not known to the police. It would appear that because of the differences between English and Scottish justice systems, there was no easy communication between the police services of England and Wales and those of Scotland. This will surely be remedied in the near future.

We hope the foregoing is helpful to your enquiries. Please feel free to contact this office further if you need any more information.

Yours faithfully

XXXXXXXXXXXXXXXXXX
    Senior Social Worker

The letter gave Brenda's birthdate – exactly four years younger than the date Tracy gave to the police, the court, the prison, local social services, the hospital and us. The person we all knew as Tracy would have been thirteen when she first came to London to escape her dreadful experiences at the hands of her mother's partner, in foster homes and in residential care in Birmingham. She endured a year of abuse in prison from the age of fourteen and died in terrible, horrifyingly violent circumstances before she reached sixteen. Each of her three pregnancies was verified by various health authorities.

To say I felt sick would have been an understatement. To attempt to resume a normal day's work was futile. I tried, but my heart wasn't in it. Richard was alone in the coffee room. He listened to my account of the whole sorry story, without his normal jovial interjections.

Afterwards, he got up in his pained, ungainly, arthritic manner, went to the kitchen and came back with a cup of coffee which he thrust into my hand. Because of Richard's infirmity, we always plied him with stimulants and it was an accepted rule that he was exempt from the coffee-making and washing-up rota. But this time, he took charge, and with that one act he told me he understood. We sat in silence for a while.

"I think you probably know by now, Wally, that we all have stories to tell, and every now and again one of us gets dragged through the wringer, but I have to say that in the short time you've been here you've had more than your share of trauma and grief and we're all amazed at your resilience.

If it's more than you can stand, take a break. Don't try to be a hero and brave it out. Go for a swim, or spend a few hours at home. No-one would think any the worse of you for it. Or if you want to just come and sit in my office for a while, I'd be happy to have your company. Nothing I can say can alleviate the agony

I'm sure you must be experiencing, but *I* know – and I'm sure our colleagues *all* know – that feeling of helpless inadequacy when something goes completely wrong. It's not your fault."

After half an hour or so I began to castigate myself for what I saw as my self-pity, and went to tell Chris the news. We closed the file together and I gave it to him for safe keeping ready for the police when they needed to refer to it. No-one was ever convicted for any crimes against that poor little girl, let alone her murder. It remains an unsolved crime.

Philip Quick was never charged with murder or drugs offences. I never saw or heard of him again.

36. The Butcher's Mum

When dealing with seemingly hardened criminals I'm often touched - even moved – by their tenderness toward their families, particularly their mothers.

Most male offenders can be tracked on a career path of criminal activity. According to the Home Office, all data on offending, when gathered together using common statistical methods, produces a near-perfect bell curve showing that the bulk of offending begins at around the age of sixteen to seventeen, peaks between twenty-two and twenty-three, and by twenty-four is in decline so that by the age of twenty-nine or thirty, most males have learned how to live without resorting to criminal behaviour. There are, however, some exceptions.

According to his file, The Butcher was almost my age, though he looked ten years younger. By practically any yardstick he was a handsome, agreeable, highly entertaining character who, despite his rough, gravelly voice, seemed to have not an ounce of vindictiveness in him.

He was a large man well-built, with what remained of a frequently-broken nose, creating the impression that one might not want to meet him in a dark alley. From his appearance, one would certainly try to avoid arousing his anger.

When compiling a report for his appearance at Old Street magistrates' court I noticed from his list of ample previous convictions (which extended to several pages) that he had never been on probation. Though serious, his offences never involved violence and did not include burglary of private homes or property. I did not rate him as a danger to the public – merely a serious risk to financial institutions. Asked if he could explain this, he said

"When I was first nicked everyone got put away. Probation existed, but only for minor offenders like middle class milk bottle thieves. Proper theft, handling stolen goods or deception got immediate prison sentences. I did approved school aged thirteen and Borstal training also as a juvenile but as soon as I got to be an adult, the court saw those an' I got a couple of quick jail terms. After that, as soon as a beak (magistrate) sees you've done time, it's automatic. Bird every time."

I made this point in my report. Since The Butcher's latest offence was deception on a fairly minor level, I proposed a short probation order – and got it. So, he visited my office on a regular basis and regaled me with East End stories.

"I was a really scrawny kid," he told me when I asked how he got his nickname. "I was hard to manage at school and got sent away to special boarding schools. I didn't go much, bunked off a lot, but when it was legal to leave, aged fifteen, I was apprenticed to a butcher. It only lasted about six weeks. But by then I 'ad learned, if you don't want people to pick on you, tell 'em what you do. I'd say to 'em 'Look, leave me alone, right? You wanna pick a fight with a butcher, that's your lookout!' No- one ever bothered me after that."

Shortly after his probation order began, he called up one day to ask if he could change his appointment. "I got a job interview in Croydon, can I come late?" I told him we have one evening a week for late reporting for those in work who can't come during the day. "Oh that's great cause if I get this job I won't get back here till about seven o'clock. Will I still get to see you?"

"Only when it's my turn on the rota for late reporting," I told him. He got the job and continued to report on Tuesday evenings as required. When I met him one evening in my office, I asked him to tell me about the job. "I used to be a floor layer, but my boss sold the business. Now he's unavailable (acherly, 'e's doing serious bird) so his wife's running it an' changed the type of work to industrial cleaning."

"I spend my time wiv me best mate in a service cradle danglin' off a twenty-two storey building cleaning winders o' the top eighteen floors. The work is great, it's a job for life, and no-one bothers us. Now the weather's hot, we strip off and just do it in our boxer shorts and safety harness. You should see the way some of them office birds look at us when we press ourselves against the glass stretchin' for the top corners. Lucky for them they're locked in."

I was surprised, therefore, when he turned up at my office unannounced one rainy Thursday afternoon.

"Mr. Butcher, nice to see you, what brings you here?" He always grinned when I called him Mr. Butcher – not by his real name.

"Once the rain sets in on the side we're working on, we can't do the winders. We still get paid though. I didn't want ter spend all my dosh in the pub so I thought I'd come and see you."

"When we first met you told me you drank rather a lot. Isn't that risky on your present job?"

"Definitely would be if I still did it. Since I started, I only drink on the week-ends when I don't see my kids. Otherwise I'm dry all week. Still go to the pub and play snooker though.

"Now I'm not drinking, I only drink halves o' shandy while me mates get pissed on pints, then late in the evening I play the winner for high stakes. It's like taking sweets off kids.... and I'm not that good at snooker: it's just that when they can no longer stand upright, they can't hit the ball straight. Sad, innit? Legal though! They can't touch me for it!"

"I 'ad to 'elp me mum coupl'a' weeks ago. She lives on the ground floor of my block. Social Services told her she could get a grant for new bedding - she's incontinent, you know - so I 'elped 'er fill in the form, sent it off and last week she got a Giro-cheque for seventy-seven quid.

"I said I'd go to the post office to cash it for her. Good job she didn't go, I 'ad to wait thirty-five minutes in line. I was chattin' to everyone. It was a real laugh in there just like a street party in the old days. Mum couldn't 'ave managed standing up all that time! No loo there, either! Then it's my turn, innit. I 'anded over the cheque."

"You got identification?' 'e said without lookin' up."

"Whaddaya mean?" I said "I lived 'ere forty-seven years. You 'eard us all chattin'. These people known me since I was knee 'igh! This Giro's for me mum. They all know me - and me mum."

"No Identification, no payment."

"Everyfink went quiet. They all knew no-one gets in my way, so you know what I did?"

My heart sank. *(Oh, no! He's come to tell me he's been re-arrested for punching a post office clerk, or smashing the window at least.... I thought to myself.)* "I stood up tall – 'e's really small, this geezer - 'e thought I was gonna smash 'is winda." Without missing a beat, he continued.

"I took a deeee-e-e-ep breaf, turned around, wen' 'ome, come back, same people, same queue, still 'adn't been served, more chit-chat, another twenty minutes and I pushed in the giro-cheque, my own ID, a 'andwritten letter to 'im from my mum, her pension book and a letter addressed to me at 'er address. 'E said nothing - didn't even register e'd seen me 'alf an hour earlier. All 'e said was: 'Seventy-seven pounds.... How would you like it?' "

"Five pence fuckin' pieces" I said. The whole crowd fell about laughin'. Do you know why? 'Cos they all know – and so do you 'cos I know you read the file – almost all my previous was for cashing dud cheques between £5,000 and £10,000 at banks and building societies all over London and not once, not ONCE was I ever, EVER asked for proof of identity!"

———

37. A Pause for Breath

Inevitably, some of the probationers began to shine. Frank Grover and Jeffrey Kenton attended their appointments – as well as group meetings and activities sessions – almost without fail. Still inseparable, they filled the rest of their time going to N.A. (Narcotics Anonymous) meetings morning, afternoon and evening, day in, day out. With their consent, the DDU continued to report their blood and urine test results, always drug and alcohol free. The tests weren't even necessary – the improvement in their physical appearance and performance during activities was visible for all to see, and was a source of great encouragement to others in our client group.

Craig Denham was also a hero. Already drug-free for many months when placed on probation he felt he could survive without N.A. meetings like the ones he had attended in Brixton Prison, though he did occasionally attend local meetings as much to give encouragement to other members as anything else. He began looking for work in his trained occupation as a veneer preparer but when, as a result of the diminishing furniture and joinery trade in Hackney, he had no success, he found stable work casting garden ornaments in concrete. At the group meeting one day he told us all of his latest invention. It arose after he read news of a sailing ship with a concrete hull.

"We could do that in our workshop" he told his boss.

"Not much call for sailing ships in Hackney," came the reply with Craig pointedly adding the 'aitch' that he habitually omitted. He told us how he thought for a while before coming up with,

"Wait a minute! What's 'Ackney famous for? It's the murder capital of England. We could make coffins. And if they don't sell, they could be plant tubs for gardens or balconies in blocks of flats. There's lots of stiffs in 'Ackney, an' lots o' flats an' all, so me boss said 'Let's give it a try and see what happens'."

I wondered if his boss was related to mine, always willing to try something new. Craig was a bit of an artist.

"I drew a model and we copied it in concrete. We shaped it, smoothed it, waterproofed it, gave it a tight-fitting lid, created slots in the sides for the straps - to allow it to be lowered into a grave - and we stood back to admire it. It was a sight to behold. Then we contacted some local funeral directors who came to admire it. They liked it and liked my extra idea that it could be made simple or ornate, ancient looking or modern. One said "I'll be able to tell my clients 'Your Grandad will be preserved forever in one of those! We'll sell a lot o' them'."

"Unfortunately we didn't sell any at all in the end. It wasn't just that it took nine people to lift the bloody thing even without a body in it. Worse than that was, it was so heavy even trying to put it down gently, we let it down with a thud and it broke apart, shattering into hundreds of pieces! 'E made me sweep it up and threatened to dock a day's wages. We laughed about it after, though."

The weekly client group seemed to be progressing well. Although attendance was somewhat erratic, with numbers varying from three to eleven, there was a hardcore of half a dozen people who made it to my office most Tuesday mornings. Of the four members who had been regular class 'A' drug users, three remained 'clean' while the other who had a minor relapse, reported it to the others one morning and they immediately gave him moral support, encouraging him to attend N.A. meetings with them and to spend time with them as a way of keeping clear of risky places.

Staff at the DDU were always willing to step in and give extra counselling in times of crisis. Kathryn 's attendance at the group improved with the addition of other female members. Diane particularly gave her confidence and Kathryn became completely drug-free, though continued to binge on alcohol from time to time. By the time her probation order ended she had no further arrests and had been sober for about four months.

Two of the 'Tuesday Regulars' were also loyal participants in the Wednesday afternoon activities group. On one such adventure, Sylvester announced that he'd booked a five-a-side football match against Camden police the following day but had lost three of his players. He was touting for volunteers. As luck would have it, Frank and Jeffrey were both there that afternoon and jumped at the chance. Craig Denham gingerly joined in and Sylvester had his team. He gave them instructions to bring a towel and trainers and arranged to meet them at the probation office with his trusty old minibus.

I was on court duty that day and forgot all about it.

On the following day, Friday, I had planned a day without client interviews in order to clear a growing backlog of paperwork. Of course, the phone kept ringing for all sorts of reasons. I was beginning to get very frustrated when it rang again.

"Frank and Jeffrey in reception for you, Wally. Oh, and Craig Denham too, just walked in."

"Oh, June, they don't have an appointment and I'm snowed under." I heard her talking to them through her reception desk window. June was a remarkable woman. She had that uncanny ability to charm everyone. She knew that she was the first point of contact with the Hackney Probation Office for anyone who walked through that front door. It made no difference if it was the Chief Probation Officer, a police officer, a colleague from another office, a client on probation, a parolee on a life sentence or a homeless person looking for warmth, shelter, money – or all three. Whether telephone callers or visitors, she spoke kindly to everyone in her smooth, gentle voice. And it was noticeable that, however agitated, however distressed or angry, whatever difficulty they had with English, June's patience and sheer good humour would calm her visitors so she would be able to have a civil conversation and establish their needs.

"They seem to be very excited about something and want to tell you. They promise not to keep you for long."

"Oh all right then..." I was turning into a curmudgeon. Resentfully, I went down the stairs.

"Mr. Wally, Mr. Wally, we won, we won!"

"Won what?"

"Our five-a-side match against the police. We won six - three!" It was Frank talking of course, but Jeffrey, normally silent, was beaming.

Then in a surprising burst of glee, Jeffrey said "We couldn'a done that a year ago when we were still on smack. But even so, I was knackered after the game. An' the police were great – really cool. They took us for a beer afterwards. We 'ad orange juice 'cos we're not drinking. Sylv didn't have any 'cos he was driving. But it was a terrific afternoon. We wanted to say thank you."

"They put me in goal because I was wearing gloves." added Craig. "I never played five-a-side before. It was wicked. It's reminded me why I got off the gear." I chastised myself for being such a misery and refusing to come down to reception. The looks of accomplishment on their faces were more than recompense for the interruption. I reminded them that it was Sylvester who got them into the game, then I weakened and offered them tea or coffee.

"No thanks, Wally, we know you're busy – your receptionist told us you wouldn't be able to come down but we're glad she persuaded you. She's a real gem, that lady. She always recognises us and chats. She treats us like we're real people. She's one o' the reasons we come 'ere. We're all going to N.A. now. Gotta go. 'Bye."

Funny how some seemingly insignificant interludes make such a difference to the job.

38. High Visibility

That autumn I interviewed a juvenile – under eighteen-years- old - for a series of thefts from vehicles parked in car parks below office buildings in the City. He was to appear at the local Youth Court for sentence. Other members of this youngster's large family were known to colleagues, but this appeared to be his first court appearance. There were no papers available from the Crown Prosecution Service and, in the absence of relevant information, I did the best I could.

Aged seventeen, Ryan Shepmore came across as a bright if naïve young man who had lost his way. His eleven older brothers were, he told me, all unemployed but though he wanted to go to school, they insisted he seek work as they were trying to do. He also told me he was coerced into these offences and promised not to do it again. Hampered as I was by the absence of documentation, and pressed for time by the volume of other work that was coming my way, I made no effort to check his story. Stupidly, I believed him and recommended a probation order as a suitable sentence, believing that I might help him get into education to train for a trade.

Luckily the Youth Court Magistrates were having none of it. Unknown to me, and not recorded on the original court papers, young Mr. Shepmore asked for twenty-two similar offences to be taken into account, and the court learned from the prosecution that the twelve brothers were all involved in a conspiracy to steal valuable spare parts and expensive accessories from luxury vehicles and sell them in local street markets. As they were all adults, they had all been convicted of conspiracy to steal at Crown Court, with varying lengths of prison sentence.

Because the Youth Court needed to establish the outcome of the main trial of the adult leaders in this conspiracy, proceedings took a little longer to organise. It was accepted that this young man had indeed been coerced by his brothers, who, to their credit, were at pains to impress on the Crown Court that their youngest brother was indeed a reluctant participant. This meant that by the time Ryan appeared for sentence, some of the brothers had already been released, though the ringleaders served much longer terms. Ryan was given a six-month custodial sentence at a young offenders' institution. Having served time on remand he declined probation contact during his sentence saying he'd be out in no time.

Imagine my surprise, then, to be asked four months later to visit him in Hollesley Bay Colony Young Offenders Institution in the misty marshes of East Anglia to prepare a report prior to his release. I booked a visit but remained baffled. Surely, I thought, he should have been released two or three months prior to this request? There was no legal visits' suite; my interview was to be held in the family visits area.

The only other time I'd conducted an interview in the main visiting facility was when I met another client at Holloway prison. It was noisy and chaotic; hardly suitable for getting acquainted with a young offender whom I was to supervise on his release. But this turned out to be an entirely different arrangement. Not only were the inmates all too young to have their own children to visit them but their visitors were for the most part subdued adults – disappointed parents, disapproving foster carers, disbelieving social workers and disenchanted probation officers.

Eventually Ryan appeared wearing a bright orange high visibility jacket. He seemed not to recognise me and said he had no memory of our earlier meeting on which I based his court report.

"Why are you still here?" I asked him.

"I only got here last week."

"But you were sentenced in September. It's now January. If you got six months you should have served only three and been released by now."

"Yeah, well I went home for Christmas, didn't I?"

"How did you manage that?"

"Two of my brothers came to visit me after I'd been here a month, Joseph and Elias. Five minutes before the end of visiting time, I went to the toilet. Three minutes later Elias followed me in and gave me his baseball cap. We had the same colour sweaters. A minute or so later I walked out wearing his cap and joined me other brother, Joseph – I sat in Eli's seat, not my chair. The officer called time, got all the visitors to line up and be counted out of the visits area and loaded us all onto the special bus and off we went to Woodbridge Station. Elias waited in the bog until two hours later when an officer came in and found him apparently unconscious on the floor. There was a right old row, but Elias wasn't in trouble. He was in the crapper pretending to be ill and waiting to be found........."

"Where did you go?"

"I went home of course. Elias had given Joe his bus and train tickets for me to use. I got home before he did 'coz he had to hitch-hike." He seemed surprised at my silly question.

"But that must have been in October. When did they pick you up? How did they find you?"

"It was only last week, they came to the flat, just knocked at the door and said ' Ryan Shepmore? Get your things, you're coming with us.' And that's why I'm wearing this stupid bright orange jacket; I'm an escape risk. It got me a lot of respect back on the wing, though... and on the street back in Hackney!"

39. Flashback

Frank and Jeffrey were exemplary probationers. They had, by now, completed an unblemished year since being placed on probation around the same time as another previously successful probationer now, sadly, in prison. In one of our weekly group meetings, during open discussion about questioning people's motives, Frank reminded me of an incident I had forgotten. Looking back in my notebook, the brief entry brought it all back to me. It was early on in their probation order. Frank and Jeffrey both continued to attend N.A. meetings. One day, Frank approached me for funding to allow him and Jeffrey to go to an NA conference in Bournemouth. Probationers were always asking for money and requests were usually rebuffed, but just occasionally there would be a request for something that might justify a small advance. I had heard there were sources of funding for some "deserving causes" (a phrase I disliked then and still do) and thought it might be worth applying for the fares to send these two earnest young men away for four days... if, that was, I believed them. Because of my inexperience, I raised the matter in the coffee-room to get advice.

"He's having you on, Wally." That was Marnie. "He's back on heroin and you'll be feeding his habit."

"Reports from the DDU confirm his blood and urine samples are clear. They both seem to be doing well," I replied.

"Don't believe him. Don't give your clients money," she insisted.

"If they're doing well, Wally, I see no problem with it. You seem to have checked up on them. How's their reporting? Regular? Punctual?" I nodded. "Might be an idea to check with N.A. that there is a conference, get the dates and accommodation arrangements. See if there are any delegates expected from

Hackney and then make your decision. If it sounds all right apply to The Sheriffs' and Recorder's Fund." Once again, Richard's sage words saved the day and a thorough telephone check revealed that not only were the conference details correct, but there were to be four candidates from Hackney, two of whom were Frank and Jeffrey. In complete contravention of any confidentiality rules (if they ever existed!), the conference organiser's secretary confirmed their names and told me that free accommodation had been offered by well-wishers and that all they had to find was their fares. The conference was three weeks hence.

With a tiny office located in the Central Criminal Court in the City of London, The Sheriffs' and Recorder's Fund is a charity established to assist in the rehabilitation of offenders. It received its original contributions from judges at the Old Bailey but now receives charitable donations from a much wider spectrum of contributors. Their annual report for 2019 began...

The Sheriffs' & Recorder's Fund

In 1808 the two Sheriffs of the City of London set up a fund to help prisoners living in appalling conditions in Newgate, and their families. In 1931 the Fund merged with the fund set up by the Recorder of London to assist offenders released on probation. The Sheriffs' & Recorder's Fund still plays a vital part in preventing re-offending.

The fund invites and considers applications from probation officers and social workers for small donations that might meet vital needs for those recently released from custody or on probation. It was a long shot and I applied by completing the simple form to the best of my ability.

A week later Chris, still juggling management of two teams, called me into his office to announce he had received a cheque for Frank and Jeffrey's fares from the Sheriffs' and Recorder's Fund. I wrote to each of them reminding them of the next group meeting – but not mentioning the arrival of their grant. When the meeting day arrived, June called my office to tell me they were first to appear so I went down to reception to welcome them. As I came down the staircase into the reception area, Frank and Jeffrey both stood up and shook my hand in greeting.

"Well, boys, I have some good news; you've got your fares to Bournemouth." Jeffrey's eyes turned into full moons and his mouth opened to a wide, smiling gape. Frank stepped forward, put his arms round my chest and lifted me up in a huge bear hug, returning me to the ground with a sudden plonk! He hadn't expected such weight! (My colleague, Mick, was in June's office at the time of this conversation. He couldn't hear it, of course, but through the reception window he saw Frank hug me and pick me up. Later he said to me, "You must have done something right, Wally!")

The inseparable two thanked me profusely. Cautious about giving them hard cash to buy the tickets, I asked them how they felt about me issuing them with travel warrants between London and Bournemouth. I knew that probationers and parolees were often reluctant to use travel warrants, feeling, mistakenly, that it highlighted the fact that they weren't trustworthy or they were on their way back to prison. They were both entirely relaxed about it, satisfying me that they were not seeking to find their next hit.

They were understandably overjoyed and their positive moods came across in the crowded group meeting that followed. It was a busy session with eight people attending. Diane and April were the only two women. Diane looked older than her thirty-nine years. She wore her appearance with confidence and authority – which she used to great advantage. I was astonished then, when Diane commented to Frank: "You and Jeffrey are doing so well.

You must feel really proud. It must make you feel good about yourself?" To which Frank replied:

"How can I feel good about myself now I've woken up to all the pain and distress I caused those I stole from? I committed my offences against family, friends and strangers. No-one trusts me now. Yeah, we're doin' our best, but even when I've got a smile on my face, I still feel like shit." A sea of nodding heads caused discussion to veer in the direction of assuaging guilt. One person, Kenny, remained quiet. Diane came back in:

"We all know now that guilt will be with us for a long time but trust is something you have to earn. Luckily, in this group we're on our way. Wally's door is always open. He always tries to fit anyone in. If he says he's too busy to see you, you'll know it's true. When someone is pleased to see you it makes you feel good, don't it? When you feel good you can overcome those urges and that guilt. What about you, Kenny? We never hear from you in these chats."

"Well, like, I 'aven't got that far yet." Kenny, startled at being brought into the limelight, hesitated, then clearly decided to go for his maiden speech: "Look, it's, well, like......... OK, I'm ashamed, yeah, but ashamed that I'm not as good as you an' Craig an' Frank an' Jeffrey. I try to clean up but I keep relapsing and can't seem to stop. I 'aven't told anyone about it, but my mum knows. She don't know 'ow to 'andle it – an' nor do I. I never registered at the DDU but I'm ready to try, but my mates say they're useless." I was even more astonished to hear Jeffrey, normally silent, jump into the conversation:

"Kenny, I know who your mates are. They would say that, wouldn't they? An' of course, you know why they don't wanna see you succeed. But now you've got a strong team around you. We go every week even though we no longer need methadone. We still 'ave urine tests. You could come along with us and we'll introduce you. If they're seeing us and you're wiv' us, they're not going to turn around an' say 'Come back in six weeks Kenny' are they?" Kenny brightened and turned to me.

"Djou fink it's a good idea?"

"Yes, Kenny. And I think that, thanks to Diane, you've just reached a turning point and I also think you know it. You've been sitting here silently for weeks now, taking it all in but saying nothing. That's OK, but today what you've just said, in effect, is 'I trust you all. I can share my secrets and I'm ready.' So, yes, why not fix up a meet with Jeffrey and Frank and see what happens? Tell us all about it at our next group if you like. And now, I have to go to court this afternoon, so we'll call a halt there. See you all next week."

I turned back to my desk and began looking at the jobs ahead of me; the buzz of conversation went on and no-one made as if to move. It was a full twenty minutes before I had to usher them all out and don suit and tie to make my way to Snaresbrook Crown Court. At that moment, I decided I wouldn't give Frank and Jeffrey travel warrants; I would give them cash to buy their own tickets.

The past year had justified my faith in them which, in turn, increased their own motivation. Not everyone on my caseload produced the same exemplary performance, but most people made considerable progress and improved their own lives immensely.

One memorable group meeting in my office, with nine people present, stays in my memory. There were four women and five men. Frank and Jeffrey were joined by Martin and new client Keith, all of them trying hard to overcome a serious drug dependency, though at different stages of accomplishment. Keith was still seventeen, not yet an adult in the eyes of the law, and told me he reckoned if he could beat the heroin urge now, he would have a long life ahead of him, unlike some of his neighbours in the same council estate whom he thought were heading for an early grave. Diane was there making light of everyone and everything and another woman, thirty-year-old April, recently placed on probation for deception – possession and misuse of a stolen credit card. I was spending time showing Craig Denham how to use the computer, now a central part of the weekly client group. Being male, I naturally find multi-tasking difficult! While talking and coaching Craig at the computer, however, sitting sideways-on to the group I couldn't help overhearing some of their conversation across the room.

"...but what's the point of probation?" asked April. "I mean, yeah, I'm glad I didn't get banged up again, but, well, I dunno, I'm still 'ere and I 'aven't changed. Still drinking."

Diane jumped right in. "When did anyone treat you as a human being?" Non-plussed, April just blinked and stared at her. "You're no different from me," Diane continued, "You 'ad a tough childhood, I bet, and you drink and you shoplift to support your addiction. Who are you copying?" Silence. "Well, come on, who showed you how to live like you do?"

"No-one. My mum drank and my stepfather was a paedo."

"Well there you go. That's your answer. Did you go to friends' homes when you were small?"

"No, no-one would play with me."

"Just like everyone in this room. Your life is broken in pieces. Probation gives you the chance to meet someone who can help you put it together again. I got an old car now but it's always goin' wrong, a right ole banger. What do I do? I find someone to fix it."

Diane lowered her voice, "People like this bloke 'ere help us to mend our lives. Whoever listened to me before I came 'ere? It's worked so far for me, and look at Jeffrey and Franklin 'ere..."

("Oi, don't call me that!")

"But you only got to come in reception," Diane continued, "and you realise you are among different people. It starts with that June lady. She's a blinder. They all treat us like we matter. And if we're smart, we'll learn that that's the way to get on, not be a slave to booze and benefit."

" 's true, Di'," Frank was back in the conversation, "Should'a seen me an' Jeffrey a year ago."

"How can you be a slave if you're not working?" April asked Diane.

"Look, you ain't gonna be free till you can get your own job, your own pay packet, and not have to keep looking over your shoulder to see if Old Bill's gonna nick you. Doesn't matter what you do, cleaning, machining in a sweatshop, bein' a waitress in a cafe or even something physical like gardening. You could learn hairdressing – I know you done that in Hollywood – I clean people's houses and flats and I like it."

"Aren't you worried you'll nick stuff?"

"I never nicked stuff off people, only shops – and usually big shops. Yes, it was a bit 'ard at first but after a while I 'aven't found it a problem. It's a relief not 'avin' to walk around with frozen meat down me pants. But when someone in one o' those big 'ouses shows they trust you, you begin to feel different about things... an' different about yerself. The buzz I get from getting me own money is still a buzz. You'll find it'll work for you, April, if you give it a good try."

"Ooo-o-oh, I dunno.. . I really want to but, well... But 'ow did you get started?"

Diane lowered her voice again, "It was 'im over there. When I talk, 'e listens. I mean, really listens. Made me realise I'm not so stupid after all. 'elped me realise I'm not just a jailbird. I got some talents, an' now I got pride. Takes a little time, but if you really wanna do it, it works. Start believin' in yerself, darlin' an' yer on yer way up."

40. No Bed of Rose's

It was far from normal for everything to run as smoothly as it seemed to have done with Frank and Jeffrey. A large majority of probationers and parolees found themselves in court as a direct or indirect result of drugs or alcohol. According to recent Home Office figures, substance misuse underlies around eighty per cent of crimes in the UK, whether it be dealing in, or possession of, controlled substances, theft, deception or fraud, as a way of obtaining money for drugs or alcohol, or violence as a result of using mind-altering substances of any nature including drink. Driving offences with too much alcohol in the bloodstream are also included in this group. Matrimonial and domestic violence, too, is often attributed to alcohol or drug misuse. Dealing with the cause - and trying to encourage prevention - therefore requires a considerable proportion of the probation officer's working hours. Spotting problems was not always easy.

One giveaway sign of possible relapse was non-appearance for appointments or group meetings. If people phoned up ahead of time with some reasonable explanation, that was permissible. If I sometimes had to change their appointments due to my other commitments, why shouldn't they be able to do the same? An occasional missed – or forgotten – date was also understandable, though I would make it clear that rules are supposed to be followed.

But when absences became frequent or regular it was time to take sterner action. The ultimate sanction, of course, was to return them to court for breach of probation and request re- sentencing. At first, I regarded such an act as an admission of failure on the part of the probation officer, but when Richard pointed out that the mere adoption of breach proceedings was a demonstration of the decisiveness – and the power – of the probation officer (and evidence to the court of the officer's competence) I began to modify my view.

One of my female clients had missed several appointments but had turned up a few times on the wrong dates merely to sign in. This fact was all that saved her from immediate breach proceedings. She called in again after lunch one day, without appointment, just as I happened to come out of the coffee room door into reception. Leaning forward to speak through the reception window, she had her back to me, as she was talking loudly to June through the safety glass.

"Yeah, I was s'posed to be 'ere yesterdi to see Mr. Wally, but I didn't 'ave the bus fare."

"OK Rose, I'll see if I can find him. He's not in his office at the moment. Hang on a sec. I'll get the signing-in book and while you're doing that I'll phone around and if he can fit you in you can take a seat." June could see me while she was saying this loudly enough for me to hear, and I assumed she was telling me so I could duck back into the coffee room if I chose to.

'Nice one June,' I thought, 'but no, I'll see Rose.' We went up to the office each armed with a cup of tea.

"I didn't think you'd see me."

"Is that what you'd prefer? You've missed a few appointments lately."

"Have I? I've come here a lot and signed in at reception 'cause you're never 'ere."

I knew what this meant. She was avoiding me, but trying to comply with the terms of the probation order by proving her attendance. When interviewing in my office I normally sat in an easy chair facing my client across the coffee table; on this occasion for some reason I sat in my desk chair sideways on to Rose. I didn't want to begin a dispute and she looked as though she was heading that way.

"Rose, what's wrong? You were doing so well." She looked startled.

"How do you know? Does it show?" It did. She would always come to the group meeting looking as though she had taken some trouble with her appearance. Her eyes would sparkle with enthusiasm and her voice was chirpy with little squeaks of delight when there was laughter. Today she was dowdy and her voice was flat. Her eyes were 'pinned', a clear indication of heroin use. (The pupils shrink to pinpoints to restrict the admission of daylight to the retina.)

"Tell me what happened Rose." I sipped my tea trying to sound calm and unperturbed.

"This bloke...... Um... Well, I met a new bloke and I really fancy him, but he's still on the gear. I thought I could help 'im get off it 'cos I was doin' so well. I'd been clean for eight months now – no methadone, no weed, nothin'. We went to bed together and one thing led to another and he was 'omeless so we started living together but I couldn't help him and 'e got me back on it again. 'E tried to get me to go on the game for 'im but I refused. I never did that when I was usin' an' I'm not gonna start for 'im or anyone." There was a pause, a lull-before-the-storm-silence which I didn't want to break. Then, like an explosion –

"Oohhh Fuck!...... Fuck! Fuck! Fuck! – orright I'll tell you.... I'm useless! I'm a failure! It's all over.... I been arrested again. I nicked a bottle of scotch to sell to pay for my drugs. I'm in court next Thursday. I know I'll go to jail now I broke my probation?"

"What will you plead?"

"Guilty of course. What's the point of denying it?"

"Well that's good Rose, because then I can write a report and tell the judge about all the good things. You gave up drugs without treatment, you found yourself a flat and started at college two days a week. Are you still going?"

"Well autumn term starts next week. Can't see them letting me back if I'm like this."

"But you thought you could conceal it from me?"

"Well, least I'm not injecting this time, that's one good thing."

"OK Rose. That's important. It seems to me you've still got plenty going for you. Where's the boyfriend?"

"I kicked 'im out. Problem is, I still fancy 'im."

"Local fella?" She gave me a name which I recognised as someone I'd had dealings with on office duty, one of Marnie's clients. "So, Rose, you've done some things right: you've got rid of the cause of the problem and you've come to see me. What's your plan? You have some choices to make."

"Isn't it automatic? Won't they just send me to prison?"

"Not necessarily. I'll be asked for a report and if I say you were doing well but faltered a little, and I thought probation should continue, they'll probably follow my recommendation. What can you offer them? What might make the judge decide against custody?"

"Well, I never went to drug dependency at the 'ospital. One of my mates was tryin' to 'elp me and said it was good. She gets counsellin'. My ex told me 'e went to a residential rehab but 'e got kicked out. He thought it was good at first but 'e only said 'e'd go to avoid prison. Once 'e got there 'e fucked off an' they wouldn't let 'im back. Serves 'im right. Trouble is, 'e's very sexy, but 'e's not a nice person. I could never live wiv' 'im again. 'E's not an idiot even though 'e does stupid things, but e's bossy, got no manners, eats like a pig and doesn't care about anyone else. E's not sleepin' in my bed again, I'll tell yer that." Her tone then changed:

"I wouldn't mind going to rehab – but then I'd lose me place in college." I took these little dropped clues as encouraging signs that she was already talking about positive options – rehab, college.

"Right, Rose, who's your solicitor?" She told me his name – fortunately one of the competent ones – and said she had an appointment the next day. . "Good. This is what you might want to do. Tell him you want to plead guilty. Also say you're on probation and you were doing very well until about two months ago. Let him know who your probation officer is and that you've told me all about it. Ask for a Pre-Sentence Report and the court will delay sentence for three weeks while we look at your options...."

Rose interrupted, now almost crying, "But I've shown that I'm a failure. Why would they want to give me another chance?"

"Rose, you're not a failure, you haven't failed yet – you hit a bump in the road, you're still trying and you just need a little more time to succeed. Relapse is a normal stage of recovery – ask anyone in the group." Her real tears told me that this is probably what she wanted to hear but didn't dare believe. She tried to smile. Her nose was running so I held out the tissue box. This allowed her to mop up, blow her nose and smile properly mouthing the words "thank you" as if she hadn't the courage to say them aloud in case she cried again.

"Why not come back to our Tuesday group. We've missed you." Gentle words were probably not what she'd expected to hear. She smiled and nodded, pressing her lips tightly together as if to stifle more crying. "We'll need another meeting for the court report interview but we can fix that when we know the court has requested it." Rose picked up an orange from the fruit bowl as she got up to go, holding it up as if to ask if she could have it. I nodded and went downstairs with her. I was out of breath when I got back upstairs to my office and hurried to my desk where the telephone was ringing insistently... It was June.

"Wally, I was surprised to see you saying goodbye to Rose. You're expected at Pentonville Prison in twenty minutes...."

41. Not Manny

HMP Pentonville is a relic of Victorian justice. It was originally built in the 1840's to house convicted men awaiting deportation to Australia. Like many failed bright ideas incorporated in our justice system, the design of four 'wings' radiating from a central building enabling maximum visibility with minimum staff was a concept imported from America. It remains a failure and the prison is frequently lambasted and shamed by staff, press and government inspectors not to mention by the inmates. All to no avail, of course....

The purpose of my visit was to interview a man who had pleaded guilty to seven counts of burglary and asked for thirty- nine similar offences to be taken into account. This strategy, commonly adopted by offenders, means that if they can "clear the books" of all the offences they remember committing, they cannot later be arrested and convicted for the same matter. The police encourage this act because it enhances their clear-up figures at little or no cost.

It was widely suggested by many of my clients (and not just a few police officers) that defendants would agree to a few "extra" TICs, (other offences taken into consideration at the time of sentencing so they cannot be prosecuted later). Offenders have been heard to argue "There's no real difference between 23 and 27, or 31 and 39. The sentence is going to be the same an' if it helps the Bill (police) - I've nothing against that. We all got our jobs to do!" Or, "It does wonders for my 'street cred' if people know I done twice as many jobs as I actually did, without getting nicked for 'em." Of course the "bonus" TICs must be reported and documented as crimes previously unsolved.

The unspoken additional reason is that in addition to enabling the police to enhance their figures, offenders sometimes agree to phoney TICs as a means of 'trading' for other privileges or benefits such as lower level charges (say, handling stolen property instead of burglary) or being given bail instead of a custodial remand. The courts, of course, also encourage this course of action since it lightens their workload in the long run. This time, though, the magistrate remanded him in custody for reports despite the defence counsel making a plea for bail. The bench was quick to point out that the last six of the seven main offences occurred while the perpetrator was on bail for the first.

Terry Underhill arrived in my interview booth with a smile. I asked him if I had recorded his name correctly with his middle name as Emmanuel. "Yes, but don't call me Manny," he replied. "I usually answer to 'Manno'." Acknowledging that he knew he was 'going down for a long stretch', Manno, was open in our discussions saying with neither bravado nor remorse, that burglary was his profession and he enjoyed it.

Now, aged twenty-five, he claimed he'd been doing it for fifteen years. As a child, he was never considered to be the perpetrator of crimes, some of which he reported to the police himself and so by the time he was old enough to be a realistic suspect he had become highly skilled in what he did. He told me he enjoyed travelling upstairs on buses. That enabled him to see potential target properties and, in the flash of time it took a bus to drive past a building, he could see a possible entry point and an exit. "Never go out the way you came in." he told me, in case I was thinking of taking up his profession. "Old Bill are usually pretty lazy. If they've seen you go in, or someone reports seeing you, they'll often wait for you to leave before nicking you." But, I wondered, why does he do it? Is it substance dependency? His reply surprised me.

"Nope. Drink and drugs interfere with my work. I don't do either. Sometimes I put some of the proceeds on a horse or a dog, but I'm not addicted to gambling. No, if I'm addicted to anything it's the buzz – the thrill of entering a building, perhaps with people still in it – even working – and moving about unseen and unheard.

"Once, on a very hot night, I went in the open ground floor window of a flat in Dalston. There was a couple in bed so hard at it they didn't see me creep past their bed into the living room. Then I heard a key in the front lock. Someone opened the door quietly, went straight into the bedroom where the couple was making one helluva row, and caught them red-handed. I didn't wait for the final act but I suspect it was curtains for the bloke in bed with the man's wife."

"I don't usually do domestics – only businesses normally but this one winked at me." I was riveted by his candour. "Stealing something is only a way of proving my presence, showing that I've been there. Well, that and maintaining a reasonable lifestyle, I suppose."

For one whose education was as disrupted as he described, Manno was eloquent. A habitual truant from Hackney schools he was moved to a residential school out of London but always found ways of escaping and returning home. The last time he absented himself, at the age of fourteen or so, no-one came looking for him, so he started work with several short-term casual jobs but didn't like it. "There's nothing available now with an income that would interest me," he concluded. He was definitely not interested in a probation order or community service and unhesitatingly told me that he would not comply with any order placed on him by the court.

"Naaa-a-a-h." he grinned, when I mentioned the prospect of probation. "Let me do the bird. I'll take a rest an' then get back to work."

"I will probably need to mention the possibility of probation in the report. But you'll get a chance to read it when you arrive at court."

"I won't even bother. Can't read an' write, y'see? That was one of the reasons they sent me to special boarding schools. But the schools said I was too bright to be there an' they weren't able to teach at my level. They was all ESN (educationally sub-normal) they called it then; learning disabled I think it is now. That's why I bunked off all the time."

In my report I explained that though the Probation Service had a number of successful programmes for serious offenders, many of which demanded a high degree of restriction of liberty, there were two major arguments militating against such a course. The first was that he would need to be on bail for a thorough assessment to take place, but since six of the seven current offences took place when he was on bail, that might not be a good idea. Perhaps more importantly, any participation in such specialised activities required a great deal of motivation and determination on the part of the offender – which was clearly lacking in this particular case. It was no great injury to my pride to acknowledge that, whatever his needs, they were outside my area of competence.

I had to convey in my report that though, in principle, it was always a good idea to consider a community sentence rather than a custodial one, Mr. Terry Underhill was an exception to this laudable aim. Indeed in terms of protecting the public from his irresistible urge to commit burglary, he should indeed be locked up for a very long time. But it's never a good idea to word the report in such a blatant way as to invite him to come looking for me to take his revenge on his release from prison - and of course, no judge or magistrate would ever disclose that it was the probation officer's recommendation that earned the defendant a long prison sentence.

As luck would have it, I was on court duty when Manno came back to court. The court went silent for several minutes as the magistrate read my confidential report. Imagine, then, how shocked – and horrified – I was to hear, even before the defence solicitor stood up to speak, the magistrate say to him:

"Mr. Underhill, I was ready to consider a probation order or community service, but in the light of the contents of this report, I now consider an appropriate sentence to be much greater than this court will allow. I therefore decline to pass a sentence and you will be remanded in custody to appear at Inner London Crown Court for sentence where a judge can impose a sentence in excess of that I am empowered to pass in this court." In other words, the magistrate just told Manno that I had persuaded the court to send him to jail for a long stretch!

I wanted to hide from this man who had appeared so personable in Pentonville. As he turned to the side to make his way out of the dock, Manno looked in my direction and I was transfixed by his gaze, completely unable to avert my eyes. Once again, I was shocked: this time it was because he smiled broadly at me and winked, with that Cockney sideways nod of the head that says:

"It's OK."

42. A Risky Experiment

After a stimulating visit to Belmarsh prison for a court report interview I had an idea. The inmate had pleaded guilty to domestic burglary – always a dead certainty for a custodial sentence – yet there was something about this young man that made me think a probation order might work. He had entered the enclosed porch on the ground floor of a house converted to four flats. His intention, he told me, was to break into each flat. But in the lobby was 'a rather nice bicycle' as he put it.

"It was locked up," he explained, "but I thought I could manage to undo it. While I was concentrating, the owner and his dog came back, saw me fiddlin' with 'is bike in 'is front porch, flagged down a police car outside in the street and I was nicked bang to rights." (Yes, they still say that!)

Vincent Wray was an engaging young man who lived with his wife Sarah. She married him because she thought she could get him off heroin. "She nearly bloody succeeded but I crashed after about a year. Been back on the gear for seven months till I was nicked. I've been goin' to N.A. here in Belmarsh and I'll keep that up during my sentence though there's plenny o' drugs in 'ere." I asked him if he was interested in getting help from the DDU.

"Yeah, but that's a long way off. Gotta do me bird first."

"Have you thought about a probation order?" I asked.

"No, did it once before I got married. I was useless. The woman never gave me a chance. First time I missed a couple of appointments I was back in court and before I knew it, I got the order changed to a custodial. I was only a kid. They wouldn't give me another one. Got custodials ever since. Once they see you done bird that's it."

"How long ago was that?"

"Dunno. Think I was about eighteen-years-old."

"And now you're?"

"Twenty-seven."

"How many prison sentences since?"

Four, six... I lost count."

"Have you grown up in the meantime?"

He smiled a warm, sheepish smile. At that point I witnessed the dawning on him that I was serious.

"Some of me mates are on it. They don't go individual like. They go to a group and they support each other. Three of them are off it – totally! Fucking lucky bastards. If I did that, I think I'd be OK. That, the DDU – and my wife."

"Who are your mates?"

"Frank Grover, Jeffrey, don't know 'is second name and Mickey.... erm, I forget." I shook my head slightly as if to say 'don't know 'em'. I gave him my talk about probation being a two-way street and giving as much support as I could in return for real effort, but not putting up with nonsense. He said he was up for it.

"Well, Vincent, I'm not convinced it'll work. I'd like you to write me a letter and tell me what you said this afternoon. Your brief can show it to the judge – but I must get it in good time. I want to know you mean business. You've got my address from the appointment letter."

"I can't write or spell."

"If you can talk, you can write. It doesn't matter about the handwriting or the spelling. No letter, no deal."

The prison officer called time and Vincent and I shook hands – he more vigorously than I. A plan was hatching.

His court date was two Tuesdays hence. I would have the report written by then. I had time to tell the group that Vincent was in court – they all knew him and were sorry he was facing a jail sentence. They liked him and said he's extremely funny, always making sharp jokes.

"He nearly got away from drugs," they said, "all on his own. His wife's a heavy lady." I wondered what her weight had to do with it and said as much.

"Na-a-a-a..." they all giggled "It means she's strong, forceful, great personality."

"Domineering" said Diane. "She makes me look like a Sunday School teacher!" Laughter all round. "But why are we talking about Vincent an' 'is wife when 'e's in the nick?"

"Because he's in court next Tuesday and I'm planning to be there to present my report to the court, so there won't be a group meeting."

"Oh good. Can we have the week off?"

"Or could we have the meeting here without you?"

"Cor, yeah!"

"I want Mr. Wally's chair!"

"OK, I'll take over the computer".

"Oh no you bloody won't!– it's got to be still there when 'e gets back! " More laughter.

"No, you can't have the meeting here without me," I interrupted, "but you could have the meeting with me."

"How, if you're not gonna be 'ere?"

"I want to show the court what probation can do. I have seven seats in my car. You've all made fantastic progress since you were placed on probation. It's time the world knew about it. Those of you who know him could join me in a trip to Inner London Crown Court in support of Vincent. If the judge calls on me to speak, I'll tell him what we do on probation and ask you all to stand up. If Vincent manages to avoid a custodial, we can bring him home."

"Shall we dress up smart, like?"

"It would probably help. Especially if you're all sober. Should be quite a performance. We'll leave at one o'clock. Anyone up for it?" They all noisily agreed and I was relieved when the letter from Vincent arrived a couple of days later and I put it in the file.

———

Dear Mr. Wally

Thank you for coming to see me yestaday. You made me fink that I could succeed an get off of drugs if I tried harder and wiv help from the Drug Unit at Hackney Hospitle and a probation oficer and my wife I'm shure I could do it.

I've stayed clean while I've been on remand so that's nearly three months without any drugs at all and if I can do it in prison where there's lots of drugs, I think I culd do it in Hackney.

I been expecting to go to prison but if I got probation I would really work hard to do it rite this time. I'm older this time an see the sence in it. But if I do get a jail sentence, will you please come and visit me? I can write you and let you know where they send me after court.

Thank you again,

Vincent Wray

43. Crown Court for Sentence

Five smartly dressed people turned up at the office to support Vincent. My car was a five-seater with a lift-up occasional rear seat for two more passengers. After leaving on time we arrived in court well in advance of our deadline. Frank, Jeffrey and Micky were kept in order by Diane and April who by now were becoming good friends. They all sat in the public gallery and sat next to a woman they clearly knew. I took her to be Sarah, whose efforts had nearly succeeded in helping Vincent overcome his addiction. I hadn't reckoned on an extra seat being needed – but thought to myself we could cross that bridge if and when we came to it.

Fortunately there was one case for sentencing before Vincent, which gave me a chance to compose myself and adjust to the frightening formality of the Crown Court environment. I took my place at the probation bench with the Crown Court Duty Probation Officer whose name I knew but whom I had not previously met. A barrister approached him asking for a copy of the report for Vincent Wray. My colleague indicated that I had the report and the barrister asked me to discuss the case with him outside the courtroom.

During our discussion I told him I had proposed probation – whereupon he raised his eyebrows, closed his eyes and slowly shook his head. I said that I had received a letter from Vincent and had brought a shining sample of recovering substance misusers who were present in the public gallery. I told the barrister I was willing to be called to the witness box. Unimpressed, the barrister looked at me witheringly.

"You'll have a hard time with this judge. Make sure you call him 'My Lord' " was all he said.

As we re-entered the courtroom, a court official was addressing the clerk saying that the defendant for the first case was in prison transport which had been delayed. Could proceedings begin with case number two?

The large courtroom fell silent as the usher called for everyone to stand, at which point the learned judge, in red robes, entered from a door to the rear of the bench. We all remained standing until he took his seat. That first impression often tells you all you need to know. Everything about the judge's appearance shouted PRISON! His steel-grey hair and, peering over half-moon reading glasses, frowning eyebrows, the same colour as his wig, the intimidating red robe and sash all designed to terrify anyone required to interact with him. It certainly worked on me! The clerk addressed the judge quietly; then aloud, he said:

"We begin the afternoon with case No. 2, My Lord." after which some more quiet conversation ensued between them probably in explanation of the change of plan.

Then: "Mr. Vincent Wray" repeated by the usher at the rear of the court. Vincent entered the courtroom through a door from the custody area and proceeded to the dock, standing to attention holding his suitcase containing his belongings. He gave his full name and was invited to sit down while the prosecution outlined the case against him. The judge asked to see the not inconsiderable list of previous offences and scowled at the number of pages even before reading it. He then invited defence counsel to speak but, as if to put him off his stride, fired an opening shot across the bows of the young barrister.

"I have read the report and I have to say that I am not in agreement with the author. This is a serious offence and merits a serious deprivation of liberty."

Defence Counsel began by reminding the judge that Vincent had pleaded guilty at the first opportunity at Old Street Magistrates' Court and that the local magistrate had committed the case to Inner London Crown Court for sentence. He described his client as a former drug dependent person who had relapsed and committed the offence in pursuit of money to purchase heroin. There followed an eloquent prepared address on why Vincent might be permitted to escape a custodial sentence: no property was actually lost, Vincent Wray had previously almost succeeded in overcoming long-term drug misuse without outside help; he had a supportive wife, a job and a flat; it was three years since his last offence. The judge cut him short:

"Yes, yes, yes, but that could be said by most counsel about their clients. I'm still not convinced that this airy-fairy report carries any substance. The Home Secretary believes that the public deserves to be protected from this kind of behaviour and I must say that in this case I agree with him." He glowered at the defence barrister who continued without hesitation.

"That is a perfectly valid point of view, My Lord, but a custodial disposal would protect the public only for the duration of the imprisonment. It seems to me that the author of the report believes that a longer-term solution might be achieved through a probation order. The report states, quite accurately, that, far from encouraging Mr. Wray to change his ways, imprisonment seems to have led him to offences of escalating seriousness. On the other hand, quite apart from the legally enforceable terms of probation, the report sets out additional stringent conditions to which Mr. Wray has agreed in writing. Mr. Wray has written an enthusiastic letter of commitment to the probation officer showing his eagerness to comply with an order if made and his willingness for a condition of treatment at the DDU to be attached to such an order."

"But what evidence do you have that this person," ruffling the pages noisily, he looked back at the report as if seeking the name of the author "...Wally Henry, can support his preposterous claims? What kind of name is that, anyway? The report gives no indication of whether the author is male or female." He was visibly irritated.

"He is male, Your Honour and he is present in court. Perhaps you might wish to hear from him?"

"Oh.... Very well," the judge sighed as if to say 'if I must' and made great show of reluctance by turning slowly and laboriously toward the witness box. I took my place in it. Invited to take the oath, I chose to affirm. The usher handed me a card which I read aloud:

"I do solemnly, sincerely and truly declare and affirm that the evidence I shall give shall be the truth, the whole truth and nothing but the truth."

"Mr. Henry, I see that probation has already failed once. What makes you think you can do any better?"

"My Lord, while no disposal carries any guarantee, I believe I can demonstrate some success for some probationers. Mr. Wray is almost ten years older than when his first probation order was made. It's clear to me that five custodial sentences have done nothing to help him. You have seen in the report that I am insistent on relevant treatment at Hackney DDU, but in addition many recovering drug and alcohol users on my caseload voluntarily attend a weekly group held in my own office for mutual support in overcoming dependency. Though it is no panacea, so far it has been successful enough and five of the members of the group have asked to attend court today. May I ask them to stand? I feel they may be the evidence you require."

"Where are they?" He leaned forward as if to scan the horizon, peering everywhere except the public gallery. Five, no, six beaming, gleaming members of assorted shapes, sizes and colours got noisily to their feet in the visitors' gallery. Sarah stood with them. The gold coloured rims of the half-moon glasses glinted as the judge peered over them and scowled, first at them, then at me. To them he merely said "You may sit down." Turning again to me he said:

"Counsel alluded to a letter." His meaning was clear. I handed the original from my file to the usher, who delivered it to the judge via the clerk. There was silence while he read it, apparently laboriously, head half turned away, frowning, implying the handwriting and mis-spelling were offensive to him.

As if scandalised, without looking up, he asked: "Mr. Henry, do you always allow offenders to address you by your first name?"

"My Lord, if used respectfully, I have no strong feelings about people's mode of address. The handwriting and spelling of the letter suggest this was no easy task for Mr. Wray and I choose to believe that Mr. Wray is earnest in what he writes."

"You are manifestly entitled to your very unusual views Mr. Henry, but I don't share them." And then, peremptorily, "Thank you." I was dismissed. The usher took the letter from the clerk and returned it to me. The Red Judge didn't wait for me to reach my seat at the probation bench before addressing poor Vincent quaking in the dock.

"Mr. Wray....?"

"Stand up Mr. Wray" the usher said to him. Vincent looked ashen. Our team in the gallery looked dejected.

"Mr. Wray, you are going to jail, which in my view is the only just disposal for your offence. To prove that I am right, and your idealistic probation officer is wrong......" There was a long pause and he ruffled some more papers. *(Oh, no, I thought, how long is he going to get?)* ....I am going to make a probation order for two years. I require progress reports at six-monthly intervals and, should you fail to maintain the conditions of your order, or worse, re-offend, you will be returned to Crown Court. I have reserved this case to myself. If I see you again in my court you will receive the prison sentence I was prepared to give you today. Is... that... clear?" These three words the judge almost bellowed.

"Yes, your honour, sir" whispered a dazed Vincent Wray.

"Very well. You may go." He peered at the gallery again. Nodding courteously to our trusty team he said: "Thank you for coming."

"All stand. Court will rise." was the usher's signal for the judge to depart. I felt numb after my encounter with him. Turning his swivel chair to his right as he stood to leave, facing me and, unseen by anyone in the court who now had other things on their mind, lips closed, he smiled at me, at the same time nodding slightly, momentarily closing one eye in what was clearly a deliberate wink as he did so.

As soon as the Red Judge departed, the court buzzed with chatter and the supporters in the team gave what sounded like a cheer. We all gathered in the public area to wait for Vincent to complete minor release procedures in the custody suite. He emerged with an enormous grin:

"Wow, Mr. Wally, I never seen you in a suit before, thank you. You did all this for me? If it wasn't for you and this lot, I'd already be in the prison van. Thanks guys."

"You may be right, Vincent, but your brief had something to do with it as well. And so did our team – you all look great." When we all got back to the car, Diane went straight for the front passenger seat. April, Frank and Mickey shared the rear seat. Jeffrey offered to squeeze into the remaining boot space thus allowing Vincent and Sarah to share the folding double 'occasional' seat. The journey through City of London traffic was like a party. On arrival at their home, Sarah and Vincent invited us all into their flat for a cup of tea. I declined and left them to celebrate while I returned to the office.

So ended another successful group meeting with a bit of theatre thrown in!

I had to get back to the office for supervision with Jackie. She had been critical last month so I didn't relish the thought.

44. The Wages of Honesty

Supervision time. I debated whether to tell Jackie that I was bang-up-to-date with my record keeping, my client supervision plans, court reports and client activities. I was beginning to learn that too much openness yielded consequences.

Our good-natured conversation must have lured me in. Commenting on our previous conversation where she had berated me for lapses in what she described as "basic professional practice" Jackie opened with:

"I've noticed, Wally, that your records are showing great improvement. That's very good, highly commendable, but everything comes at a cost: is there something you've let slip in order to accomplish that?"

"No Jackie, certainly not."

"What about your supervision plans, they were a bit adrift last month."

"Bang on target."

"Pre-Sentence Reports?"

"Full up to the top – all complete, including two Crown Court reports."

"Any non-reports?" (When clients don't show up for their appointments, a nil report is submitted and sentencing is usually adjourned for another three or four weeks for a second try.) I shook my head.

"Court duties?"

"A few people owe me exchanges – I did more than my quota to help out." I should have recognised I was beginning to sound smug.

"Office duty?"

"Same thing." I stupidly didn't see it coming.... I shouldn't have boasted.

"Well, Wally, that sounds terrific. You see? It wasn't so hard was it?" Jackie paused and smiled. "Erm, could I ask you to do another couple of reports this month? One's a parole report for a young offender, the other the local Magistrates' Court for a female."

GOT ME ! ! !

The first available appointment for the young man serving his sentence was a couple of weeks hence, but since the report for the female was due shortly, I made two quick appointments for her to visit my office for interview. Unusually, in cases of fraudulent benefit claims, the Crown Prosecution Service was not involved. Such cases were brought by counsel for the Department of Social Security. My letter went out the same day as my supervision session.

Crystelle Young arrived early and, since the previous client had failed to attend, I showed her to my office as soon as she arrived. She had clearly taken some trouble with her appearance. Though she seemed slightly nervous, she carried herself with considerable poise. She sat upright, not leaning back in the easy chair opposite mine.

"Tell me why you think you're here. How did all this happen?"

"Well," she explained, "I look after my mum. I'm on benefit – I have a book of weekly vouchers. My son is twelve and has some problems. My mum does too, really. We live on the eighth floor of a high-rise building and she's no longer able to go out. But I'm allowed to work a few hours a week without affecting my right to benefit." That seemed to be the extent of her explanation. I asked why she was arrested.

"I don't know. I don't understand it. We don't have much money and mum only gets a pension and even with my benefit it's not nearly enough to get by. I decided to get some part-time work and asked at the 'social' (the benefit office where she signs on weekly) if I was allowed to work. The young lady said yes, up to fifteen hours a week. After that I will start to lose benefit. So, I got a job with a shoe firm selling shoes part-time in their shop in the High Street. They agreed I could work fourteen hours a week. I must have been quite good at it because I got bonuses for good sales – I don't know how they worked it out. I got tax and National Insurance deducted and now I've been dismissed I've got a P45 but they won't let me sign on for unemployment benefit because they say I was working illegally." Mrs. Young was holding back tears.

"Is there anyone else in your family?"

"No," then after a few seconds' pause, "My dad died twelve years ago in 1979, the year I got married. I was twenty-three, then my husband disappeared when our son was three. Police never found him but he was a violent drinker and I suspected he was still alive and I got a divorce after five years. I spent most of my life looking after my mum. She is arthritic, asthmatic, blind, deaf and diabetic." I gasped inwardly. "When my son was five-and-a-half he was abducted after school. I thought then it was by my husband but it turned out it was by a known local child sex abuser who's still in prison for that and other offences. The police were wonderful to us. But since then, my son has developed severe psychiatric symptoms, including panic attacks, nervous breakdown and attempted suicide. He's often subjected to bullying at school."

"So, you look after your infirm widowed mother, your son, who has many very real difficulties and you still manage to find some time to keep busy at work? That must be an awfully punishing agenda for you?" Then, foolishly, in a vain attempt to lighten a somewhat difficult conversation, I asked her whatever did she do in her spare time? I was unprepared for her response as she quickly, though not maliciously, put me in my place.

"I look after the lady next door. She's 87 and has lived alone for the past thirty years. Her husband was a taxi driver and died of a heart attack in his late fifties. She was always so good to my mum and me."

"Do you or your mum receive disability allowance? Or do you get a carer's allowance?"

"I don't know what they are and I've never been told about them. I wouldn't even know where to apply for them." My original anger while reading the prosecution papers changed to anger with the bureaucracy.

Curious as to how Mrs. Young could have misunderstood the regulations, I telephoned the Benefits Agency, as an anonymous enquirer, while she was still with me in the office. I was completely taken aback to be told by the duty worker on the general enquiries counter that if I were claiming unemployment benefit or income support, I would be permitted to work up to fifteen hours a week without affecting my claim. Only when I pressed my enquiry did he then go on to say that the maximum amount I was permitted to earn depended on my circumstances. He still did not explain that the maximum sum that would be disregarded would be £15 per week after which benefit would be reduced pound for pound on a sliding scale. His explanation then became so complicated that I had to consult the Hackney Probation Money Advice Officer for clarification.

What the Benefits Agency neglected to tell me was that it was necessary to tell them each week the amount earned, though since Mrs. Young had a book of vouchers, and never knew the amount of her wages until they arrived, it would have been difficult to adjust her weekly payment except well in arrears. The enquiry clerk told me on the telephone that if as a claimant, I were to convert from part-time work to full-time, I would receive a one-off payment of £1,000 from the Benefits Agency. Mrs. Young had alluded to this in her taped interview of which I'd read the transcriptions, so I therefore had no difficulty believing that she, too, made the same enquiry as I did.

It became clear that a second interview was unnecessary, but I did ask Mrs. Young if I may make a short home visit. She assented and I was relieved, if a little distressed, to find everything exactly as she had earlier described. By coincidence, the next-door neighbour was outside her front door on the communal balcony as I arrived and the warmth of the cheerful exchange of cockney banter between her and Mrs. Young would have told me all I needed to know.

Mrs. Young clearly had her hands full and, in my view, no doubt needed – and benefitted greatly from – the company and stimulation of workplace surroundings to enable her to continue her perpetual domestic responsibilities. Though I did not believe her to be intellectually gifted, I did form the opinion that she was a disciplined person, a devoted daughter, a committed mother and a valued neighbour. At no time did I gain the impression that she was dishonest.

Telephone enquiries to the relevant police station yielded confirmation that Mrs. Young's son was indeed abducted for several weeks and seriously sexually abused. Moreover, not only was the perpetrator jailed for that and other offences, but more matters had come to light in the meantime, which almost certainly meant that another long custodial sentence would follow the current one.

After ceasing work, Mrs. Young's income support voucher book was cancelled for eight weeks – a total of £565.20 - withheld from the family, money which the family needed but which she did not receive. The file showed that, while investigations for this matter were in progress, she had offered to repay at the rate of £10 per week, an offer that was neither accepted nor rejected. The total overpayment of £3,619 allegedly over-claimed was in my view (and in the opinion of our Money Advice Officer) illusory. Mrs. Young would have been entitled to a weekly £15 "disregard" with her benefit having already been reduced pound for pound by the remaining £35 salary. Thus, of the true over-claimed amount of £1,820, the Benefits Agency had already recovered £565 during the two months of their enquiries leaving only approximately £1,255.00 still owing. During this period, the three generation family survived solely on Mrs. Young senior's meagre state pension.

My report told the court that Mrs. Young was so traumatised by this experience I did not think it would recur. The relentless demands of caring for her mother, her son and her neighbour which she met so tirelessly seemed to me to be a direct contribution to society, reducing significantly the demand on community resources that might otherwise be called for. I further stated that in my opinion, a sentence of community service (unpaid work was a common sentence for blatant benefit offenders) would be not merely unnecessary but grossly unfair while a period of probation supervision was not called for. I asked the court to make a conditional discharge and to instruct the Benefits Agency to adjust their demand to a just sum or cancel the outstanding balance.

The magistrate followed my recommendation to the letter.

45. Marcus Benjamin

Some days later I found myself driving to the Young Offenders' Institution in Aylesbury, Buckinghamshire. Marcus Benjamin had been sentenced to one and a half years imprisonment for his involvement in drugs related offences with three other males who, as adults, were convicted in the Crown Court.

Before the visit I had been able to contact his aunt, with whom he planned to stay on release, and also to contact the social worker in Islington who helpfully gave me access to some of her records but wisely gave me the contact details of her colleague who had worked with Marcus for several years previously.

From the outset Marcus Benjamin seemed eager to impress on me that he was ashamed of these matters and regretted his part in them. It was his first brush with the law and he chastised himself for being so easily influenced by "bigger boys" just to "look big like them". Marcus told me earnestly that, once at liberty, he would steer clear of his co-defendants and others like them. This was the reason he had chosen to live, on his release, with his aunt in Hackney, away from his own territory in a neighbouring borough.

I learned from wing staff in the Young Offenders' Institution (YOI) that he had been attending education classes during his time at Aylesbury. He told me he enjoyed reading and named some of his favourite authors, describing some of the books and asking my opinion of them. He came across as an able young man who realised he would have much to gain from a course of study, perhaps in further or higher education. As if reading my mind, he then stated exactly that, and asked if I would be able to help him should he get parole."I would certainly try," I told him, "but I have to warn you I'm pretty new in this job. I'm still feeling my way around."

"That's OK, I'm cool with that," replied Mr. Benjamin instantly, "I'm pretty new at bein' without drugs on the out – though I managed while in here. I figure if I can do it here, I can do it anywhere." I asked him how he did that.

"Everyone tries to get jobs – cleaning, kitchen, visits room. Those are the ones who get the drugs – meeting others on the wing or around. I realised the best way to stay away from all that was to go to education. Some of the teachers are great – it's like bein' entertained all the time and you get to learn something. School teachers never treated us like adults. We were never listened to; no-one ever thought we had opinions that might be interesting."

When, prior to my prison visit, I had visited his aunt, she told me she was a social worker in another borough, helping disaffected youths find motivation. She was an agreeable and charismatic person and I found myself wishing she worked in our team. She was disappointed he had got himself into trouble but, in a way, she thought Marcus was lucky to have been arrested the first time he tried crime and said she knew he would overcome this 'false-start' as she described it.

"If anyone would learn from this experience, Marcus would," she said, "I know it."

Throughout our animated conversation, Marcus was constantly on the move which made me feel he had great physical energy and I raised the subject.

"They told me I had ADHD" he said. I can never remember what it stands for but that's why they sent me away to boarding school: they thought I was unmanageable." When I turned the discussion to the topic of physical pursuits, he told me of his athletic achievements while away at school. I told him of our weekly sports activities group and he brightened. Could he, he asked, join the group - or what would he have to do to be a member?

Marcus's own family, I learned, was fraught with its own problems. He had been in local authority care since early childhood, having been placed with a series of foster parents. Eventually he was sent to a boarding school, described as having Attention Deficit Disorder, but he said he was clearly "much brighter than the other kids" who were all there because, he said, they were described as educationally sub-normal (ESN).

I certainly did not assess that the 'ESN' label could be applied to him. My report stated that if he were released on parole, by moving to Hackney, living with his aunt, attending the probation office and seeking a course of education, he would have every opportunity to turn his life around. Few of my earlier parole reports had offered the possibility of such positive outcomes.

Every child in care has a social worker and after my return to the office I contacted the social worker who had worked with Marcus for many years. Miss Seely told me that, regardless of the London borough in which he chose to live, he would almost certainly be eligible for nomination for housing under the 'Adolescent Quota' – a provision for young people leaving local authority care – a privilege which, ironically, would be likely to disappear if he remained in custody until his final date of release.

Marcus Benjamin appeared to me to have learned much from his time spent in custody. In my parole report I told the Parole Board that if released under supervision he would be encouraged to continue learning how to live as an adult, within the law, in a society that, especially to members of minority communities, is not always friendly and accommodating.

As his supervising officer I would help him to continue the studies he had commenced during his sentence, for which he showed promise. He would attract probation support in finding accommodation and eventually employment and in the meantime would be eligible to participate in the physical, sporting, education and leisure activities available through our probation office.

The sooner he could be released, the longer the term of supervision that would be available to him. A long period of supervision would be appropriate and I would support his application for release on parole licence.

The parole review process takes a long time – sometimes several months – and unusually, Marcus began corresponding with me. I was relieved, therefore, to learn he was awarded parole and, as planned, came to live with his aunt. He was an assiduous client and a delight to work with, never missing our appointments. Even when he had successfully completed his period on licence with flying colours he would occasionally stop by the office to greet me and, if I were available, chat about his life.

"I passed my tests an' that at college," he told me proudly the last time he came to see me after a long gap in his visits. He was sporting a new pair of expensive-looking trainers. "an' I got a great job as a mechanic in a fancy private hire car garage. It's great. I'll get my own wheels one day, you just wait and see." He noticed my jaundiced glance at his extravagant footwear. I raised one eyebrow.

"Yeah... My first week's wages..." Screwing up his face, he explained with a wry grin, "...an' I got a receipt for these!"

It was to be many years before our paths crossed again...

NOT THE END

Coming soon,
also by Wally Morgan...

Only Yomi

A Story of
Drugs, Sex and Police Corruption

Wally Morgan
Probation Officer

With help from
contemporaneous notes

Just when he thinks he's beginning to get the
hang of the job, his star probationer gets a
four-year stretch in jail.

Where did he go wrong?

And, on the lighter side...
It Was an Accident
by JEREMY CAMERON

An 'inspirational probation officer' in Walthamstow for twenty years until he left in disgust at the government messing with his job

Nicky Burkett, still incarcerated at the end of *Vinnie Got Blown Away* is released on to the streets of Walthamstow in ***It Was an Accident***. He wants to go straight. Noreen wants him to go straight and she won't go near him if he doesn't. He tries. But events and people conspire against him. He is offered "work". He is attacked. His mates are attacked. He runs to Jamaica and is attacked again. Then the fight back begins.

A wonderful thriller...an absolute cracker, superb narrative voice.
The Independent.

Ingenious, his street-talk sizzles with wit and invention... Engaging, eventful and original
Literary Review

ALSO By Jeremy Cameron

Vinnie Got Blown Away

Wider Than Walthamstow

Hell on Hoe Street

Brown Bread in Wengen
Sleazy, violent and laugh-out-loud funny
(Amazon)

Printed in Great Britain
by Amazon

73322891R00200